Truth, Power and Lies

Truth, Power and Lies

Irish Society and the Case of the Kerry Babies

TOM INGLIS

UNIVERSITY COLLEGE DUBLIN PRESS

Preas Choláiste Ollscoile Bhaile Átha Cliath

First published 2003
by University College Dublin Press
Newman House
86 St Stephen's Green
Dublin 2
Ireland

www.ucdpress.ie

© Tom Inglis 2003

ISBN 1 904558 01 1 hb
ISBN 1 904558 02 X pb

CIP data available from the British Library

The right of Tom Inglis to be identified as the
author of this work has been asserted by him.

Typeset in Ireland in Adobe Garamond, Janson and Trade Gothic
by Elaine Shiels, Bantry, County Cork
Text design by Lyn Davies
Printed in England on acid-free paper by
MPG Books Ltd, Bodmin, Cornwall

For Olwen

Contents

Acknowledgements

I would like to begin these acknowledgements by thanking those who have examined this case before me. In particular, I would like to thank Justice Kevin Lynch. His tribunal report was a most unusual legal document, written in a very clear and accessible manner. Although I believe the report was flawed, it was an earnest and honest effort to determine the truth about what happened. I would also like to thank those who wrote books about the case, specifically Joanne Hayes for *My Story*, Barry O'Halloran for *Lost Innocence*, Nell McCafferty for *A Woman to Blame*, and Gerard Colleran and Michael O'Regan for *Dark Secrets*. It is no coincidence that some of the leading journalists of their generation wrote about the case. I would also like to thank Gene Kerrigan who wrote extensive and very insightful articles for *Magil* magazine at the time, and Deirdre Purcell who reported on the Tribunal for *The Sunday Tribune*. Finally, among journalists, I should like to thank Don Buckley and Joe Joyce whose investigative reporting first broke the story in October, 1984.

Having read all the secondary material, I realised that if I was going to write anything about the case I would have to read the Transcripts of the Tribunal proceedings. This proved difficult as they were not part of any official archive. But I was fortunate to encounter Tom Goff in the Department of Justice who was most helpful in making a copy of the transcripts available for me to work on in the UCD Archives Department. My thanks to Seamus Helferty and other members of that department for all their help.

I talked with many people who were involved in the case directly and indirectly including Pat Mann, Steve McDonagh, and Brian Curtin. I am particularly grateful to Pat Mann who made his offices available to me to work in when I was in Tralee. I was fortunate to be able to speak with some of the gardaí involved in the case, as well as some of the lawyers involved in the Tribunal. I respect their desire to remain anonymous.

Within the academic sphere, my friends and colleagues in the Department of Sociology have been very supportive and encouraging in listening to my arguments and reading my papers. I am also grateful to the Amsterdam School for Social Science Research, where I spent a period of sabbatical leave in 1999, and to the friends and colleagues there who read my material and listened to me talk about the case. Others who have listened and read over the years include Paul O'Mahony, Carol MacKeogh, Dave Caffrey, Eugene Murray, Manus Charleton and David Blake-Knox. I owe a special debt of gratitude to Michael Cussen, Aileen MacKeogh, Michel Peillon, Cas Wouters, Hilary Tovey and Aogán Mulcahy who read and made detailed comments on earlier drafts of this book. Earlier versions of some chapters were published elsewhere. Chapter 1 is modified and expanded version of 'Telling Stories about Irish Women' which appeared in *Auto/biography* 6 (1) 1998: 23–30. Chapter 10 is a revised version of 'Honour Pride and Shame in Rural Ireland' which was published in *Amsterdams Sociologisch Tijdschrift* 28 (4) 2001: 495–512 and, finally, Chapter 14 is revised and expanded version of 'Sexual Transgression and Scapegoats: A Case Study from Modern Ireland' which appeared in *Sexualities* 5 (1) 2002: 5–24. I am very grateful to *The Kerryman* for permission to reproduce the photographs that appeared in *Dark Secrets*.

I wish also to acknowledge the generous support of the National University of Ireland and the Academic Publications Committee of University College Dublin for the grants they awarded to aid the publication of the book.

This book maintains a lasting and good relationship with UCD Press. I am very grateful to members of the Editorial Committee, particularly Finbarr McAuley. I should like to thank Barbara Mennell for her great skill, kindness and diligence, and Stephen Mennell for his support and encouragement. Finally, but most importantly, family is what matters most to me and I would like to thank Olwen for her love and curiosity, and Arron for his affection and humour – as well as for the cover design and all his help with the map, diagrams and photographs. Last, but always first in my life, I thank Aileen for her wonderful, enduring love and for reading me so well.

Tom Inglis
Dublin
May 2003

The Hayes family

The Hayes Family Farm
(Bought in 1907 by Robert Stack)

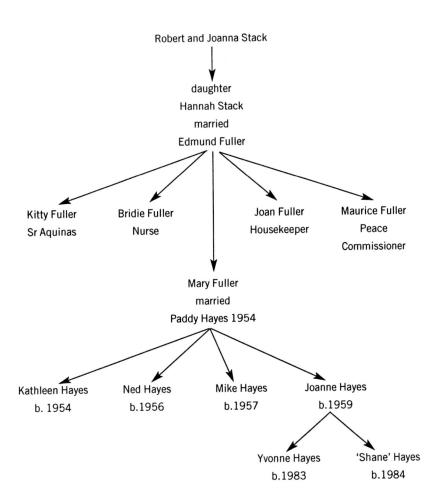

Robert and Joanna Stack

↓

daughter
Hannah Stack
married
Edmund Fuller

Kitty Fuller
Sr Aquinas

Bridie Fuller
Nurse

Joan Fuller
Housekeeper

Maurice Fuller
Peace
Commissioner

Mary Fuller
married
Paddy Hayes 1954

Kathleen Hayes
b. 1954

Ned Hayes
b.1956

Mike Hayes
b.1957

Joanne Hayes
b.1959

Yvonne Hayes
b.1983

'Shane' Hayes
b.1984

The Gardaí

Det. Superintendent John Courtney

Det. Sgt Gerry O'Carroll

Det. Sgt Joe Shelly

Det. Garda Vincent Flood*

Det. Garda P. J. Browne

Det. Garda John Harrington

Det. Garda Brendan McArdle

The Kerry Gardaí

Superintendent Daniel O'Sullivan
(Tralee and Kerry District)

Det. Sgt Timothy Callaghan
(Tralee)

Det. Sgt Paul Downey
(Killarney)

Sgt Paddy Reidy
(Cahirciveen)

Sgt Martin McCarthy
(Tralee)

Det. Garda Pat Casey
(Tralee)

Det. Garda Dan Coughlan
(Cahirciveen)

Det. Garda Con O'Sullivan
(Tralee)

Det. Garda John Sullivan
(Killarney)

Garda Liam Moloney
(Abbeydorney)

Garda Noel O'Connell
(Tralee)

Superintendent John Sullivan
(Cahirciveen)

Det. Sgt Kevin Dillon
(Tralee)

Sgt Mossie O'Donnell
(Ballyferriter)

Sgt Michael Coote
(Rathmore)

Det. Garda Stephen Brew
(Listowel)

Det. Garda Frank Considine
(Killarney)

Det. Garda Tim Mahony
(Tralee)

Det. Garda Michael Smith
(Tralee)

Garda Tim Collins
(Dingle)

Ban Garda Ursula O'Regan
(Tralee)

Garda John O'Connor
(Cahirciveen)

*Not granted legal representation by the Tribunal of Inquiry (see TR, p. 169)

Abbreviations

References to the following publications are given in the text in brackets:

TR   *Report of the Tribunal of Inquiry into The Kerry Babies Case* (Dublin: Government Publications, 1985).

TT   Transcripts of the Public Tribunal of Inquiry into the Case of the Kerry Babies. References take the following format: Day 7, page 64 is given as TT, 7/64.

CHAPTER ONE

Telling stories: truth is stranger than fiction

My mother told me to tell the truth and not to tell tales, but what happened in County Kerry in 1984 is an extraordinary story that will be recounted for generations to come. It is a mythical tale of people living in troubled times, when Catholic Ireland was yielding place to a new social order. It has all the hallmarks of a Greek tragedy – love, sex, birth, infanticide, scandal, shame, allegations, contestations, and courtroom drama. And yet it is a story about modern Ireland, about a people breaking free from a repressive culture of self-denial and the suppression of sexuality, to a culture of expression and self-fulfilment. It is easy to tell the story; it is harder to tell the truth about what actually happened.

The story has been told many times before.[1] It revolves around Joanne Hayes, a young woman making her way in the field of sex and romance, who falls in love with a married man. How do we understand her passionate affair, lived out in rural Catholic Ireland? Contraceptives were out of the question, though in any case she wanted his children as well as his love. She stood well outside the traditional approach to marriage and the family. She became pregnant, but this ended in a silent, lonely miscarriage at work in June 1982. Soon she was pregnant again and this time gave birth to a daughter, Yvonne. Joanne Hayes was not the classic Irish single mother. She was different. She did not hide away or give up her baby for adoption. She went public. She continued to live on the family farm and reared her daughter with her widowed mother, spinster aunt, two bachelor brothers, and single sister. How do we see and understand such a bold and transgressive figure? How was she seen and understood then?

Things then began to go horribly wrong. When she became pregnant for the third time, she was effectively abandoned by her lover. This time she reverted to type and behaved as a traditional woman who had become pregnant outside marriage. There was no pride or joy, only shame. She did not go to the doctor. She hid her bulging stomach behind large, bulky clothes. Her family all lived the same lie, saying nothing to each other. How can you describe the forces that drive people to live in silence, ignominy and shame?

Sometime late on Thursday night 12 April 1984, all hell broke loose. She went into labour. What exactly happened after this is not known. She insists that she left the house around midnight and gave birth to a baby boy alone in a field. She said that she broke the umbilical cord with her hands, and that the afterbirth came very soon after. She said she was very confused about what happened next, but she tried to stop the baby from crying, and the baby died. She went back to her bedroom. The next morning she got up early, went outside and placed the body of the dead baby in a couple of plastic bags. She walked some distance from the house and put the body in a water hole.

Whatever happened that night was the beginning of an emotional storm that would rock not just Joanne and her family, but the whole of Irish society. What was supposed to be another quiet, concealed pregnancy and birth – a traditional Irish solution to the problem of sex outside marriage – became a national scandal. The following day, the body of another newborn baby was found stabbed to death near Cahirciveen, about fifty miles away from the Hayes farm in Abbeydorney. Two weeks later on 1 May 1984, Joanne Hayes and her family were brought in for questioning by the Murder Squad, an elite corps of the gardaí (the Irish police) based in Dublin. Within twelve hours, Joanne Hayes and members of her family had given signed statements confessing to the murder of the Cahirciveen baby. In the early hours of the following morning, at a hastily arranged court hearing, Joanne Hayes was charged with the murder of her newborn baby boy. Her aunt, brothers and sister were charged with the concealment of the birth of the baby and of helping to dispose of its body.

Later that day, the body of Joanne Hayes's baby was found on the farm. The gardaí, never doubting the reliability or veracity of the confessions, concluded that she must have given birth to twins. Subsequent blood tests showed, however, that the two dead babies had different blood groups. The gardaí devised different theories to explain this. The preferred theory was that Joanne Hayes had sex with two men with different blood groups within a short time and became impregnated by both. While the Murder Squad wanted to pursue the case, the Director of Public Prosecutions insisted that it should be dropped. The charges against the Hayes family were withdrawn in October 1984. But Don Buckley, a freelance journalist, had received a copy of the

Garda File and Report. He and Joe Joyce wrote a major piece about the case in *The Sunday Independent*. This snowballed into a major media investigation. Eventually, following the failure of two internal garda inquiries, the government decided to hold a public tribunal of inquiry. It was expected to last six weeks; it lasted six months. When the Tribunal Report was published in October 1985, it criticised the gardaí for the way they handled the case, but ultimately exonerated them from any wrongdoing, particularly from extracting confessions through any form of abuse or intimidation. On the other hand, the Tribunal castigated members of the Hayes family as liars and perjurers and essentially blamed them for everything that had happened to them.

And so a private, tragic story from Kerry became part of national history. It is not just a story about Joanne Hayes, but of Irish society in the 1980s. The past may be a foreign country; things might have been done differently then. But to understand who we are today, to understand contemporary Irish society, we have to reflect critically on how the past is embodied in us. For this is not just the story of one unfortunate woman. It is a story about Irish women, about honour and shame, about Ireland awakening from the Catholic Church's monopoly over sexual morality, about the state and what happens when people turn a blind eye to the way the police operate, of the way the legal field operates, and of the synergy between police, lawyers and judges. This case reveals the way the established orders in society produce truth, and how the state symbolically dominates society through maintaining a monopoly over the means of producing the truth. It also demonstrates how the truth produced by state functionaries can be resisted and challenged. In Foucault's terms, power produces knowledge; consequently institutions and experts who claim to speak the truth should be treated with wariness and critical reflection. Most of all this is a story about modern Ireland and its painful transition from a deeply conservative and traditional society to one that is liberal, modern and deeply individualist.

Stories, Kearney tells us, are 'as basic to human beings as eating'. They are what 'make our lives worth living'. They give answers to 'the great unanswerable questions of existence: Who are we? Where do we come from?'[2] Ireland has a rich tradition of storytelling. Much of what is known about Irish social history comes from personal stories, mythical tales, songs and poems. These stories provide a knowledge and understanding of ordinary people and their struggles to survive. They are stories of fantastic characters, great escapades, noble deeds and extraordinary feats. The ordinary becomes extraordinary. Over time, these tales become the means by which people read and understand themselves and the world in which they live. They are parables.[3] Many mythical tales are about how ordinary people became heroes, fell on bad times, and became the victims of cruel and evil men. They are moralistic in their reminders of the frailty of the human condition, of the beauty, vagaries and cruelty of life, of how power and powerlessness corrupt (for example, people who do not have power are often forced to lie, cheat and steal to survive) and how continually reliving the past is necessary to avoid repeating its mistakes.

As part of the preliminary research for this study, Eoin O'Mahony and I conducted a telephone survey of over a hundred people throughout the country selected randomly from the Register of Electors (see Appendix for a description of the survey and the findings). What is remarkable about the results is how many people remembered the case, how much they remembered, and the often strong opinions they expressed about it. The survey results demonstrate that the Kerry babies story has become inscribed in memory, working at the level of feelings and emotions. It is part of a generation's collective memory and consciousness which, in turn, is a primary ingredient for any story to become mythical.

Stories of ordinary people

The stories told about Ireland tend to revolve around great men – Tone, Emmet, O'Connell, Parnell, Pearse, Collins, de Valera – who have attained mythical status. They fought the heroic struggles that shaped the course of Irish history. All of this fits in with the mythical view that great men make great history. It places the emphasis on human agency, and leaves aside structural forces such as state, church, gender and class, and long-term processes such as the development of capitalism. To counteract this mythical view, alternative stories are needed to present a different picture and understanding of life, of men and of power. These alternative stories, which resist the dominant ideological interpretation, keep history and people alive. As Kearney puts it:

> Without mythology, our memories are homeless; we capitulate to the mindless conformism of fact. But if revered as ideological dogma, and divorced from the summons of reality, myth becomes another kind of conformism, another kind of death. That is why we must never cease to keep mythological images in dialogue with history. And that is why each society, each community, each nation, needs to go on telling stories, inventing and reinventing its mythic imaginary, until it brings history home to itself.[4]

Mythical figures are neither arbitrary nor without symbolic power. Myths reveal the past, but do so in a way that dominates the present. To overcome the symbolic domineering effects of myths, it is necessary to ensure that stories are told not just about the legitimate and powerful, but also about the ordinary, the dominated, and the illegitimate.

Biographies and autobiographies have a crucial function in telling different stories, creating different perspectives, and rewriting history. Foster, however, warns us to be careful. Personal stories tend to dramatise or romanticise the past. He argues that many contemporary Irish autobiographies are 'gauged for an audience in search of reaffirmation rather than dislocation – or enlightenment'. They are written 'in order to reconstruct the borders and defences which apparently protected our innocence before the onrush of the modern tide'.[5] Biographies written in a sociological manner can, however, help to overcome the gap between, on the one hand, structural descriptions and analyses of states, institutions and organisations and, on the other, the personal, subjective experiences of ordinary individuals. In other words, biographies can help link a macro perspective which emphasises the economic, political, social and cultural structures within which individuals live their lives, and personal accounts which reveal the logic of the thinking and practices of people's everyday lives.[6]

Telling the truth

The problem with telling stories is that they often become associated with telling tales or telling lies. This is because stories have more to do with meaning than truth.[7] Artistic licence allows characters and events to be embellished. But, as Kearney writes, 'if fiction is free to recreate the past *as it might have been* . . . history has an obligation to recount the past *as it actually was*'.[8] This raises issues central to the understanding of what happened in the Kerry babies case. The first is how can we determine 'the truth' of an historical event? This was the task of the Tribunal.

We can, for example, establish as fact that Joanne Hayes gave birth to a baby and that the baby died. But how the baby died became central to the way the Tribunal determined the facts of the case. Not only were there differences in what people said happened, but also in the way they described the same events. In describing an event, particularly in the context of police questioning or cross-examination in a court of law, much depends on who is talking, what is left unsaid and, within what is said, on the choice of words, and the way they are combined into sentences and an overall description.

This raises the fundamental difficulty of how events in the real world correspond with statements made about those events. For example, towards the end of the Tribunal Report, Mr Justice Lynch stated that Joanne Hayes 'did away with her baby'. This is a careful choice of words. It implies that she killed her baby, but that is not what he said. Moreover, his statement has to be read in the context of other statements, particularly the scientific evidence of the state pathologist, Professor John Harbison, who could not be certain in his post-mortem report that the Tralee baby found on the Hayes's farm had attained an independent existence.[9] This relates to another problem at the heart of understanding the Kerry babies case. Leaving aside the personalities involved, it was the Irish state that initiated the Tribunal and instructed Mr Justice Lynch to produce 'the truth' about what happened.

Three issues here relate to the central role of the state. First, the foundation of a state is dependent on its developing a monopoly of the legitimate means of violence, which it does primarily through the army and police. In an equally fundamental way, however, the state is also dependent on developing a monopoly over the means of producing the truth.[10] Second, the Kerry babies case was, in effect, about one arm of the state, the judiciary, producing the truth about another arm, the executive – in this case the police. The Tribunal found that while members of the Hayes family were liars and had perjured themselves giving evidence, the gardaí were credible and guilty of nothing more than exaggeration or 'gilding the lily'. This, I will argue, was because the gardaí were experienced in giving evidence in court and in being cross-examined. The Hayes family were completely ignorant of the juridical field, of the operation of the law, of the best way to present their case and to give evidence (see chapter 11). Third, and most importantly, the truth produced by the Tribunal has the force of law. What Mr Justice Lynch determined to be true, limited and controlled the production of other alternative, resistant truths. It limits our ability to reflect critically about what really happened then (see chapter 12). Is it possible to work within the official truth that has been produced, to provide an alternative version of events, without being sued?

Even if we manage to avoid being sued, there is still the problem of relativism. As we shall see, despite Mr Justice Lynch's pronouncements there are still two other versions of what happened – Joanne Hayes's and the gardaí's. They still insist that they told the truth. Does this mean that in producing an alternative version of events, we simply end up replacing one story with another?[11] Do we end up in a relativist *cul de sac* in which there are no standards of truth? The answer to these questions is an emphatic no. To arrive at a justifiable explanation of what happened we need to examine the mechanisms through which truth was extracted, the standards that were employed, see what was omitted and overlooked, and what other standards might also have been applied. Events like the Kerry babies case, as Kearney writes, pose the problem of how we move from individual testimonies about what happened to some collective understanding 'without succumbing to the illusion of some absolute scientific consensus'. He has advocated an ethic of discourse or free public discussion. Such an ethic

> could explore the necessary conditions for a narrative counting as historically true – for example consistency of memories, coherence of testimonies, credibility of witnesses, confirmation of referential evidence, public sharing of truth-claims, appropriateness of narrative genres, effectiveness of account, moral persuasiveness of justice-claims, etc. – while acknowledging that no one of these criteria is sufficient in itself.[12]

Such procedures can bring us closer to a shared understanding or consensus truth about what happened. I argue, however, that they have to be balanced by a critical reflection of why things happened the way they did. Such reflection can begin by putting the people and events into a broader social structural and long-term historical perspective. This is what lies at the heart of a sociological approach.

Sociology has its own ethics and standards, working at two ends of a continuum. At an abstract, general level it develops theories and concepts about society and social life. At a more concrete level, it makes and tests statements about the empirical world.[13] If I said that the number of Irish women who went to Britain for an abortion in 2001 was four times higher than it was in 1984, it would be a statement about the empirical world, which could be tested for validity and reliability. Had only abortions been counted in each case? Had miscarriages, for example, been included? Was the method used to gather the data accurate and reliable? That is, were the same questions used, or the same records kept in different clinics and hospitals? Once the measurement is made, links or correlations can be made between data – for example, whether the number of women from Kerry who had abortions was lower than in the rest of Ireland.[14]

Some theories and concepts about Irish social life cannot be tested in the same way. The social codes, manners, rules, strategies and tactics of everyday life for instance. These are very real[15] and have a material, constraining effect on people's lives, but are not amenable to measurement as are Irish women who have had abortions. To understand the Kerry babies case it is necessary to understand the facts of everyday life in Ireland and Kerry at the time, and the tactics employed in the struggles for power, love, friendship, honour and respect. We have to develop an understanding of the logic by which this tactical life operated. This understanding has to be linked to objective structures, particularly to the different fields of social life.[16] These fields – religion, sex, love, sport and law – have different languages, discourses and rules,[17] linked to different ways of reading and understanding social life which in turn create an almost automatic, often unreflective, way of speaking and behaving. The effect is that social fields such as religion produce practices that have their own *habitus* and logic.[18] In other words, one could say that the rules regarding sex outside marriage in Ireland in the 1980s could not be researched in the same way as gathering data about abortions, yet they were facts of life. They had a very real existence which limited and constrained people.

A sociological explanation of the Kerry babies case depends, then, on examining the validity and reliability of empirical statements as well as developing an understanding of sexuality, honour and shame, the rules of everyday social life, the nature of lying, the way the state operates, the role of the media, and so forth. The explanation in this book of what happened is different from that produced within the parameters and rules of the juridical field, as it is produced within the rules and strategies of sociology.[19]

Stories about Irish women

In order to prevent history going stale and what Kearney calls 'mindless conformism', it is important to tell stories which challenge the myth that great men have made Irish history. Part of this struggle involves producing stories about Irish women.[20]

It is no coincidence that many of these stories have emerged only in the last thirty years. It was the struggle for social, political and economic emancipation – the struggle against patriarchal conditioning – that enabled these stories to be told. Critical reflexivity and greater detachment are linked to the development of a relational perspective. Irish history is seen more in terms of changing relationships of power, dependency and domination.[21] To understand what happened to Joanne Hayes, it is necessary to understand the position of women in Irish society, how they were seen and understood, and the stories that were told about them.[22]

One of the few places where women did have power – albeit moral rather than political or economic – was in the home, as 'desexualised, quasi-divine' mothers.[23] Most women ended up as unpaid servants working in the kitchen of Irish social life, where they were expected to become living representations of Our Lady. It is no coincidence that women who succumbed to this sacred, mythical image were written out of history while those who challenged or vilified it, for example unmarried mothers, were often 'rescued from' society.[24]

Resisting dominant truths and challenging dominant methods of revealing sociological truths involve focusing on the lives of ordinary men and women. The practices and struggles of day-to-day living and of the structures of power within which people operate have to be considered.[25] This means looking at everyday life, and how people lived in their homes, schools, fields, workplaces, communities and the various institutions and organisations within which they operated.[26] Most important of all, it requires building a picture of women's position in social life, their values, beliefs, attitudes and practices and the tactics which they use in their daily struggles. This must include sexuality for, as Ward argues, it is through identifying the constraints placed on their sexuality in each historical period that women's true status in society can be measured.[27]

Telling stories about Irish women helps to create 'a distinctive sense of cultural self-identification and self-imagining'.[28] They can help to show, in C. Wright Mills's terms, the intricate connection between the pattern of our own lives and the course of history. We can only become fully aware of our own experiences and life chances by becoming aware of the experiences and life chances of others.[29] To know ourselves we have to face ourselves and what was done in the past. As Kearney concludes, sometimes, in some places, it is important to let go of history, at other times, in other places, it is important to remember the past in order to try to ensure that it never happens again.[30]

Retelling Irish history, then, necessitates critically reflecting and challenging the way women were seen and understood – how they were represented within Irish culture, particularly in religion, education and the mass media. The symbolic domination of women through the various stories told about them becomes embodied in a female habitus, that is the semi-automatic, second-nature way in which women are seen and understood. This habitus becomes central to the way women see and understand themselves, whether as compliant and docile, or transgressive and troublesome.[31]

To understand what happened to Joanne Hayes we have to explore this Irish female habitus and the way in which, traditionally, women had to be sexually attractive but modest, and how this was linked to being sexually available but chaste. Embodying this habitus, and the double standards of Irish sexuality, became central to being seen as a good woman, to succeeding in social and occupational life and to making a good marriage and home.[32] As Bourdieu pointed out, women are more inclined to adopt the legitimate and dominant language about themselves when they have to specialise in the logic of marriage and the sphere of consumption in order to advance socially.[33] In the last twenty years the traditional conception of Irish women has changed dramatically. Almost half married women work; more than three in ten women who give birth are not married.[34] The retelling of the past necessitates a rereading of events like the Kerry babies case in light of the present existential story of Irish women. To retell the story of Joanne Hayes is a reminder of what happened to a woman who resisted and challenged the female habitus of the time.

Stories about Ireland

The story of the Kerry babies provides an insight into the ordinary everyday life of rural life in Ireland towards the end of the twentieth century. A detailed, microscopic analysis of this particular case reveals and illuminates what was happening in the rest of Irish society at the time.[35] One of the unintended consequences of the Tribunal Inquiry and the books and articles written about the case is that they provide a wealth of ethnographic material about the hopes, concerns, interests and struggles of people living on a small farm. We can see how they are caught in changing times and circumstances. It gives us a picture of family and gender relations, of the way men dominate women, of how husbands and fathers dominate their wives and children, and of double standards in sexual relations. At the same time, we can see the tactics that women use to control men, how mothers control their sons and daughters, and sisters their brothers. However these struggles were resolved on a day-to-day basis, there were larger, historical processes at work which had been inherited from previous generations. None of the Hayes children married. This was not untypical behaviour; throughout the last century Ireland had one of the highest proportions of bachelors and spinsters in any Western society.[36]

We also gain an understanding of how structural transformations in Irish society, particularly the economic growth of the 1970s and the concomitant increase in employment opportunities, affected life on a small family farm. With more people finding work in local towns such as Tralee, farming became a part-time activity. Having a job brought new opportunities to consume, to venture out into the world and to explore new pleasures. It led to a transformation of self, of the way people read, understood themselves, their family and community. People who were able to hold on to jobs, particularly when the recession came in the 1980s, not only had a better income, they were also able to command greater respect, have themselves taken into account more seriously, and exert their will over others.

These social and economic changes were linked to changes in the wider culture. Irish society was becoming less formal and authoritarian. The gap between men and women and social classes was beginning to narrow. There was no longer the same sense of fear about challenging and resisting the authority of the established élites. The monopoly that the Catholic Church had developed over Irish morality through the nineteenth century and most of the twentieth began to fragment. There was still a very high level of belief and practice – up to nine in ten Catholics in rural Kerry would have attended Mass once a week in the 1980s. But young people were increasingly distancing themselves from the Church's moral teachings, particularly in relation to sexuality. They were beginning to make up their own minds about what was right and wrong. This was not an easy journey; it was full of contradictions, personal turmoil and family conflict. More young people might have begun to have sex before and outside marriage, but they were playing a high-risk game of pregnancy – a form of Irish roulette. Even if they wanted to use contraceptives, many chemists did not stock them and, even if they did, they were available only to married couples. If a woman became pregnant, abortion was not only illegal, but also – after the divorce referendum in 1983 – unconstitutional.

The Kerry babies case provides an insight into what it was like for a young woman in rural Ireland to fall in love with a married man, to become pregnant by him, and to give birth to his children. A tidal wave of change was taking place in relation to births outside marriage. The Victorian practice of locking away sexually deviant women and forcing them to give their babies up for adoption had probably reached a peak in the 1950s. Yet was still difficult for a single mother to avoid shame and attain honour and respect. It might have been possible with only one child, with blame being attributed to ignorance of the facts of life or being caught out by male charms, but two children would have suggested not just carelessness but wanton disregard for moral decency. The case also shows how sexually transgressive women in Ireland became isolated, marginalised and oppressed. It demonstrates how when shame became unbearable, when the stigma of being a single mother became insufferable, women were forced into lying about their condition, and how others shared and lived their lie. It also provides an understanding of how shame can so suddenly turn to anger and rage, ending in tragedy.

Half-hidden behind the Kerry babies case but essential to understanding it is the brutalisation of Irish society and the rise in violence and criminal activity that took place during the 1970s, some of which can be linked to the conflict in Northern Ireland. It shows what happens when there is a challenge to the state's monopoly over the means of violence, of how sections of the gardaí were not only given free rein to deal with the rise in terrorism and violent crime, but also expected to achieve results. It shows what happens when a team of skilled interrogators, used to obtaining confessions, encounter people who have never been inside a police station, let alone rigorously questioned. We also gain an understanding of how the force of law operates in court; the legal rules and procedures, the legal mentality, the strategies of presenting the best case possible, giving evidence and dealing with cross-examination. It also shows the close connection between law and morality, not just in the formation of legislation, but in the enforcement and interpretation of the law. The law may, formally, be objective and impartial, but inevitably those who operate the law – judges, barristers and solicitors – have different social origins, are of different social class, and read, understand and interpret the world differently from most of those who appear before the court.

We also gain an understanding of the important role the media play as the fourth estate, as a watchdog over the state and public institutions. Without the investigative journalism that broke the story, and the rigorous pursuit of politicians, it is unlikely that the case would have ever gained public notoriety. Without the media, the Hayes family's allegations of abuse and intimidation against the gardaí might never have gone beyond the family and local community.

At a wider level, this story explains how the establishment and the structures and discourses of power operate, of how throughout history in times of crisis and rapid social change minorities and marginalised members of society are made into scapegoats and, in particular, how deviant women – especially those who are sexually transgressive – come to be designated, castigated and cast out as strange, exotic, others. There are many coincidences and unusual twists of fate in the Kerry babies case – two newborn babies being found dead around the same time and, more importantly, having different blood groups. Yet given the strategies by which states, organisations and those in power operate, it was no coincidence that an ordinary woman and her family were plucked from obscurity to become national figures.[37] To understand what happened, we have to understand how the forces and mechanisms of power, particularly of the state, produce and maintain the truth. But the Kerry babies story also shows how, through changing relationships, through increased equality between classes and the sexes, through critical reflection, and through retelling the story, we can relive the past, see how power elites and the state operated then, so that we do not make the same mistakes, and the will to truth can overcome the will to power.

The storyteller

There are two sides to storytelling. The first is that the storyteller is irrelevant. The story becomes a text that can be read, interpreted and understood independently of the intentions of the storyteller. The text becomes an independent record that speaks for itself. We do not need to know anything of the intentions of the author. The author, so to speak, is dead. Almost like tarot cards, the meaning of the story emerges from reading the way the words and sentences have been combined.[38]

One of the remarkable things about the Tribunal Report is that it does not read as a dry, legal document. Although the task of the Report is to relate the facts of the case, it has the narrative structure of a tragic love story. We are introduced to the Hayes family, and to Joanne Hayes. In the next chapter, 'The Affaire', we are introduced to Jeremiah Locke and the relationship that developed between him and Joanne Hayes at work. Love affairs are extremely difficult to describe, let alone analyse. How does one get inside the hearts and minds of the characters and disentangle the turmoil of emotions and feelings?

The important point to emphasise is that texts can be read and interpreted differently from the intentions of the author. But it is often important to know the interests of the author and from what social position he speaks. Mr Justice Lynch was interested in establishing the facts of the case. He was satisfied that his interpretation of the affair was beyond reasonable doubt. It is important to know the social position from which he writes. It is not so much that he is Kevin Lynch, a professional middle-aged, married man, living and working in Dublin, whose father came from County Kerry, but that he was a High Court Judge, that he operated within a legal field, that he wrote within a legal discourse, and that he had the power to declare the truth. I also have an interest in telling the truth.

My interest in telling this story

Like many others, I was taken aback when the reports of the Tribunal of Inquiry began to emerge. I followed these over the first few weeks, but began to lose interest once the technical scientific evidence began about winds, tides and currents, and when, day after day, each of the gardaí who gave evidence seemed to tell the same story. I was busy at the time writing *Moral Monopoly,* and soon after left sociology to work in adult education for a number of years. It was only when I returned to sociology in 1992 that I began to investigate the case in more detail. I cannot remember exactly when or why I became interested in the case. It may have been prompted by the publication of Paul O'Mahony's article.[39] At the time I was also beginning to think and write about Irish sexuality. It seemed to me that Irish sexuality had been avoided by sociologists, and that the Kerry babies case would be a good place to begin. The more I looked the more I discovered that the case raised many questions about the role of the police in society, particularly when the state's monopoly over violence is threatened. I soon realised that by looking at this one particular case in depth, whole aspects of Irish society began to emerge. It was a type of sociological DNA, as if an in-depth analysis of one event could reveal the mentality and structure of Irish society during the latter half of the twentieth century.[40]

There are other interests. One of the reasons I am a sociologist is to help me to understand how I came to be the way I am. In trying to understand myself, I try to understand the culture and society within which my sense of self became constituted. How have my nationality, gender, family, education, religion, class, suburban upbringing and the media influenced who I have become, the stories I tell about myself? But the stories of growing up in middle-class suburban Dublin during the 1950s and 1960s, going to university, becoming a lecturer in sociology are too obvious. There is much in how we look at and understand others that is ours, that reveals to us our sense of self. While Joanne Hayes and I grew up in the same Catholic Irish society, with much the same rules and practices, and although we both experienced the winds of liberal individualism sweeping through our lives, many would say we have little in common. However, to understand who I am, I have to understand the 'other' in my life – that which I am not.[41]

There is a notion that only women can fully understand what it is to be a woman, and that since men have for millennia symbolically dominated and colonised women, only women should write about women. I believe this to be false and dangerous. It is false because if we accept that gender is socially constructed – a story we tell about ourselves – then to understand our gender identity, we have to understand what we are not, and how we see and construct others. It is dangerous because if this is taken to its logical conclusion, only the Irish can understand the Irish, teenagers what it is to be a youth, and so forth. This is the slippery path to solipsism.

Throughout the book it will be evident that I have difficulty with the way Mr Justice Lynch constructed the truth about what happened. I believe that much of what he had to say about the case was right, but I also believe that much of what he said was wrong. Similarly, I believe that much of what other commentators and analysts had to say, including Joanne Hayes herself, was right, but that for various reasons they omitted some aspects and did not put the pieces of the story together in a way that I find satisfactory. I do not have any startling new revelations in this book. I am intrigued that the gardaí still insist on their version of the story, that Joanne Hayes still insists on her version, and that Mr Justice Lynch is adamant that he has told 'the truth' about what happened.

But there is a personal as well as sociological side to my interest in telling the story. My son Luke died after an accident in our home some years ago. In the days after his death I found myself telling the story of his death over and over to family, friends, colleagues and acquaintances. In constantly retelling the story, I came to understand better what had happened and to come to terms with it. Each time I told the story I realised I was highlighting a different aspect; something important had happened which I had previously missed or misjudged. I covered the same territory each time, but in a different way, from a different angle. No one version of the story was ever the same. There were some incidents which, like key ingredients, kept being included, but since they were never put together in the same way, never produced the same story. For a while I searched for the ultimate cause of the accident, but I soon abandoned the scientist's approach. I decided that even if I had carried out a microscopic analysis of the events and moments before his death, I would never discover the definitive truth about what happened. In fact, it seemed to me that concentration on the minute details – the positive empirical struggle to find out precisely what happened at each crucial moment – lessened my understanding about what had happened to me or my family.

Power produces knowledge and a coroner's inquest was held to discover the truth about what happened. This turned out to be a perfunctory legal exercise in which some ingredients of the story were selected and cast in stone as the state's recorded truth of what happened. It centred on the medical scientific description of the cause of death: coming down the stairs he had slipped from arms that held him; he had landed on the back of his head; he had started to bleed internally. It was the power of the state, using a positivist legal and scientific approach, which ultimately determined the publicly recorded truth about what happened. I realised in the days after the inquest that whereas power in general produces truths through the legal system, the state power, having a monopoly of the means of symbolic violence, produces 'the truth'.[42]

I also realised that the undermining and elimination of a hermeneutical, sociological, psychological understanding of what happened was not an accident. It was part of a much broader system of power in which truth, by being reduced to positivist scientific and legal truth, becomes absolute. The truth about what happened was defined by juridical power. But it was more than that. It was the way the legal proceedings seemed to ignore the personal, communal meaning and logic of what happened. It was, in Bourdieu's terms, a symbolically violent event in which the logic, understanding and practices concerning what had happened were supplanted by the force of law.[43]

I write, then, as a sociologist who is interested in the connection between power and knowledge, specifically about how power announces truth, and how we can develop an alternative, resistant truth. But like all those who have written before me about this case and sought to seek its truth, I am constrained by my social position, by the logic and fallacy of scholasticism and by the theoretical and methodological approach I use.

This, then, is a sociological biography. It is a story about what happened to a woman and her family, about how the state entered their lives. It is told in the belief that a microscopic description and analysis of this story, of what happened in one event in Irish history, can illuminate what happened to the whole of Irish society during the latter half of the twentieth century. In the first half of the book, I tell the story up to the beginning of the Tribunal. I then tell the story as developed by the Hayes family during the Tribunal. This is followed by the case presented by the gardaí to the Tribunal. I complete the first part by describing and analysing the events as constructed by Mr Justice Lynch. These various versions of the story are problematic. Who is telling the truth about what happened? Maybe we cannot reach any conclusion beyond there being nothing more than different versions of the same story, including this socio- logical one. Maybe all we end up doing is telling stories. But not only do I believe that some stories are better than others, I also believe in telling the truth.

PART I

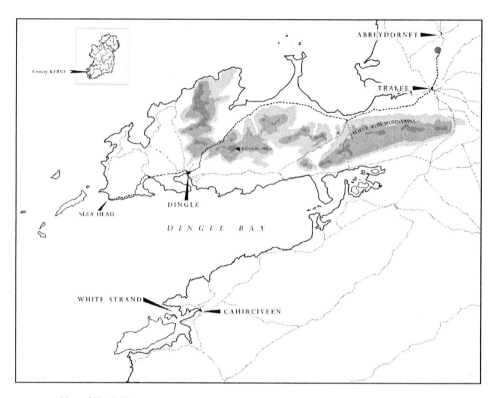

Map of North Kerry

CHAPTER TWO

The investigation

The Kerry babies, if you like, was a catharsis, it was symptomatic of a dead Ireland, of an Ireland that no longer exists in such a short period of time. It was a witch hunt, and I was a victim of a witch hunt as some of my colleagues were. (Former Det. Sgt Gerry O'Carroll on *The Joe Duffy Show*, RTÉ Radio 1, 22 January 2001)

Finding the Cahirciveen baby

On Saturday evening, 14 April 1984, John Griffin went out for a run. He lived near White Strand in Cahirciveen, County Kerry. He was a part-time farmer and part-time builder. That afternoon he had been helping to build a new Garda Station in Cahirciveen. He was a member of the local athletic club. He combined running with keeping an eye on his cattle.

It was shortly after eight o'clock in the evening. He ran down to the water's edge. It was getting late and the light was fading. As he came to the end of the small strand, he noticed something caught in the rocks. It looked odd, but he kept running. He thought it was a doll. But the hair looked different. After he had checked on his cattle, he went back to have a closer look. The doll looked more like the body of an infant. He looked, but did not want to touch. He decided to get help. He ran two miles over to his brother-in-law, Brendan O'Shea's house. The two men drove back down to the beach.

As they stood looking at the body in the moonlight, they were still not certain what they had found. The baby was lying face down, wedged in between the rocks. They wondered how it got there. They looked around and saw a grey fertiliser bag lying on the beach close by. There were two other bags inside it. They decided to go to the gardaí in Cahirciveen.

Garda Enda McGill was in charge of the Cahirciveen Garda station that night. When Griffin and O'Shea reported their finding, he asked Garda Pat Collins to go back with them to White Strand. Garda Collins examined the body. He noticed that there were two black marks on the baby's back, but since it was facing down he could not tell if it was male or female. He also noticed that the bag was for 0-7-30 fertiliser, that it was tied at the top, but had a hole in the bottom. Inside the fertiliser bag, he could see a brown plastic shopping bag, and another clear plastic bag.[1] Garda Collins told Griffin and O'Shea to return home while he waited for Sergeant (Sgt) Patrick Reidy.

Sgt Reidy was at home enjoying his evening off watching television when Garda McGill phoned. In fact he and his wife had been out with their dog earlier that afternoon on White Strand. Reidy phoned the local undertaker Tom Cournane and suggested that he collect him at the station. The two men drove to White Strand in Cournane's ambulance. They dislodged the baby from the rocks and wrapped it in a white sheet. They placed the body on the stretcher they had brought. On the way back to the ambulance, they crossed a small stream. Cournane stopped. He took the baby off the stretcher and, pulling back the white sheet, knelt down. He dipped his hand in the stream and with the river water he baptised the dead baby boy, declaring out loud, 'I baptise thee in the Name of the Father, the Son and the Holy Spirit. I call thee John.'[2]

It was not unusual to find plastic bags, dead dogs or even human remains on the beach. A woman once found a frogman's flipper with a sock still attached to it. When she took it home to show her children, she discovered bones inside the sock. The guards traced the flipper and sock to a diver on Valentia Island who had drowned seven years previously. It had taken seven years to travel the two or three hundred yards from Valentia Island to White Strand.[3]

Tom Cournane and Sgt Reidy took the body of the baby boy back to Cournane's Funeral Home in Cahirciveen. On the way, they discussed what they had found. Since Jack Griffin had said the body of the baby was dry when he first discovered it, they assumed that it had originally been in the fertiliser bag, but had broken free when the bag was holed on the rocks. When they got back to the funeral home they noticed cuts and marks on the chest of the baby. At first they thought that these might have been caused by birds or sea creatures, but some of the cuts were deep and looked more like wounds. Sgt Reidy went back to the station and contacted his superiors in Tralee and Dublin. He was told that the State Pathologist, Dr John Harbison, was nearby in County Cork. It was arranged that he would carry out a post-mortem in the Isolation hospital in Killarney. Sgt Reidy and Cournane took the body there on Sunday morning.

Dr Harbison began his examination at noon. Four hours later he concluded that the baby had died from 28 stab wounds, four on the right side of the neck, twelve on the front of the neck, and twelve on the chest. The most important were two large wounds to the chest where the heart had been stabbed. The baby had also sustained a broken neck. The air passages were not obstructed and there was no evidence of strangulation, but there was evidence of internal bleeding and this suggested that the baby's neck had been broken while it was still alive. Harbison noted the absence of blood in the chest cavity. This was unusual given the number of stab wounds. He decided that this was probably due to the body lying face down in the sea for some time. On the other hand, the absence of excessive water indicated that the baby had not drowned. He believed that the wounds had been caused by a sharp pointed knife or stiletto type instrument. The number and nature of the wounds suggested that they had been inflicted during a panic frenzy. Experience suggested that it was a case of infanticide and that it was probably carried out by the child's own mother in a temporary state of derangement. The umbilical cord had been cut flush with the skin. This contravened standard medical practice – there would be no room for a clamp in the event of unexpected bleeding – and indicated that the birth had not occurred under medical supervision. However, the baby had been washed. Harbison estimated that the baby had been born three or four days prior to his examination, and had died within a day or so of its birth. He took samples of muscle and lung tissue from the baby. These would be needed if it was necessary to establish definitively that the baby had not drowned. He did not take a blood sample.[4]

Reidy and Cournane took the body back to Cahirciveen. The next morning, Monday 16 April, Cournane phoned the local scout leader and the local convent. At four o'clock, the small white coffin was taken to the cemetery. The funeral cortege was followed by hundreds of local schoolchildren. Wreaths were placed on the grave. They came from the local girl guides and boy scouts, and from pupils in the local Christian Brothers' School. A simple plastic cross was placed on the grave with the inscription 'In memory of Me, The Kerry Baby'.[5]

The investigation begins

Later that evening the gardaí held their first conference. The gardaí in Kerry had encountered cases of infanticide and abandoned babies many times before. Under the Infanticide Act 1949, the deliberate killing of a newborn baby was a criminal offence.[6] However, the custom and practice in County Kerry was for women who were admitted to hospital and seemed to have given birth, but denied having done so, to be treated sympathetically, quietly and discreetly.[7] But this was obviously a brutal murder which had to be treated differently.

There was no obvious immediate family that could be linked to the dead baby. It was decided to carry out a house-to-house inquiry in Cahirciveen town, and within a half-mile radius of White Strand. A questionnaire was drawn up to discover if there were any likely suspects in the wider county area and 1,500 copies were distributed. Doctors, nurses, midwives and social workers in the South Kerry area were contacted and interviewed. It was also decided to check out and compile a register of all those known to be involved in extra-marital affairs, single women with children, and members of families in which there were violence or known instances of incest. The small red car which Jack Griffin had seen leaving White Strand on the Saturday evening turned out to belong to a husband and wife from Cork who had been touring the Kerry area at the time. The fertiliser bag was discovered to be one of 100,000 manufactured in Cork in November 1981.

In technical terms, the investigation centred on identifying and tracking down 'any woman who might have been pregnant and who was no longer pregnant and to the whereabouts of whose baby there was uncertainty'. (TR, p. 28) The gardaí learnt of a woman in such circumstances. When they called at her house they discovered that she had given birth to a baby with her mother's assistance and that all three were alive and well, although living in very poor circumstances.

> This girl was therefore also eliminated as a suspect for responsibility for the Cahirciveen Baby and the only matter which remained to be done in relation to her was to notify the doctor, the Public Health Nurse, the Priest, and the Local Housing Authority that they urgently required assistance and better housing. (TR, p. 28)

This shows how close was the relationship between state agencies, particularly gardaí, doctors, public health nurses and social workers. The gardaí do not act solely as law enforcement officers. They often act in a social welfare capacity. Indeed, during the Tribunal, Garda Liam Moloney said that he saw himself as a social worker and in his view this was very good for police duty. This also demonstrates that the gardaí investigating the crime were not hostile to unmarried mothers; rather they were sympathetic to their plight, particularly when they withdrew from society and behaved in a suitably remorseful manner, even when they abandoned or killed their babies. It is also interesting to note how, almost automatically, the local priest was seen to be part of the rescue service. All of this is important as it gives a clear picture of how *local* mechanisms of power operated in Ireland at that time. What happened, of course, is that *state* mechanisms of power became involved, with devastating consequences.

The investigation also included gardaí checking out hospitals in County Kerry. When Garda Noel O'Connell called at St Catherine's Hospital in Tralee on Tuesday 14 April, Joanne Hayes was in one of the wards. Staff at the hospital were suspicious that Joanne Hayes was not telling the truth; they had encountered similar cases before. As they saw it, she might have been living in denial about being pregnant, she might have given birth in tragic, traumatic circumstances. They felt she needed time and space. They also considered themselves more competent at helping her to talk and thus find out what had happened. Consequently they told Garda O'Connell that they had no patient who fitted the description of the woman he was looking for.[8] Unsurprisingly given the reaction of medical staff in St Catherine's, the investigation was not making much progress. In rural Ireland, particularly in County Kerry, there has always been ambivalence about helping the gardaí with certain types of crime, notably those involving close-knit families and communities. There is a gap between the public and the private, between the state and the local community. It is as if the local community decides the issues on which the state has jurisdiction in their area.

The investigation was not helped by the fact that when a questionnaire arrived at the local garda station in Abbeydorney – where the Hayes family lived – asking whether there were any suspects in the area, Garda Liam Moloney replied 'nil'. This was despite the fact that he knew that Joanne Hayes was having an affair with Jeremiah Locke, that she had given birth to a child by him and that, again acting more as a social worker, he had called out to see her house to plead with her to stop the affair. Did Garda Moloney simply not make any connection between Abbeydorney and an event in Cahirciveen fifty miles away, or was he too living in denial and somehow, perhaps unconsciously, protecting his own patch?

The Murder Squad

There were many coincidences in the Kerry babies case, and it was perhaps coincidence that led Detective Superintendent John Courtney and the Murder Squad to become involved in a case of infanticide. The Murder Squad was the name given to the Investigation Section of the Garda Technical Bureau. The Bureau is based in Garda Headquarters in Phoenix Park in Dublin. It consists of scientific and technical experts in forensics, fingerprinting, photography and mapping. The Investigation Section was a body of detectives specialising in tracking down and interrogating people suspected of having committed serious crimes.

Superintendent Courtney was from Kerry. He had been home on leave in Anascaul the weekend the Cahirciveen baby was found. He had talked about the case with Det. Sgt Mossie O'Donnell, a close friend who was on the investigating team. He suggested to O'Donnell that when sending out the questionnaire it would be a good idea to ask whether any local girls living in Dublin had been home that weekend. When he returned to Dublin he discussed with a superior the idea of sending someone from the Murder Squad to help in the investigation. It was agreed that Det. Sgt Joe Shelly would go down. He was accompanied by Det. Garda John Harrington whose role in murder investigations was primarily administrative. Two days later, they were joined by Det. Sgt Gerry O'Carroll – from Listowel, County Kerry and second in command to Superintendent Courtney – and by Det. Garda P.J. Browne, a leading figure in the Murder Squad, also from Listowel. The case of the Cahirciveen baby's murder led to the involvement of the three senior members of the Murder Squad, all based in Dublin, but all originally from Kerry. It might have been the case that the Cahirciveen murder was so unusual and so brutal that regardless of any other commitments it would have attracted the involvement of the Murder Squad. Or it might have been that the leaders of the Murder Squad felt that such a violent crime was an evil that they could not tolerate, especially in their own back yard. Whatever the reason for their involvement, it immediately shifted the investigation down a different track and into a higher gear. If the Murder Squad had not become involved, the case would probably have been left unsolved, or quietly resolved among the local players in the grey area between health, social welfare and law enforcement.

As soon as the detectives arrived from Dublin there was an improvement in the procedures used and the records kept in the investigation. The terms of the search for suspects changed. It now included any female who had left the area since the incident. Assistance was to be sought from local clergy who were asked to make an announcement from the pulpit the following Sunday. Then three days after Shelly and Harrington arrived there was a breakthrough. When Det. Sgt Kevin Dillon contacted St Catherine's Hospital on Friday 27 April, he was told that Joanne Hayes had been admitted after apparently having a miscarriage. The doctors, however, believed that she had given birth.[9]

That night, Murder Squad detectives O'Carroll and Shelly drove from Cahirciveen to Tralee Hospital. They examined the evidence against Joanne

Hayes. She was saying that she had had a miscarriage although a scan indicated that she had given birth to a full-term baby. But there was no baby. They went with Sgt Dillon to Abbeydorney and spoke to Garda Liam Moloney.

Joanne Hayes was a single woman who lived with her mother Mary, her sister Kathleen, her brothers Ned and Mike and her aunt Bridie in their family farm on the Abbeydorney to Tralee road. The family had lived in Abbeydorney for generations. Joanne Hayes was 25 years old. She had started work as a receptionist in the Sports Centre in Tralee in 1978, the same year Garda Liam Moloney came to work in Abbeydorney. For the first year or more, he used to call out to the Hayes house to get Maurice Fuller, who was a Peace Commissioner, to witness or sign documents. Liam Moloney told the others that it was well known that Joanne Hayes had been having an affair with Jeremiah Locke, the groundsman at the Sports Centre. He was a married man, four years older than Joanne. Joanne Hayes had a daughter Yvonne who had been born the previous May. Everyone knew that Jeremiah Locke was the father.

Liam Moloney phoned the house and was told that Joanne Hayes was in hospital and had lost her baby. More than ever before, Joanne Hayes became the prime suspect. It was at this stage that Superintendent Courtney, Head of the Murder Squad, was asked to come down from Dublin and join the investigation.

Later that night, detectives Dillon and O'Donnell spoke to John Creedon, the consultant gynaecologist at St Catherine's Hospital. He gave little away, spoke of patient confidentiality, and refused them access to the medical records. But the two detectives did not give up. They interviewed him again on the following Saturday and Sunday. He told them that there was strong evidence that Joanne Hayes had given birth to a baby. But he was very doubtful about making any connection between Joanne Hayes and the Cahirciveen infanticide. He told them that they were on the wrong track.

Superintendent Courtney arrived in Tralee on Sunday 29 April with Det. Garda P.J. Browne. By the time they arrived, there were five other members of the Murder Squad already in Kerry. As well as O'Carroll, Shelly, and Harrington, there were Vincent Flood from the Photography section and Brendan McArdle from Ballistics. The evidence seemed fairly conclusive. Despite her protestations of having a miscarriage, Joanne Hayes had almost definitely given birth to a baby. But there was no evidence or mention of a baby, nor had there been any funeral.

With the emergence of Joanne Hayes as the primary suspect, the centre of the investigation moved from Cahirciveen to Tralee. When Superintendent Courtney arrived in Kerry, he and the Murder Squad effectively took control of the investigation. At the case conference that evening in Tralee Garda Station, he briefed local detectives and gardaí about the case. Arrangements were made for a swoop on the Hayes family farm the following morning, and on the Sports Centre in Tralee where Joanne Hayes had returned to her work the previous day. Decisions were made as to who was to be interviewed by whom, when and where. Nobody was going to be arrested. The Hayes family and Jeremiah Locke were being asked to help the gardaí with their inquiries. Superintendent Courtney warned everyone about the delicate nature of the investigation and the sensitivity required when questioning the various members of the family.

The interrogation

Shortly after noon on 1 May 1984, Joanne Hayes and Jeremiah Locke were brought in separate cars into Tralee Garda Station. Their questioning began almost immediately. Meanwhile, out at the Hayes farm, Joanne Hayes's brothers Ned and Mike were brought into Tralee along with their Aunt Bridie, all in separate cars. Mary Hayes and her other daughter Kathleen stayed in the farmhouse with Joanne's young baby daughter Yvonne. Det. Garda Dan Coughlan and Det. Garda Stephen Brew stayed with them. Later, Kathleen Hayes was brought first to Abbeydorney Garda Station and then, from there, to the station in Tralee.

Jeremiah Locke

Jeremiah Locke

As well as being a groundsman in the Sports Centre in Tralee, Jeremiah Locke leased a 35-acre farm with a local man. They kept sheep and horses. He had married a local girl, Mary Kenny, in 1980. They lived in a housing estate outside Tralee on the road to Abbeydorney. They had two children: Thomas was born in June 1982; the second child had been born on 25 April 1984, a week after the Cahirciveen baby was found. Since Jeremiah Locke was suspected of being the father of the dead baby, it was thought that he might have been involved in the murder and in transporting the body to

Cahirciveen. He was interviewed by Sgt Mossie O'Donnell and Sgt Downey. For two and a half hours Locke was asked about his involvement with Joanne Hayes and whether he was involved in driving the body to Cahirciveen. But he kept insisting that the only thing he knew about the case was that Joanne had told him that she had lost her baby in hospital. It gradually became apparent to the detectives that while Jeremiah Locke was being open about his affair with Joanne Hayes, he knew little or nothing about the birth and death of her baby.

Joanne Hayes

The first person to interview Joanne Hayes was the local policeman, Garda Liam Moloney. He was on his own. Part of the overall strategy was to use local Kerry gardaí rather than members of the Murder Squad to conduct the first interviews with all members of the family. The interview began around 12.35 p.m., and at first Joanne Hayes told Liam Moloney that she had had a miscarriage at home on Thursday evening, 12 April. She kept insisting on this until she broke down. They were joined by Ban Gharda Ursula O'Regan. Around 1.25 p.m. Joanne Hayes admitted for the first time she had given birth to a baby boy. 'I had the baby boy at home. I delivered the baby myself on the 12/4/'84. I panicked and hid it. The baby is dead, I buried it at home.'* She was then cautioned. Shortly after she made this statement, Superintendent Courtney came into the room. Joanne Hayes told him that Moloney and O'Regan were trying to blame her for the Cahirciveen baby's murder. But like Moloney and O'Regan, as well as not believing her story about having a miscarriage, Superintendent Courtney did not now believe her story about the dead baby being wrapped in plastic bags and hidden on the farm. He told her to tell the truth. Ten minutes later, Joanne Hayes made another statement.

> On Thursday night 12/4/'84 sometime around 1/2 eleven or Twelve o'clock, I gave birth to a baby boy of six to seven months in a field at my brother's farm. I delivered the baby myself with my own hands. I delivered the baby standing up. I panicked and then I put the baby down on some hay. I went in home and said nothing. I went to bed and couldn't sleep. I got up at 5 a.m. I sat down and had some tea and went back to bed until 7.30 a.m. I got up and went out to the baby. I put my baby into a blue and white plastic bag I think it was a bag from O'Carroll's Chemist, in Tralee. I then put the baby into a brown paper bag first

---

*Extracts from the statements made by members of the Hayes family have been taken from the Tribunal Report. Spelling and grammatical errors have not been corrected.

and then into the plastic bag, I mean. I put the baby down in the river, its a pool of water. (TR, pp. 198–9)[10]

The gardaí did not believe her. They were looking for an admission from Joanne that the Cahirciveen baby was hers. They wanted to know how the baby died and how the body got from Abbeydorney to Cahirciveen.

Joanne Hayes

Joanne kept on insisting that she had given birth alone in the field. She kept pleading with her interrogators to let her go and she would take them to the pool. At 2.30 p.m. Liam Moloney, with Brendan McArdle from the Murder Squad, went out to the family farm to look for the baby. They were replaced in the interrogation room by Det. Sgt Gerry O'Carroll and Det. Garda P. J. Browne of the Murder Squad. Joanne Hayes kept repeating the story of having given birth alone in the field, of the baby dying, and how she went back inside the house and had left the body outside until around 7.30 a.m. Then when she went back out to the field, she put the baby in the plastic bags, walked down the field, climbed over a gate with a bedstead and put the bags with the body in a pool of water. Again Joanne Hayes asked to be allowed to go to the farm to show the detectives where she had hidden the baby. But permission was refused; Superintendent Courtney was almost 100 per cent certain in his own mind that Joanne Hayes was the mother of the Cahirciveen baby and responsible for its death. He did not want any respite in the interrogation which might prevent him from obtaining a confession. The main reason perhaps was that Joanne's brother Ned had in the meantime given a confession which directly implicated her in the Cahirciveen murder.

Ned Hayes

Ned Hayes was 27 years old. He was unemployed. He had worked as driver in Kiely's Bakery in Abbeydorney and in Fitzgerald's wholesale drinks firm in Tralee. He was involved in amateur drama, read literature, and studied history. He was on the local GAA selection committee. He liked a few pints. He was the only one to have previously been inside Tralee Garda Station, having being caught and charged with drink-driving some months previously. Along with his mother and sister Kathleen, he lived in the Hayes's county council cottage about a hundred yards away from the farmhouse. On the night the Tralee baby was born he had been on his own in the cottage. His mother and Kathleen were staying up in the farmhouse.

Ned Hayes was interviewed by Det. Sgt Dillon and Det. Garda Mahony. At the beginning, Ned denied any knowledge of Joanne being pregnant, having a miscarriage, or a baby. He then admitted that his mother had told him three months previously that Joanne was pregnant. Around 2.30 p.m., they said he suddenly declared that 'whatever happened, happened in the house'. Then he went silent for fifteen minutes and eventually said 'I will tell the truth. Alright, I know she had a baby'. He began to describe what happened and, most importantly, made references to the baby being stabbed and the body taken to Slea Head to be dumped in the sea; this directly linked what had happened in the Hayes family home that night to the Cahirciveen baby.

The search at the Hayes Farm

Meanwhile Garda Liam Maloney and Det. Garda Brendan McArdle had searched the fields at the back of the Hayes farmhouse. They had found nothing. When they arrived back, they were instructed to go out and conduct another search. Because of what Ned Hayes had been saying, however, the focus of the search this time was in and around the house. Again they found nothing. O'Carroll and Browne confronted Joanne Hayes, telling her that while they accepted she had had a baby, she was not telling the truth about where it was and how it had died. The failure of the searches convinced them that Joanne Hayes was the mother of the Cahirciveen baby.

At around 8 p.m. there was a dramatic development. Detectives Smith and Coote, who had been out in the Hayes farmhouse interviewing Mrs Hayes, arrived into the room where Joanne Hayes was being questioned. They had with them the family carving knife, a bath brush and a turf bag. Joanne Hayes became hysterical. O'Carroll said that she shouted out that she was insane, a murderess, that she had stabbed the baby with the knife, that she had beaten it with the bath brush and that the baby was taken away in a turf bag similar to the one she had been shown. Not long afterwards, O'Carroll and Browne began to take Joanne Hayes's second statement:

The Hayes farm at Abbeydorney. A – where Joanne claimed she had given birth to the baby. B – where the Tralee baby was found.

I am cautioned that I am not obliged to say anything unless I wish to do so but anything that I do say will be taken down in writing and maybe given in evidence. I started to go out with Jermiah Locke who worked in the Sports J.H. Centre in Tralee with me as a groundsman. I knew he was married. Its exactly the 26th October, 1981 I first started to go out with him. He told me that he wasn't getting on with his wife. I fell deeply in love with him, and we were very intimate from the very beginning. Around May, 1982 I became pregnant by Jermiah but around the Bank-Holiday in June I think it was the Sunday I lost the baby. I wanted to be pregnant. I thought from the beginning that Jermiah Locke would go away with me and that we would live together happily ever after. I remained going out with Jermiah and on the 19th May, 1983 I had a baby girl in St. Catherins Hospital in Tralee. I called the baby Yvonne. I still thought that Jermiah would go away with me especially after having the baby for him. Jermiah only saw Yvonne twice and that also upset me. I stayed going out with Jermiah and I still loved him and he said he loved me and that he might go away with me eventually. I became pregnant again for him last year and I had my last period in August, 1983. My mother and all the lads at home were upset about the first baby, but they accepted it and they decided to help me to rear it. They were all very upset when I became pregnant again and I was thoroughly and absolutely ashamed of myself and I tried to hide it. I wore tight clothes and I tried not to let it show. On the 12th/13th April, 1984 I was at home in the farmhouse in my own room, the baby Yvonne was in the cot. Sometime during the night I started to go into Labour and a baby boy was born. I was in my own bed in my own room in the old farmhouse. My Auntie Bridie Fuller was present at the birth and delivered the baby. Michael my brother was in the house at the time. The baby was alive and crying and my Auntie Bridie placed him at the end of the bed. She left the room to make a pot of tea and I got up and went to the toilet. On the way back to the bedroom I picked up the white Bath Brush and I went to the cabinet in the kitchen and picked up the Carving knife with the brown timber handle. These are the items i.e. the White Bath Brush and the Brown Timber-handled carving knife, I have been shown here today by Detective Garda Smith and Coote. I went back to the bedroom and I hit the baby on the head with the Bath Brush. I had to kill him because of the shame it was going to bring on the family and because Jeremiah Locke would not run away and live with me. The baby cried when I hit it and I stabbed it with the carving knife on the chest and all over the body. I turned the baby over and I also stabbed him in the back. The baby stopped crying after I stabbed it. There was blood every where on the bed and there was also blood on the floor. I then threw the knife on the floor. My Mother, Auntie Bridie, Kathleen my sister and my two brothers Ned and Mike ran into the bedroom. I was crying and so was my Mother, my sister Kathleen and my Auntie Bridie. I told them I would have to get rid of the body of the baby and then my two brothers said they would bury it. I told them to take away the baby from the farmyard and they said they would. Everyone was panicking at this stage. The boys then brought in a white plastic bag and they put the baby into it and then they put this bag into a turf bag similiar to the one Detectives Smith and Coote showed me earlier on this evening at the Station. The boys then left in our own car with the baby. I heard the car leaving the back-yard. I was feeling sick and depressed and upset, soon afterwards the afterbirth came and I put into a brown bucket beside the bed. I then changed the sheets and I put the bloody sheets on the floor until the following day. I then took my baby Yvonne into my bed and Bridie remained on in the house, all the others left and went to our cottage about a hundred yards away. I got up around 5am and I took the brown bucket with the afterbirth in it and I went out the front and I put the afterbirth into the old hay beside the well. I went back up to the house and I went to bed again. I woke up again at about 7.30am and my brother Michael was back in the house again. I started to clear up my bedroom after that. I gathered up all the sheets that had blood on them and the brown handled carving knife and the white bath brush. I washed the knife and the brush and put them back in their proper places. I then washed the sheets. All day Friday I was bleeding heavily and feeling bad and my sister Kathleen went up for two neighbours, a Mrs. Mary Shanahan and Elsie Moore who is a Nurse. I was then taken to Doctor Dalys Surgery in Elsie Moores car along with Mrs. Mary Shanahan. I told the two neighbours that I had a miscarraige. I told Doctor Daly I had a miscarraige. Dr. Daly examined me and told me that I hadn't lost the child and that I was four months pregnant. He gave me a letter for St. Catherines Hospital, Tralee to go in as soon as possible. I didn't go into hospital that night as I did not want to leave Yvonne. On the next day Saturday the 14th April, 1984 my brother Ned took me into St. Catherines Hospital. I was examined by a doctor, a lady doctor, a tall very thin lady with black hair. This lady doctor told me after examining me that I was pregnant. She didn't say for how long. I had told her I thought I had a miscarriage. I was kept in the hospital until the following Saturday, when I was discharged. Since the night that I killed my baby there was never any talk about it in the house. When the body of the baby was found at Cahirciveen I knew deep-down it was my baby. I was going to call him Shane. I am awful sorry for what happened, may God forgive me. I have this statement read over to me and it is correct. I don't want to change any of it. (TR, pp. 200–2)

Det. Sgt Gerry O'Carroll told the Tribunal that when Joanne Hayes made this statement, he believed that they had solved the murder of the Cahirciveen baby.

Kathleen Hayes

At 29 years, Kathleen was the eldest of the Hayes children. After leaving school she worked in a laundry in Tralee until in closed in 1982. She was then unemployed but helped her brother Mike with the farm work. More recently, she had been looking after Yvonne while Joanne went to work in the Sports Centre.

On 1 May 1984, Kathleen was at home with her mother. She was interviewed by Det. Garda Coughlan and Det. Garda Brew. At first she said she did not know that Joanne had been pregnant. She then said that on the night in question she had heard Joanne go outside and, on her return, say that she had had a heavy period. A short time later, Kathleen was asked to go to Abbeydorney Garda Station. There she told the detectives that at 10.00 a.m. the following morning she had gone outside and on lifting up some hay saw something that gave her the shivers. But she would not say what it was. At around 6 p.m. she was asked to go to Tralee Garda Station, where she was questioned by Det. Sgt Callaghan and Det. Sgt O'Donnell. They told her that they were investigating the death of the Cahirciveen baby. Despite three hours of questioning they made no progress. They were replaced by Garda Liam Moloney, the local guard, and Det. Sgt Mossie O'Donnell. Then there was a dramatic turn of events. Moloney said that when he returned after leaving to get tea and sandwiches, Kathleen suddenly announced 'I was with Mum and Mike when Joanne had the baby'. He said she then went on to say 'Joanne stabbed the baby. I got her the knife.'

Her final statement gave a clear account of what happened.

The Hayes family.
Joanne is in front with
daughter Yvonne.
Behind, left to right,
Ned, Mary Hayes,
Kathleen and Mike

It was about 1.45 a.m. at this time. I lay down on the mattress on the floor and Joanne was in bed and Yvonne was inside her in the bed. At about 2 a.m. on 13/4/'84 Joanne called me and asked me if I was asleep, I answered her, she said 'I think I am having a baby'. I got up and I called my Aunt Bridie who came up to Joanne's bedroom. Bridie then called Mam. My brother Mike who is sleeping in the same room as Mam also got up; I took Yvonne from Joanne's bed and put her into her cot. She was asleep when I put her into her cot. Joanne was having labour pains and Aunt Bridie went to assist Joanne in having the baby. My Mother and brother Mike were present in the room when the baby was born. The baby was crying after birth. It was a baby boy. Joanne was upset when the baby was born and she was crying. I said 'the baby was a fine little lad'. My Aunt Bridie cut the umbylical cord with a scissors. She placed the baby at the end of the bed on the bed clothes. I went to the kitchen and got a basin of luke warm water and gave it to my Aunt Bridie. She washed the baby and washed Joanne. There was blood on the sheets in the bed. My mother, my brother Mike was also present when the baby was born. My mother was upset and she said 'one of his children was enough to have' meaning Jeremiah Locke from Shanakill, Monavalley, Tralee. We all knew he was the father as he was the father of her first child, Yvonne who will be one year old on 19th May, 1984, he is a married man. I took the basin of water down to the kitchen and when I returned Aunt Bridie was gone to her room and my mother and Mike were in the room with Joanne and the new baby. Joanne was crying and was crouched over the baby in the bed in a kneeling position and she was chocking the baby with her two hands. She was shaking all over when she was doing this and the baby was screaching while she was choking it. No one tried to stop her from doing this to the baby. Joanne asked me to go down to the kitchen to get the carving knife from the drawer in the cabinet. I got the knife for her and I handed her the knife. Joanne then stabbed the baby with the point of the carving knife in the chest about six or seven times. She was in a temper when she was stabbing the baby. I have been shown a carving knife 'Prestige' make by D/Gda. Smith and I now identify the knife [K.H.] to Garda Moloney and D/Gda. Smith as being the knife that I handed to my sister Joanne when she stabbed the baby in the bedroom on Friday morning 13th April, 1984 at approximately 2.45 a.m. My mother, my brother Mike and my Aunt Bridie and myself [K.H.] were present in the room when Joanne was stabbing the baby with the carving knife. The baby died from the chocking and the stabbing and it was dead when my mother and I left the room to go up to our other house which is about 150 yards away from my house to call my brother Ned who is sleeping there. It was 3 a.m. when we went to call Ned. It was dark and I was using a flash lamp to give us light on the way up. We knocked up Ned and I told Ned to come down Joanne had a baby and that the baby was dead. Ned hopped out of bed and came down to our own house after us. He went to Joannes room and he saw the dead baby with stab wounds on Joannes bed. Joanne was in the kitchen when Ned came to the house. After Ned had seen the baby he was very upset. He said 'why did you kill the baby'. We were all upset at that stage and we didn't know what to do. We thought we might bury it on the farm. Mike said will we bury it back the field but Mon and Aunt Bridie were against that. So then we decided we will have to dump it some where. Mike went to the back kitchen to get a turf bag and I went to a drawer under the Television and got a white plastic bag with two handles, like the ordinary shopping bag you would get in Supermarkets. I held the white plastic bag and Ned put the dead baby into it. We done this in the bedroom and then Ned put the white plastic bag containing the baby into a turf bag which Mike had got in the back kitchen. I have been shown a bag by D/Garda Smith and I believe that it was a bag of similar colour and material as the bag in which the white plastic bag containing the baby was put into. The bag containing the baby was then brought out to the back kitchen, by Ned and Mike tied the bag with a piece of twine. Ned then took out the bag and put it into the booth of our car. Ned, Mike, and I left our house at about 3.50 a.m. in our car a Blue Ford Fiesta Reg. No. 822–ZX we drove through Tralee on through Dingle town for about six miles and we stopped at a place where the road runs beside the sea, and Ned who was driving got out and opened the booth of the car and took out the bag containing the baby and threw it into the sea. It was about 5.30 a.m. on Friday 13th April, 1984, when Ned threw the bag into the sea. You could see the water from the road where we were parked and when the bag was thrown in, it sank, and re-surfaced and flooted on the water. We arrived back home at 7 a.m. Ned drove the car that morning when we were disposing of the baby. I was in the front passenger seat, and Mike was sitting in the back seat. (TR, pp. 207–9)

Mike Hayes

At 28, Mike was a year older than his brother Ned, a year younger than Kathleen, and three years older than Joanne. He had finished school at primary level. Mike lived in his own world. He was seen as slow but, at the same time, nobody's fool. He was deeply interested and committed to his work on the family farm, particularly with the cows. The detectives who interviewed Mike Hayes had a difficult time. He would admit things and then retract them.

They nevertheless managed to get a reasonably clear and coherent statement from him.

Mike Hayes said that Kathleen went and fetched the brush from the bathroom. Then she went to the kitchen for the carving knife and brought it up to Joanne in the bedroom where she stabbed the baby and beat it with the bath brush. He said he and Ned dug up a stone to put in the bag – Ned made no mention of this. There was again a difference about the bags used. He said the main bag was a blue manure one. He said the baby was first wrapped in newspaper, then placed in clear plastic bag, then in a brown shopping bag. He said that only he and Ned went on the trip to Dingle.

Mary Hayes

Mary Fuller was born and reared on the family farm. When she married Paddy Hayes he came and lived on the farm. Her brother Maurice, a bachelor, and her sister Bridie, a spinster, also lived on the farm. Her other sisters were Sr Acquinas, a nun in the Mercy Order, and Joan, a priest's housekeeper in County Kildare. She too had never married.

Mary Hayes was interviewed at the family farmhouse by Det. Garda Michael Smith and Det. Garda Michael Coote, who had not been at the briefing the previous evening and knew little or nothing about the case. At first Mrs Hayes was insistent that she knew nothing about Joanne's pregnancy or birth. However, when Det. Sgt Callaghan arrived at the farmhouse around 6 p.m., he told Smith and Coote about Ned's statement. He asked the two detectives to put that version of events to Mrs Hayes. She then made a second statement:

> I remember [M.H.] Tuesday night 10th April, 1984 at 7 p.m. I knew Joanne my daughter was ill as she was loosing a lot of blood around and I knew she was about to have a baby. In the house with me was my sister Bridie Fuller who is a retired Nurse, who lives with me [M.H.], my son Mike and daughter Kathleen. At about 2.30 a.m. The following morning 11/4/1984 Joanne had a baby down in her own room. Bridie, Mike and Kathleen was with her. After the child was born Mike and Kathleen came down from Joannes room to tell me in the kitchen about the birth of the child and they left Bridie alone with Joanne. About five minutes later Bridie came down to the kitchen to tell me to go down quick and see the child and Joanne, Kathleen and Mike came with me and in the bedroom I saw Joanne lying in her bed and the baby was at the bottom of the bed. I saw that the baby was dead and its body was marked, I saw a white toilet brush beside the bed and Joanne used that brush to beat the child. I then

left with Kathleen to call my other son Ned who was in bed above in our other house which is about loo yards away. [M.H.] Before I left to go up for Ned Joanne was crying out aloud and was very upset. I saw her with the toilet brush in her hand. When I arrived back down with Ned Joanne had calmed back down. I said to Joanne 'you will have to bury the child' and Mike or Kathleen said we will bury the child on the land. I said the child cannot be buried on the land. Ned and Mike went to the back kitchen where they got a turf bag and put the child into the bag. I told Mike and Ned that they would have to bury the child. They left Mike and Ned with the child in the bag and drove out of the yard at about 5 a.m. They Mike and Ned returned at about 7 a.m. and said that they had buried the child. I did not ask them where. We all decided not to talk or tell anybody about it. (TR, p. 218)

This was the first reference that had been made to a brush. Coote went to the bathroom and brought back three or four brushes, and Mrs Hayes identified the bath brush in question.

Bridie Fuller

Bridie Fuller had emigrated to England and trained as a nurse. She qualified in 1942 and after the war she went to work in Kuala Lumpur in Malaya. She had returned to Abbeydorney in 1947 and after her father died took up work in St Catherine's Hospital in Tralee. She was a well-known and respected woman but towards the end of her career had become an alcoholic and was forced to retire early. By 1984 she had become somewhat senile and a semi-invalid. She suffered a stroke in the summer, 1984.

Bridie Fuller maintained the same line throughout nine hours of questioning in Tralee Garda Station. During this time she strenuously denied knowing anything about Joanne being pregnant, let alone that she had had a baby. Just after 10 p.m. Bridie asked to see Joanne. This was agreed. During the meeting, Joanne said to Bridie, 'Tell them I killed the baby I don't want to see anyone, just put me in jail. I made a statement telling them all about it and what happened. . . . You were in the room Bridie I told them.' (TR, p. 205) Shortly after this meeting, Bridie made her own statement:

I am telling you the truth about what happened to my niece Joanne the night her last baby was born in April of this year. I think the baby was born on the night of Tuesday the 7th of April or early the Wednesday morning. I knew Joanne was pregnant by Jeremiah Locke from Tralee but I couldn't say for certain how far she was gone. Joanne was living at the time in the farm house with her brother Michael Hayes and her daughter Yvonne who is nearly a year old. I went to bed that evening early as I usually wake at about twelve or so. I must have been awake about one and Michael was up also. I went down to Joanne's room and she was getting in and out of bed. I suspected that she was after going into labour. I sent Michael up to the cottage where my sister Mary and her daughter Kathleen and son Ned were living. Kathleen and Mary came down to our house and I told them that Joanne was in labour. Someone else went for Ned, I'm scattered about that, I think it was Michael. It was now about half past two and Joanne was at an advanced stage. We went up to see her and I helped break her waters. The baby was then born and I did the best I could to help her, it was a baby boy. I saw it move and it was bubbling with mucus. I was not in the room when the baby died, I think I made tea in the kitchen. After this I don't know what happened but I remember it was light before I got back to bed. I stayed in bed for a while and Michael milked the cows around seven o'clock that morning. (TR, p. 220)

Despite the overall similarity between the statements, there were some important differences. In her statement, Joanne said she first hit the baby with the bath brush and then went down to the kitchen to get the carving knife to stab the baby. Kathleen made no mention of a bath brush and said that she went and fetched the carving knife for her. Kathleen said that the body of the baby was put in a white supermarket plastic bag. But she made no mention of any turf bag. She did say that the bag had been tied with a piece of twine, like the turf bag found on White Strand. On the other hand, she confirmed that Mike and Ned drove out past Dingle and that Ned threw the bag into the sea from there. The only difference is that Ned and Mike said that they went alone. Kathleen, however, said that not only did she go, but that she sat beside Ned in the front passenger seat, and that Mike sat in the back. As well as these contradictions, there were errors within the individual statements – such as the date of the event – but there was substantial agreement about the main event: Joanne Hayes had given birth to a baby boy; she had stabbed the baby to death; her mother and aunt had been present throughout; her brothers and sister had confessed to driving to Slea Head to dump the body in the sea.

The charges

As the final statements were being made, Superintendent Daniel O'Sullivan phoned Dónal Browne, the State Solicitor, and asked him to come in to finalise the charges to be made against the Hayes family. At 10 p.m. the local Peace Commissioner Timothy Mahony was brought to the station to hold court. Each member of the Hayes family was brought before him separately. Joanne was charged with murdering her unnamed male infant. The other members of the family were charged with concealment of birth, and helping to dispose of the body. Joanne was remanded in custody over night. The others were allowed bail and were told to appear at Tralee District Court the next morning at 11.00 a.m.

The hearing on Wednesday 2 May 1984 was perfunctory. Joanne Hayes was remanded in custody and taken to Limerick Prison. The other members of her family were remanded on continuing bail.

The Tralee baby

The following morning the gardaí met to discuss the case. They went over the consistencies and inconsistencies. On balance the consistency of the story about the baby being born in the house, being stabbed to death, and transported to Slea Head, was greater than the inconsistency concerning who was present, who fetched the carving knife, the bags used, and who went on the car journey.

It was not until that evening that Kathleen Hayes called to the station and told Liam Moloney that she and her brothers had found Joanne's dead baby in the fields at the back of the house. He did not believe her, but he phoned Tralee Garda Station and reported the matter. Three detectives came out and went with Moloney to the farm. They went over the bedpost fence and found the pond and the body in the thicket beside it. It was exactly where Joanne Hayes had told Garda Liam Moloney to go the previous day. An hour later Superintendents Courtney and O'Sullivan came out from Tralee. The body was taken away to await a post-mortem examination by the State Pathologist.

The next day, 3 May 1984, another conference was held. This time the major inconsistency was the finding of the Tralee baby. But the gardaí were all agreed that this was easily explained – Joanne Hayes had had twins. They had been wrong to discount the first statement she made on 1 May. As she had said herself, and as Kathleen had originally confirmed, she had gone out and given birth to the Tralee baby. She said nothing to her family about this. On coming back into the house and going to bed she realised she was going into labour a second time. She was too tired and weak to get up and go back out. It was then that the Cahirciveen baby was born and killed as described in the statements. The only problem, however, was that there had been no mention or reference by Joanne Hayes or any other member of her family to her having twins.

CHAPTER THREE

Preparing the case against the Hayes family

Finding the Tralee baby posed a problem for the gardaí. There were two possibilities. Either Joanne Hayes had had twins, or the statements made in relation to the Cahirciveen baby were false. As everyone at the conference would probably have known, especially Superintendent John Courtney, to acknowledge that people had signed statements admitting to their involvement in a murder that they might not have committed conjured up an appalling vista. At the conference on 3 May 1984, none of the gardaí involved in questioning Joanne Hayes and her family seemed to have had any doubts that their statements were made spontaneously and voluntarily: the twins theory was true because the statements were true. People do not confess voluntarily and spontaneously to crimes they have not committed. It was an unquestioned orthodoxy, something which could not be doubted.[1]

John Harbison's post-mortem examination of the Tralee baby showed that it was full term and weighed about five pounds. The umbilical cord was very long. It had been cut cleanly over a foot from the body.[2] The baby had not been washed. There were bruises to the head which could have been caused during birth, or by deliberate blows. There were bruises to the neck, but they were not consistent with strangulation. There were no stab wounds. His examination of the baby's lungs was inconclusive. The gardaí who attended the examination swore they heard Dr Harbison announce at one stage 'Gentlemen, we have a separate existence'. In other words, the baby had been born alive and had died after birth. However, Dr Harbison did not remember saying this and, more importantly, subsequent microscopic examination of the lung tissue could not confirm an independent existence.

On Friday 4 May 1984, Superintendent Courtney returned to Dublin. His deputy, P.J. Browne, stayed behind to prepare the Garda File and Report, with the help of a local garda, Det. Sgt Mossie O'Donnell. Browne had been in the Technical Bureau for four years and had written fifty similar reports.

The strength of the case against Joanne Hayes and her family became dependent on the results of the forensic analyses being carried out in Dublin by Dr Louise McKenna.

The blood tests

Dr Louise McKenna works in the State Forensic Science Laboratory. This laboratory is run by the Department of Justice and employs about twenty scientists and technicians to help gardaí in their criminal investigations. On about 1 May 1984, she performed a blood-grouping analysis from a section of the lung tissue from the Cahirciveen baby provided by Dr Harbison. She ascertained that it was Group A. She did three repeat tests, and had the results verified by a colleague. Later she received a sample of blood from the Tralee baby and from Jeremiah Locke. These were both Group O. From the hospital in Tralee it was known that Joanne Hayes was also Group O. In a report sent on 28 May 1984, McKenna said that while Jeremiah Locke could have been the father of the Cahirciveen baby, Joanne Hayes could not have been the mother. In other words, the Cahirciveen baby could not have been the child of Joanne Hayes and Jeremiah Locke.

There was another problem. The forensic analysis showed that none of the material taken from Joanne's bedroom – where the second baby was supposedly born – showed any traces of blood group A. In other words, unless Joanne had had sex with and became pregnant by a man who was of blood group A (not Jeremiah Locke), or unless the tests carried out by Louise McKenna were not valid, then nothing other than the confessions linked the Cahirciveen baby with Joanne Hayes and her family. Even if either of these conditions were met, there was no evidence of a baby with blood group A having been born in Joanne's bedroom.

The gardaí searched for plausible explanations. One theory was that Joanne had given birth to a second baby of whatever blood group in her bedroom, that the baby had been stabbed to death as described in the confessions, and then dumped in the sea off Slea Head. This baby, however, had never been found. According to this theory, there would have been three babies not two, with two of the babies stabbed to death in a similar manner. One was found in Cahirciveen, but the other was still missing. Even if a baby had been born in the bedroom and stabbed to death as described in the confessions, one would have expected to find some traces of blood group A in the bedroom.

Towards the end of May and beginning of June a number of meetings took place between the superintendents involved in the case and Dónal Browne, the State Solicitor for Kerry. Browne had serious reservations about the twins theory, especially in light of the blood findings. Another theory began to be developed: Joanne Hayes had given birth to twins of different blood groups. This would mean that at the same time she had become pregnant by Jeremiah Locke she also became pregnant by another, as yet, unidentified man who was Group A. She could then have given birth to twins of different blood groups.[3]

The Garda Report and File

When someone has been charged with a serious offence, the gardaí produce a File on the case and a covering Report which is then submitted to the Director of Public Prosecutions. Det. Sgt O'Donnell and Det. Garda P. J. Browne were delegated to write the Report of what they termed 'this bizzare [*sic*], unprecedented case'.[4] The Garda Report is reproduced in the Tribunal Report. The authors were emphatic that the Garda Report 'is based solely on facts and the realms of speculation are not entered into'. Perhaps the most important task of the Report was to make the case that, as described in the statements, there had been a journey to Slea Head to dispose of the body. To substantiate this, although it was not included in his statement, the Report highlighted Mike Hayes saying that he saw a garda patrol car in Dingle as they drove through the town. This was crucial as garda records in Dingle would verify that, very unusually, a patrol car was out early that morning. How could Mike Hayes have known this unless he had been there? On the other hand, the Report ignored the large number of contradictions about the supposed journey. Why Ned never mentioned the patrol car was never discussed. No cognisance was taken of the fact that Kathleen said she went with her two brothers, while they said they went on their own. There was no mention that the descriptions given by Ned, Kathleen and Mike of the area where they had stopped to throw the bag into the sea varied significantly.

Having shown how the Cahirciveen baby was killed and brought to Slea Head, the Report then had to show how it could have travelled across Dingle Bay and been washed up on White Strand. This is a north–south direction and, given the Gulf Stream and the normal prevailing winds from the south-west and west, the expectation would be that the body would have been washed back up on the shore along Dingle Bay. To make this case of a north–south journey, the Garda Report relied on the hearsay evidence of unidentified fishermen.

> Fishermen who sail the dangerous waters of these two bays (Dingle and Doulus Bay) say that the currents flow from the Dingle peninsula side towards Inishvickallane [*sic*] and then verge towards Valential [*sic*] Island.
>
> The flow of tides in that area would then most likely bring anything in its hold towards An Trá Bán [Whitestrand]. (TR, p. 113)

Having made the strongest case possible to support the theory that Joanne Hayes had twins and that she was the mother and the killer of the Cahirciveen baby, the Report suddenly backtracked and speculated that there could be another possible scenario.

It was pointed out that the charges preferred against Joanne Hayes and her family had not been specifically in relation to the Cahirciveen baby. It was, the Report argued, public opinion and the media which had led to the speculation that the charges made against the Hayes family were in connection with the Cahirciveen baby.

> It is because these people were charged with the offences as stated that popular opinion and media sensationalism presumed that these charges referred to the dead baby found at An Trá Bán, Cahirciveen, on Saturday, April 14th, 1984. This opinion did not emanate from the Garda investigators involved in the case. They accept that it would be a most difficult task to definitely associate Joanne Hayes with the baby found in Cahirciveen. (TR, p. 114)

Almost as a safeguard, the Report argued that since the charges made against Joanne did not refer specifically to the Cahirciveen baby, they could be made to apply to some other baby. Effectively this meant that on 1 May 1984 Joanne Hayes was charged with the murder of a baby whose body had not yet been found. Consequently, when the Tralee baby was found, it meant that there had to be a third baby since this baby had not been stabbed to death. The Report argued that it was not necessary to produce the body of the third infant in order to sustain the charge of murder against Joanne Hayes. It quoted four legal precedents for this, including a Court of Criminal Appeal of 1954 which convicted a defendant of throwing a man overboard from a ship, even though his body was never found. It also referred to the case of Liam Townson who was charged and convicted of the murder of Captain Robert Nirac of the British Army, although again no body was found.[5]

The Report was adamant that Joanne Hayes had killed two babies that night in April.

> Within the file there is, I submit, evidence adduced to show that Joanne Hayes gave birth to twins, secretly hid the first-born on her mother's farm having killed it and after some hours gave birth to a second baby which she, with the co-operation of her entire family and live-in aunt, secretly disposed of the second infant's body to prevent its finding [*sic*]. (TR, p. 114)

Having made this categorical charge, the Report again backtracked. It wanted to water down the charge of Joanne killing the first baby. 'Even if she did not kill the baby by the free use of her own hands, she certainly committed a callous act by omitting to take proper care of the baby to prevent its death.' (TR, p. 117)

There was another problem. If the Report was claiming that a third baby had been killed in a similar fashion to the Cahirciveen baby, why then did Joanne say in her confession, 'When the body of the baby was found at Cahirciveen, I knew deep-down that it was my baby'? The Report noted that this was strange remark. It went on to conclude:

> As already stated the possibility exists that the baby found in Cahirciveen's Trá Bán on April 14th, 1984, is the baby of Joanne Hayes but the converse probability that it is not her baby is more likely. (TR, p. 120)

Central to all the theories and reasoning of the Garda Report was that the confessions made by Joanne Hayes and her family were beyond question. They had been made voluntarily and spontaneously. If, as the forensic evidence suggested, she was not the mother of the Cahirciveen baby, then where was the baby which Joanne Hayes had stabbed to death? This was final conclusion of the Report.

> If they at sometime submit that their statements are a tissue of lies manufactured at the whims of various experienced Gardaí [*sic*] the burning question that they can never escape from is:-

> 'where is the baby that Joanne was delivered of?'

They cannot now say it was the baby in the pool beside the stream, they had their chance to do that but could not because they did not know of it's [sic] existence but they did know that she had a baby, and they could not deliver it up for inspection because they had witnessed it's [*sic*] destruction and eventual disposition. (TR, p. 128)

Leaving aside the eclectic choice and presentation of the facts of the case, the Report is characterised by unusual literary style and choice of language to describe what it calls 'a sad tale'.[6] There are many examples of this. The Report says that it was 'a strange twist of fate' that the Tralee baby was not found until after Joanne Hayes and her family had been indicted for the murder of the Cahirciveen baby. It noted that Joanne Hayes 'was the willing concubine of a gentleman named Jeremiah Locke'. About Mrs Hayes, the Report said that she was 'the mother of this unfortunate family'. It said that Ned Hayes 'takes a drink but since the events of Friday the 13th April, 1984, he has become somewhat reliant on its utopic effect'. About Mike Hayes, it said that 'he is not endowed with great intelligence, but does possess a high degree of native cunning'. The authors reached into Joanne Hayes's mind claiming that on the night of 12 April 1984 she 'went to bed weak and weary thinking all was now past and her secret forever hidden'. Finally, it concluded that this 'sad tale' occurred because 'a young girl in her mid-twenties was scorned by the married man she loved, had children for and wanted for herself – "Hell hath no fury like a woman scorned".'[7]

The background to the tribunal

Throughout the summer of 1984 there were continuing discussions between Dónal Browne, the state solicitor for County Kerry, and the office of the Director of Public Prosecutions (DPP). Browne was adamant that there was not enough evidence to justify the charges, but the gardaí wanted to pursue the case. There was a final meeting in September between Eamonn Barnes (the DPP), his senior assistant, Simon O'Leary, and Superintendents Courtney and O'Sullivan and Det. Garda P.J. Browne. After this reportedly heated meeting, Simon O'Leary wrote to Dónal Browne and instructed him to have all the charges struck out at the next sitting of the District Court. This is what happened on 10 October.

The media had played a negligible role in the case until now. There had been reports of the finding of the Cahirciveen baby and the subsequent charging of Joanne Hayes with murder. But Don Buckley, a freelance journalist, had obtained a copy of the Garda File and Report. He wrote a long feature article on the case in *The Sunday Independent* (14 October 1984). During the week, the

Irish Council for Civil Liberties said there would be serious implications if the gardaí continued to question Joanne Hayes until they obtained confessions that corroborated the known details of the Cahirciveen baby's death. The case was featured on *Today Tonight*, the main current affairs programme on RTÉ, the national television station. Barry O'Halloran, who wrote a book on the case, *Lost Innocence*, was at that time producer for *Today Tonight*. During the programme, Joanne Hayes said:

> It was the Guards that made the statements. We just agreed with them at the end. They convinced themselves that we did do it. They were saying the statements and we were just agreeing with them. They were writing down the whole time. Why I signed my statement was because they told me they were going to make mother charged with murder as well and put my little girl into an orphanage and going to sell the farm as well.[8]

Joanne Hayes said the 'harassment and insults were something else'. Her sister Kathleen told the reporter that they all cracked under the strain and said whatever the gardaí wanted them to say. Her brothers Ned and Mike made allegations of physical abuse. Ned said: 'I was belted there on the kidneys and also I was put down lying down on the ground and my head pushed back like that and one of them had his knee down there.'

Given that there had been previous allegations of gardaí ill-treating people in custody and forcing them to make confessions, the Hayes case had the necessary ingredients for a major news story. On the *Today Tonight* programme, Senator Sean O'Leary commented:

> I hope it turns out for the individual gardaí concerned that the people in this case were not abused . . . questioning in a garda station is so oppressive that people may believe they are confessing to things that they haven't done, particularly cases where they may have in the past, done something like what they are now accused of having done. It is where it is close to the truth but not quite the truth that you are going to have a lot of pressure on people to forget the details and just admit the crime.[9]

On the same day as the *Today Tonight* interview, it was announced that there would be an internal garda inquiry which would be expected to explain why the gardaí persisted in their efforts to have members of the family stand trial. It was also announced that the Cabinet had given Michael Noonan, the Minister for Justice, permission to set up a judicial inquiry if the internal garda inquiry proved unsatisfactory.[10] The following week Michael Noonan said that 'the possibility of criminal charges, perhaps very serious charges against individual members of the force will arise'.[11] There were two internal inquiries into the allegations. The first by Superintendent John Moore was quickly superseded by one of Chief Superintendents Hugh Sreenan and John Reynolds. Members of the Hayes family wanted guaranteed immunity from prosecution as a result of participating in the inquiry. This was refused and so they declined to give direct evidence. Instead they made formal statements to their solicitor Pat Mann. At the same time, members of the gardaí were given legal advice that they should participate in the inquiry with extreme caution.[12]

In her statement, Joanne Hayes said the Superintendent Courtney had pushed his finger into her shoulder and told her to tell the truth because they knew what she had done. Then when she told Garda Liam Moloney that she had given birth to her baby on the farm, he had said that it was all lies. She said that the gardaí had come in and read out a statement, supposedly by Ned, which stated that she had killed her baby by stabbing it with a carving knife. While this was taking place, she had felt sick and asked to go to the toilet; the detective refused, put a newspaper on the floor and told her that if she wanted to be sick, to do so onto the newspaper. She claimed that she was called a murderer and a cheeky bitch and was told that Mike would not be milking a cow for a very long time. She said that one of the detectives had said 'your baby is buried in Cahirciveen and your baby will haunt you for the rest of your life', and also that a detective had sat her on his lap and that as he made the statement she just agreed with what he was saying (TR, pp. 134–9).

Kathleen Hayes said in her statement that she was first questioned at home and then she was taken in the afternoon to the local station in Abbeydorney, where she said the questioning was interrupted by phone calls. She said that when she was taken to the garda station in Tralee one of the detectives told her to get down on her knees and to say a prayer for herself, that she would end up in Limerick Jail, and that he slapped her across the back of the head.

> He then said 'you went to Dingle that morning, didn't you?' and I said 'I don't remember going anywhere'. Det. O'Donnell then said, 'do you go to confession and receive Holy Communion?' I said that I did. He then said 'did you vote for the Pro-Life Amendment Bill?' I said that I did and he said 'of course you did'. He said, 'what will the neighbours think of you? They will not have anymore to do with you. You are evil.' He said 'that poor baby, that poor innocent baby, his face will haunt you for the rest of your life'. (TR, p. 236)

Kathleen said that one of the detectives had roared and shouted at her and that she became very frightened. She kept overhearing them talking about other members of the family who had already confessed.

> I overheard the Detectives talking so I got the impression that all the others had made their Statements and were gone home. I decided then that I would make up a story including what I had overheard. A turf bag was brought in and shown to me and I said 'that's the bag', even though I had seen in the paper that it was a fertiliser bag that the Cahirciveen baby had been in. I only said that it was the turf bag because they brought it in to me.
> I said that Joanne was crouched over the baby and she was choking the baby who was screeching. I said that we all saw that it was a boy and that Joanne asked me to go the drawer of the cabinet in the kitchen and get the knife. I then said she stabbed the baby 6 or 7 times in the chest. Garda Moloney then said 'Kathleen, you know that a woman would be very weak after having a baby'. I changed my story then and said that it was Mike who stabbed the baby but Garda Moloney said 'no Kathleen, it was not' Then I said that 'it must be Joanne so'. I said 'Liam I can't remember any of it happening' and he said 'stop telling lies'. Then Det. Smith said 'it is alright Liam'. I had to say out the whole Statement before he wrote it down then. He read the whole lot back to me then and I said 'yes, that is correct'. (TR, p. 237)

The threat of criminal proceedings made by the Minister for Justice had meanwhile prompted many gardaí, particularly those against whom there had been specific allegations, to refuse to give direct evidence to the internal inquiry. They too submitted only written statements. The internal inquiry came to no conclusion about the allegations of ill-treatment, or how it was that the Hayes family had confessed to a crime it appeared they could not have committed. On 6 December 1984, the Minister for Justice announced that a public Tribunal of Inquiry was to be held. Justice Kevin Lynch was nominated as the sole member of the Tribunal.[13] After hearing the evidence, he wrote the Report and decided the facts of the case.

CHAPTER FOUR

The Hayes family story

The Tribunal lasted 82 days, 77 of which were spent taking evidence. There were 109 witnesses and over 61,000 questions. The Tribunal began to hear evidence on 7 January 1985 in Tralee, and continued until 22 February. The Tribunal then moved to Dublin Castle and concluded on 14 June 1985.[1]

The Tribunal was established under the Tribunals of Inquiry Act (1921) as amended by a further act in 1979. Tribunals are used exclusively to investigate matters which have caused great public disquiet and which, if unresolved, might threaten the confidence of the public in some major aspect of government or administration. The Tribunal has all the powers and privileges of the High Court. The terms of reference for the Tribunal were to investigate:

1 the facts and circumstances leading to the preferment of criminal charges against members of the Hayes family which were later withdrawn;
2 related allegations made by members of the Hayes family concerning the circumstances surrounding the taking of the statements on 1 May 1984;
3 any other matters connected with or relevant to the aforesaid.

The primary purpose of the Tribunal was to establish the facts of the case. In this crucial respect, the Tribunal was not a court of law. Members of the gardaí or the Hayes family could not be found guilty of any offence, or be punished by the Tribunal. The various parties were granted legal representation. The procedure was that all witnesses were called and examined by Counsel for the Tribunal. The witnesses were then available for cross-examination by all other parties. However, the Tribunal operated in much the same way as a traditional civil court case in that it was based on the adversarial system. This Tribunal therefore proceeded with the rationale that the truth of what happened was best determined by two opposing teams, the prosecution and the defence, each presenting the best case possible for the clients. The Tribunal became effectively a legal battle between the gardaí and the Hayes family. As Mr Justice Lynch said during the Tribunal, '[t]his Inquiry is neither a criminal nor a civil trial, but insofar as one can seek an analogy with a trial it has some similarity to a civil action by the Hayes family for damages against the Guards' (TT, 15/2).

There were five legal teams, which consisted of counsels for (a) the Tribunal, (b) the Attorney General and the Director of Public Prosecutions, (c) the three Garda Superintendents, (d) the remaining 25 gardaí involved in the case and, finally, (e) the Hayes family. It could be argued that the first two teams, those of the Tribunal and the Attorney General and the Director of Public Prosecutions, were neutral. However, it could also be argued that the state had four different teams and the private citizens, the Hayes family, only one.

It is important to note that the Tribunal did not have to follow the adversarial system; it could have chosen to follow another path of inquiry. Yet the adversarial system was the way the legal profession and the gardaí were used to playing the legal game, and it seemed the most obvious one to use. Once the system had been chosen, it was left to the judge to lay down parameters within which the prosecution and defence teams could operate. Mr Justice Lynch gave the teams a huge degree of latitude, particularly those 'defending' the gardaí. He was determined from the outset that each team should be able to make the best possible case for their clients.

> [T]he overriding principle must be that the parties should be free to make their respective cases to the Tribunal whether the case be good, bad or indifferent without inhibition and without fear of adverse consequences. (TR, p. 152)[2]

Another important element in the operation of the Tribunal caused concern, and might have constrained the legal teams. Although the Tribunal could not formally punish or sanction any of the parties, it would make recommendations regarding costs. Not having the legal costs paid could be very expensive. At the end of his Report, Mr Justice Lynch recommended that the legal costs of all the parties should be paid by the state. Yet this was in doubt throughout the Tribunal and the effect of this is difficult to assess. Since the gardaí were employees of the state, even if Mr Justice Lynch had decided against them, they could have appealed to have their costs met by their employers. The Hayes family had no such recourse. The threat of having to pay their own costs might have limited the advice sought and the research conducted in presenting their best case. If, for example, legal costs were not awarded to the Hayes family, on the grounds that they had obstructed the work of the Tribunal, Mr Justice

Lynch could have made them liable for their own legal costs, which would have been enormous and could have forced them to sell the family farm.

Given that the Tribunal was run on an adversarial basis, and given that the Hayes family could be seen as the prosecution since they alleged they had been intimidated into making false confessions, the Tribunal was organised so that the Hayes family gave their evidence with the gardaí present. However, their evidence as well as the gardaí's was regularly interrupted to allow other witnesses, especially experts, to give their evidence. It was the eighth day of the Tribunal before Joanne Hayes was called.

Joanne Hayes's testimony

Joanne Hayes told the Tribunal that on Thursday night, 12 April, she started to have labour pains. She went outside. She gave birth standing up. She broke the umbilical cord with her hands. She left the baby on some hay and went back into the house, changed her clothes, and went to bed. She got up at 5.30 a.m., put the dead baby first into a paper bag and then into a Carroll's chemist bag and hid it in a water hole about a hundred yards from the house. She said that when she was being questioned she told the gardaí where she had hidden her baby, but that they did not believe her. She said that she was slapped across the face, and told that her daughter Yvonne would be put in an orphanage and her mother charged with murder. A detective came in and read a statement in which her mother said that she had given birth in the bedroom, had beaten the baby with a bath brush (which was shown to her) and had stabbed it with a carving knife (which was also shown to her).

Towards the end of the second day Joanne Hayes broke down under the stress of the cross-examination. Her counsel asked for a pause. Mr Justice Lynch refused, but when she broke down again soon afterwards, he accepted. At the beginning of the third day, Martin Kennedy asked: 'Do you accept Miss Hayes, that you find it difficult to distinguish between the truth and the untruth?' He went on to insist that Joanne was lying about the way she gave birth outside the house, and to imply that she was selfish and immoral.

> After Yvonne was born and that while you were enjoying the good life, earning good money, working everyday at the Sports Centre, enjoying your work, no doubt meeting the public, looking after the cash, answering the telephone, socialising, going to parties, your sister Kathleen then approaching thirty years of age was sitting at home minding your baby? (TT, 10/12)

Shortly after this Martin Kennedy began a series of questions about the miscarriage of her first pregnancy. She said that around five o'clock on the Sunday afternoon she felt blood running down her leg. She went to the toilet and passed a clot. She was asked to describe the number and the nature of the clots. When Kennedy was asked the purpose of such detailed questions, he said that Joanne might have transposed the events of the Bank Holiday weekend 1982 with the events of 12 and 13 April 1984.

She was taken through her account of the birth in the field in minute detail. She was asked how she broke the umbilical cord. It was suggested to her that the reason she bled so heavily was that the cervix of her womb had not fully closed, which was because she was about to give birth to another baby in her bedroom. She denied giving birth to another baby. She denied beating her baby with a bath brush and stabbing it.

On the fourth day, she was taken through the confession she made to the gardaí on the 1 May. It was repeatedly suggested that *both* of her statements were true, that she had given birth alone in the field and again later in her bedroom. She admitted that she had said she had stabbed the baby, turned it over and stabbed it on the back. She agreed that she had said that she then threw the knife on the floor. When Martin Kennedy asked her why she said this, she could not say why and Kennedy asserted that it was because it was the truth. Joanne Hayes broke down again. Her counsel asked for a break. She ran out of the courtroom crying. She was sick outside the door and went through a period of empty vomiting. Her doctor was called. She was deemed unfit to continue giving evidence and was sedated. Her sister Kathleen began to give evidence in her absence. Eventually Joanne Hayes came back in, but soon broke down again.

On the fifth day of her evidence, Joanne Hayes was asked if she knew a Tom Flynn. Her colleagues in the Sports Centre had also been asked about him. She accepted that his name was written in blue biro on the mattress of her bed. Joanne Hayes told Martin Kennedy that her Aunt Bridie had bought the mattress in a shop in Castleisland. It was suggested to her that she had had sex with some other man, perhaps Tom Flynn, within 48 hours of having sex with Jeremiah Locke. She denied this vehemently. Again she broke down. But her cross-examination finished that day. She had been asked over 2,000 questions.

Kathleen Hayes

As with her sister Joanne, Kathleen began her evidence by being taken through the statements she had made to the gardaí and later to her solicitor, Pat Mann, about her allegations of intimidation when she was being questioned on 1 May 1984. She said that her statement was a mixture of agreeing with suggestions put to her by the detectives and her own words (TT, 14/35). She admitted that Joanne was proud to be pregnant with Yvonne and had made quite a display about it. This bothered the family since it had been a scandal in the village. The family was shocked and she was very conscious of what the community would think (TT, 14/31).

She was asked about the origins of her statement that she saw Joanne stabbing the baby in the chest six or seven times with the point of the carving knife. She told the Tribunal she had read it in the country edition of *The Kerryman*. But it was pointed out to her that the only reference in the newspaper to the injuries sustained by the Cahirciveen baby was that it had a broken neck and chest wounds. Kathleen then said that the reference to the six or seven stab wounds did not come from her but from the detectives interviewing her (TT, 14/13, 56).

She described how she had been intimidated into making her confession to the gardaí. She was slapped across the back of the head, was told that the face of the innocent baby would haunt her for the rest of her life, and that she should get down on her knees to pray for forgiveness. She insisted that on the night in question she heard Joanne go outside and that she suspected she was having her baby. She shouted to Joanne if she was okay. She saw drops of blood on the corridor and a heavily bloodstained night-dress. Joanne, when she came back in, said that she had had a heavy period. They went to bed. The following morning, she said she went down the field, half expecting and half dreading, what she would find, but found nothing.

Kathleen Hayes insisted that neither she nor any of her family said anything to Joanne about what they suspected. There was complete silence in the home about the events that night. The first time they spoke about it was when they were questioned by the gardaí.

Q. Is it fair to say that not alone were you satisfied but the rest of the family were aware that Joanne had given birth to a child?

A. Yes, I think so, yes.

Q. Yet the subject was never probed in the two weeks prior to the 1st May.

A. No.

Q. Good, bad or indifferent it was never discussed?

A. No.

Q. What do you think you would have done if the Guards had not arrived on the 1st May?

A. I don't know. I don't know really what I would have done.

Q. If no investigation had commenced would it have disappeared forever and would the subject never have been broached?

A. It probably wouldn't. (TT, 15/41)

Ned Hayes

When Ned Hayes gave his evidence, he said that the first he knew about Joanne being pregnant was when Kathleen came back from the hospital and told him that Joanne had had a miscarriage. He claimed that he had been intimidated into making his confession; it was a mixture of what had been suggested to him and what he had made up himself. He had been to Slea Head three times when he had worked as a van driver, and that it was the detectives who had suggested that he had driven out there again on the morning in question. '[T]hey had me half convinced we had something to do with the baby in Cahirciveen. I was in dread of them. I was afraid of them. I was simply afraid of them' (TT, 18/98).

Mike Hayes

Mike Hayes began his evidence by telling a story which fitted in with what Joanne and Kathleen had told the Tribunal, and with what other members of the family had said before the Tribunal. He knew nothing about Joanne's being pregnant and giving birth that night. Like the others, he said that his confession was partly suggested and partly made up to suit the demands of the detectives.

It was during the second day of his evidence that the first major crack appeared in the Hayeses' story. James Duggan, junior counsel for the Tribunal, asked Mike if he understood the purpose of the Tribunal and the role of Mr Justice Lynch. Mike said it was to find out the truth. Duggan asked Mike if he was helping the Justice by telling the truth. He said he was. Then Duggan reminded him of the oath he had taken before he began his testimony; of swearing to Almighty God to tell the truth. He was asked if he remembered what would happen to him if he did not tell the truth. He said he realised it was very wrong not to tell the truth under oath.

> Q. Tell me, had any of your family anything to do with the Cahirciveen baby?
> A. No.

Duggan then said that Kathleen had testified that she and other members of the family knew that Joanne had given birth to a baby. Mike said he did not know anything about it. But then Duggan suddenly asked:

> Q. Where was the child born, in what room?
> A. It was born in the top room above my room.
> Q. Above your room. Whose room is that?
> A. Joanne's
> Q. Who was present?
> A. I don't know who was present. I wasn't there.
> Q. You weren't there?
> A. No.
> Q. Have you heard who was there?
> A. No.
> Q. Was Bridie there?
> A. No
> Q. Was Kathleen there?
> A. No
> Q. Did Joanne give birth on her own?
> A. Yes. (TT, 20/65)

After this Mike left the witness box. This appeared to be a major breakthrough. It was the first time that any member of the Hayes family admitted that there had been a birth in the house, and not outside. It was a major boost to the twins theory. Joanne, Kathleen and Ned had said that Joanne gave birth to one baby alone in the field. Now Mike was saying that there was a birth in the house. But there were inconsistencies in Mike's evidence. He said he was not there. He said he did not know who was present at the birth, but then confirmed that Bridie and Kathleen were not there and that Joanne gave birth on her own. Then he said that nobody told him about it. But he immediately then added that Kathleen told him about it. Moreover, Mike's suggestibility is evident in the last series of questions when he simply answered yes to everything. It would have been interesting if he had in this series of questions been asked something completely different such as 'And did Joanne give birth alone in the field?' Would he have said 'yes' again?

When Dr Fennelly was giving evidence, he was emphatic that Mike was 'of rather sub-normal intelligence' (TT, 54/38).

> He is more unreliable. He is very unreliable in his evidence. If you approached him in a different way he might have a different sequence. I would say that his evidence would be most unreliable. (TT, 55/40)

An indication of Mike's unreliability came from within the Tribunal itself. Mike said that he could not remember how he had made statements about the trip to Dingle since he had never been there in his life. Yet he frequently denied that the details of the trip were suggested to him and said that he made them up (TT, 20/45; 70). But if he made them up, how was it that he could describe in detail in his confession a drive over the mountains, down through Dingle, across the bridge at the end of the town, and on out to Ventry?

Mary Hayes, Bridie Fuller and Joan Fuller

Any cohesiveness left in the case presented by the Hayes family began to disintegrate with the evidence given by Mrs Hayes and Bridie Fuller. Mrs Hayes said that she did not know that Joanne was pregnant in March 1984 and insisted that as far as she knew Joanne had a miscarriage on the night in question.

> Q. Can you tell us everything you can remember, Mrs Hayes, about this particular night. We know that a baby was born to Joanne from the evidence already heard in the Tribunal?
> A. I did not know the baby was born until I heard it on the news after she was arrested in the Garda Barracks in Tralee.
> Q. When was it you first heard the news that she had a baby?
> A. The 9 o'clock news on the morning I heard it. (TT, 21/70)

Mrs Hayes was suggesting that the first she heard of there being a baby was on the radio news on the 2 May. This would have meant that her confession on 1 May was a complete fabrication, and that when the rest of the family returned from being questioned in Tralee Garda Station none of them had mentioned anything to her about a baby being born.

She said she was surprised at Mike's evidence of a baby being born in Joanne's room. 'It did not happen.' She was reminded that Kathleen told the Tribunal that she thought everyone in the house knew a day later that Joanne had had a baby. Mrs Hayes replied: 'I did not know anyway and there was no baby born in the house anyway' (TT, 21/77).

Mary Hayes's evidence was interrupted repeatedly over a number of days by the calling of other witnesses. The most important of these was her sister Bridie Fuller, whose evidence was given in Tralee Hospital where she was recovering from her second stroke. Though the Hayes family deny it, there seems to have been an attempt to get their local doctor to certify that she was not fit to give evidence.[3] The consultant physician in Tralee hospital decided that although her ability to express ideas had been damaged, she still had good comprehension.

Very shortly after she began to give evidence, Bridie said that Joanne gave birth in her bedroom and that she helped to deliver the baby. 'I remember she was pregnant and she delivered herself that night . . . I did help her to deliver herself.' (TT, 22/8)

Q. Did that mean that you gave some assistance in taking the baby out?
A. Yes.
Q. Were you able to do anything yourself in relation to the umbilical cord?
A. No
Q. What was the position about that?
A. She delivered herself alright and then she, I was able to help with the umbilical cord.
Q. What way did you help. Did you cut it?
A. Just cut it, got a scissors.
Q. Did you take the child yourself and put it somewhere or did you leave it with Joanne?
A. I took the child.
Q. You took it?
A. Yes.
Q. Where did you put the child?
A. On the bed, on her bed.
Q. Was it a girl or a boy?
A. A boy.
Q. And was it wrapped in anything?
A. Yes, she had sheets to wrap it in. (TT, 22/10)

She said she went back to her room, but later checked on Joanne and the baby. She said he was 'very chesty all the time'. She called back in another half hour and the child was worse. Joanne had passed the afterbirth, which was taken away in a bag (TT, 22/12). She said her sister Mary had come down to the room before the baby was born and that half an hour after the birth Mary and Kathleen were still in the room. By the time of her next visit, it was nearly daylight. Joanne was calmer and had been able to clean herself. This was her evidence about the death of the baby.

Q. Where did you go after leaving then?
A. I went to the kitchen again.
Q. Were there any signs of the two boys about on this occasion?
A. No.
Q. Was the child who you said was only barely hanging on to life, was it lying on the bed or in Joanne's arms?
A. It was in Joanne's arms
Q. Was it making any cry or any sign?
A. A small cry.
Q. After you went to the kitchen again where did you go next after that?
A. I think I stayed in the kitchen.
Q. You stayed in the kitchen?
A. Yes.
Q. How long would you have been – a good while?
A. I don't know how long.
Q. What was the next thing you found out or learned about the child?
A. I heard the child was worse.
Q. We have kept hearing all through the night that the child was getting worse?
A. Yes.
Q. You said it was barely hanging on to life?
A. Yes.
Q. We have heard evidence that the child died that was born. Isn't that so. What I am asking you to tell me is did you at any stage see the child again before he died or were you only told about what happened?
A. I did not see the child dead at all.
Q. You have described these six visits and with the child barely hanging on to life. You didn't see the child after these six visits?
A. No. (TT, 22/23–4)

Two days later, Bridie Fuller continued her evidence. She insisted that despite the State Pathologist's claim that there was no definite evidence of an independent existence, the baby had cried (TT, 24/12). After the baby had died there were intense discussions as to what to do (TT, 24/22). In relation to the twins theory, she was adamant that there was only one baby born that night. However she agreed under cross-examination that it might have been possible for Joanne to have gone out into the field earlier, given birth, and then come back in later to give birth to another child. But she said that Joanne had said nothing to her about this.

There were inconsistencies and discrepancies in Bridie Fuller's evidence. Most notably on the second day of evidence she said under cross-examination that she had not washed the baby. This corresponds with the State Pathologist's evidence that the Tralee baby had not been washed (TT, 24/11); but then, shortly afterwards, Bridie said that she did wash the baby and that Kathleen helped her (TT, 24/22).

Before Mary Hayes returned to the witness box, an important piece of evidence was given by another sister, Joan Fuller, who worked as a priest's housekeeper in County Kildare. Joanne Hayes had written to her – as well as to her manager Liam Bohan – while she was on remand in Limerick Psychiatric Hospital. Since the letter went missing, Joan Fuller had to testify on what she remembered about it.

> Q. Perhaps you could recollect and tell my Lord what you remember of the contents?
> A. It said: 'Dear Aunty Joan, I am terribly sorry for the worry and upset which I caused to the family I love and the family who love me' and she said, 'the baby came before the time. I put my hand on the baby's neck to stop it from crying' and she said 'I don't know what happened to me. I must have panicked. I'm terribly ashamed of myself. I will never forgive myself.' . . . Next evening I had a phone call from her . . . I said to her: 'there is only one question I want to ask you, Joanne. You don't have to answer it if you wish.' I said 'where was the baby born'. 'Out in the field' she said. I said to her: 'do you realise you could have lost your life'. (TT, 22/41)

Her sister Bridie's evidence about the baby's being born in the bedroom was put to Joan Fuller. She said that Bridie had had two strokes in the past year. 'I am not a psychiatrist, but I would say she is getting more feeble minded every day. She is not responsible for what she is saying' (TT, 22/43). Later, Joan

Fuller admitted that the previous evening in the Hayes household there had been a discussion about Mike's testimony and how he had broken ranks with everyone else and told a different story. She said the family was in disarray, and were discussing whether the game was up.

When Joan Fuller finished her evidence, her sister Mary Hayes was recalled. Owing to the calling of other witnesses, particularly her two sisters, it was now six days since Mary Hayes had begun her evidence. She could not explain how Bridie Fuller knew a month in advance of the birth that Joanne was pregnant. She then crucially altered her testimony about what had happened that night. She might not have been in bed, but in the kitchen and had heard Joanne go out of the door. This contradicted her earlier evidence. It also contradicted Mike and Bridie's evidence of Joanne giving birth in the bedroom.

Mr Justice Lynch then put a series of questions to her. He wanted to know how six days previously she had said that she knew nothing about what happened that night as she was in bed asleep. She was now saying that she heard Joanne go down the corridor in her slippers and out of the front door and that she stayed out for over an hour. He suggested to her that after the evidence of Mike and Bridie, she was anxious to place the birth outside in the field (TT, 25/24). Later, another scenario was suggested to her.

Q. Couldn't the reality of the case be that 'yes' there was only one baby. Of course there was only one baby but that baby was born not outside the house but inside. Couldn't that be so, in fairness to yourself, couldn't that be so?
A. There was no baby born inside the house.
Q. And aunty Bridie, who is your sister, perjured herself?
A. I don't know
Q. Answer the question, Mrs Hayes. Aunty Bridie, your sister, has sworn that there was a baby born inside and also that you were there and she has sworn that. Is it perjury she is telling. 'Yes' or 'No'?
A. Yes, I suppose. I don't know.
Q. You are now saying that your sister is perjuring herself. Isn't that so?
A. Yes, I suppose it is. It is Bridie that is doing it, not me. (TT, 25/28)

Mr Justice Lynch asked her about Mike and how she acknowledged that 'he is honest as the day is long' (TT, 25/29). She was reminded that when Mike was told about the importance of the oath he had taken, he had sworn that the baby was born in the top room. She was then asked 'Are you calling your son, Mike, a perjurer "yes" or "no"?'

A. I'm not because I swear by Almighty God too that the baby was not born in the room.

Q. Mrs Hayes, I want you to answer the question. Mike was reminded of what the oath was. Mike swore on his oath that the child was born in the top room above my room. Is he a perjurer for saying that?

A. Yes, he is I suppose.

Q. You have made a perjurer out of your sister and your son. Isn't that right?

A. It is, I expect correct. (TT, 25/29)

The Hayes family case had appeared to be simple. At the beginning it certainly seemed simple. Joanne had given birth alone in the field. She had later that morning got up and hid the body down by the pond. The family knew little or nothing about what had happened. They thought she had a miscarriage or lost the baby in hospital. On the 1 May they were brought in to Tralee Garda Station where they were intimidated into making false confessions about the Cahirciveen baby. If this was the agreed story of the Hayes, it was dependent on their repeating it exactly, one after another. But it was a story which was fatally flawed from the outset, not only because of the weakness of Mike and Aunt Bridie's testimony, but because it was full of inconsistencies and contradictions in the first place. The Hayes family might have told lies, but they were not professional liars. Their story was easily dismantled in the Tribunal.

Perhaps the reason for telling lies during the Tribunal was that they feared that if they admitted that the baby had been born in the bedroom, it would have given support to the twins theory and indicated that their original confessions were true. During the Tribunal they wanted to distance themselves at all costs from the Cahirciveen baby. Mary Hayes's sister, Aunt Joan, suggested this during the Tribunal.

Q. The arrival of that baby was witnessed by members of the family in the bedroom. What do you say to that?

A. I don't believe it.

Q. Why not?

A. No, we are not like that. We are simple, innocent country people who wouldn't do that to a baby.

Q. Who wouldn't have a baby out in the field?

A. We would have a baby out in a field all right but not to stab, that is my opinion just. (TT, 22/74)

Despite the Tribunal's preoccupation with the place of birth, the central element of the Hayes case was that the confessions they had made on 1 May were false, forced out of them through a variety of strategies of abuse and intimidation. After the court hearing in October 1984, they had made allegations of abuse and intimidation to the media. These were followed later by statements that they gave to their solicitor, which were used during the internal garda inquiry.

During the Tribunal, Joanne, Kathleen, Ned and Mike repeated their allegations of abuse and intimidation. Joanne told the Tribunal that Superintendent Courtney had poked her in the shoulder with his finger, that Detective Browne slapped her across the face and had sat her on his lap. She also claimed that she had been verbally abused and intimidated, that they told her that her mother would be charged with murder, Yvonne put in an orphanage, and the farm put up for sale. She said that detectives came in after Ned had confessed and showed her his confession. She also claimed that they read out her mother's confession and kept roaring at her to tell them that she had stabbed the baby (9/27; 52).

Kathleen Hayes said that she had been hit across the back of the head, told that the face of the dead baby would haunt her for the rest of her life, and that 'it is unknown how many you have killed out there' (11/82).

Ned Hayes said that he had been punched from behind, hit in the kidneys, knocked out of his chair and kneed in the back as he lay on the ground and, at one point, turned and held upside down. 'I was suddenly caught by Det. Sgt. Dillon and turned upside down and kept there for about three minutes'. He said he was told to tell the truth or he would see Mountjoy (a prison in Dublin) before the evening was out. He claimed his cigarettes were taken away from him, that he was told to kneel down and say a prayer, and was called a 'fucking murderer'. Mike said that while he was being questioned a detective caught him by the collar, and walked him round the room with his arm around his shoulder, followed by two punches in the stomach. He was told that he would never milk a cow again.

In a technical and strictly legal sense, the Hayes family were helping the gardaí with their inquiries. They were not in custody or under arrest while they were in Tralee Garda Stattion. Yet Joanne, Kathleen, Ned and Mike Hayes were all under the impression that they were being held against their will, were not free to do what they wanted and, most importantly, that they were not free to get up and go home. More significantly, Joanne Hayes claimed that she repeatedly asked the gardaí to let her go home to the farm to show them where the body of her baby was hidden, but that she was refused.

The strength of the Hayes family's position was, then, that the main players – Joanne, Kathleen, Ned and Mrs Hayes – all testified that Joanne gave birth alone in the field. Their case that no baby was born in the house was sustained by the absence of any forensic evidence to link the birth to the bedroom. Their case was also sustained by finding some hay in the bag in which the body of Tralee baby had been found. If the baby had been born in the house and put into the O'Carroll's Chemist bag, how did the hay get into the bag?

The weakness of the Hayes family position lay in the testimonies of Mike and Bridie, the changes, inconsistencies and contradictions of those family members (particularly Mrs Hayes), who said the baby had been born in the field and, finally, the forensic evidence that the umbilical cord of the Tralee baby had been cut cleanly rather than torn.

CHAPTER FIVE

The gardaí's story

The three pillars, or perhaps eggshells, on which the gardaí's case was founded were that (a) the confessions made by various members of the Hayes family on 1 May 1984 were spontaneous, voluntary and independent, (b) that Joanne Hayes give birth to twins, and (c) that there were a number of different explanations for the blood group of the Cahirciveen baby not matching that of the Tralee baby. The main explanation for the mismatch between the blood groups began to emerge during the first few days of the Tribunal.

The Tribunal began its main business with evidence from colleagues at the Sports Centre where Joanne Hayes and Jeremiah Locke worked. During cross-examination it became obvious that a key strategy of the legal teams representing the gardaí was to make out that the women who worked in the Centre were immoral and irresponsible, bad judges of character and easily fooled by Joanne Hayes who was, they suggested, the most immoral and irresponsible of them all.

The unruly pleasures of immoral women

Mary O'Riordan had worked as a swimming instructor at the Centre for five years. She said that she always found Joanne Hayes to be 'a spirited and sincere person'. Joanne had phoned her towards the end of April and told her that she had had a miscarriage (TT, 2/21; 24). During cross-examination, Anthony Kennedy asked her if she had expected such deception and lies from Joanne about the birth of the Tralee baby. Had she not reckoned how cunning Joanne could be? (TT, 2/35). Dermot McCarthy, who was the Senior Counsel representing the Hayes family, asked that his colleague not use such pejorative terms. But Mr Justice Lynch said that he was not going to limit unduly the bounds of language used in the Tribunal.

Martina Rohan, who worked as a receptionist with Joanne at the Centre, said that she and Joanne Hayes were very close friends. A gang of about eight or nine, including Joanne and Jeremiah, used to go out together, but within the gang Joanne and Jeremiah did not pair off (TT, 2/47). Like Mary O'Riordan, she was asked if she thought that Joanne was capable of deception. She said she saw no reason for Joanne to lie to her (TT, 2/52).

In his cross-examination, Martin Kennedy moved the attack on Joanne's character away from her being a liar, to her being selfish. He suggested in a question to Martina Rohan that Joanne was happy to keep her sister trapped at home minding her child while she went out to work and had a good time. He then asked if the name Tom Flynn meant anything to her. Martina said that she knew of no other man in Joanne's life other than Jeremiah Locke. Initially she did not know that their relationship involved sexual intercourse, and admitted that she was offended when she inquired from Joanne about her first pregnancy and was told that it was none of her business.

The next three witnesses who worked in the Centre with Joanne were also asked if they had ever heard of a man called Tom Flynn 'hanging around the place as a customer or anything else' (TT, 2/72). It must be remembered that the strategy of presenting the best case possible for the gardaí was dependent on undermining not only the case presented by the Hayes family, but also their moral character. By asking these witnesses repeated questions about Tom Flynn, the legal teams for the gardaí seemed to suggest that Joanne was both 'two-timing' the man she loved and able to keep a man 'hanging around'.

The task in presenting the gardaí's case was to make out that Joanne's immorality was a reflection of the immorality of the times and, in particular, of the gang of colleagues with whom she went out. Peggy Houlihan was a cleaner at the Centre. She was questioned about the morality of her social habits, especially going to the pub with Jeremiah Locke and taking a lift in his car.

Q. You knew he was a married man?
A. Yes.
Q. You knew he was having an association with Joanna?
A. Yes.
Q. Is your husband alive?
A. Yes, he is.
Q. You were going drinking with the married man who was carrying on an association with a friend of yours?
A. Not going drinking.

Q. You went to the Blasket [a pub]. You didn't go in for a box of matches.

A. He asked me if I would come in and have a drink.

Q. What drink did you have?

A. I'm not sure really. I could have had a vodka.

Q. How many vodkas did you have with him?

A. I had about two.

Q. We know you were drinking a pint of Harp.

A. Probably, I can't remember exactly.

Q. How many half-pints of Harp did you have?

A. I suppose I had three or four now.

Q. Three or four half-pints of Harp and at least two vodkas. Is that your evidence?

A. So far as I can remember.

Q. What happened then?

Peggy Houlihan said they left the pub and that she walked home on her own. It was about half past eight or nine o'clock when she reached home.

Q. What did your husband say to that?

A. I told him I was out.

Q. Out drinking with a married man. I presume that Joanna [sic] had the same quantity of drink as you had?

A. I don't know. (TT, 3/11)[1]

The implication here was that it was not acceptable for a married woman to be out in a pub without her husband, and it was not acceptable to be drinking alcohol in the company of another married man.

Sexual promiscuity

On the third day of the Tribunal, the process of undermining the moral character of Joanne Hayes's colleagues continued. This time it was in cross-examination of Jeremiah Locke. He was asked if he had made Joanne pregnant at the same time as his wife. Locke said that he could not say; he was not an expert in that. He was asked how could he have fathered five children and not be an expert. Later he was asked

Q. Are you very casual about your sexual adventures?

A. What do you mean by that?

Q. Are you very casual, in other words do you take any girl at any particular time and vent your lust on her?

A. There have been no other women. (TT, 3/77)

The implication here was that Jeremiah Locke lived in the kind of society in which men simply go over and sexually engage with a woman on the street who attracts them. The legal team were conjuring up a picture of moral decay and decadence, a depraved society in which sex could take place at any time, anywhere, even while driving a car. Jeremiah was asked about the first time he and Joanne made love. Which of them suggested it? He could not say. But where did it take place?

Q. Was it in the car or the side of the road? Did you bring her to your home while your wife was out?

A. It was in the car.

Q. What was the occasion?

A. I don't know.

Q. You don't know when. Did you pull in to the side of the road. Was that it?

A. I could have.

Q. Were you driving along while you were having sexual intercourse? Did you stop the car?

A. I suppose I stopped. (TT, 3/78)

It was at this point that the Tribunal reached the first major test of the degree of latitude which legal teams would be permitted in presenting their best case. Mr Justice Lynch asked Martin Kennedy the relevance of this line of questioning.

I am trying to establish the sexual life of this man and Joanne Hayes. If I can show to the Tribunal that Joanne had a previous sexual history which we know she did, and if I can establish that at the time she was having intercourse with others. If the others, one of the others, turns out to have a blood group A then it will be clearly established by medical testimony amongst other things, that it is not only possible but probable that twins born as a result of that union will have, one twin will have A and the other will have O. (TT, 3/89)

This was the first time that the superfecundation thesis had been laid before the Tribunal. To sustain this thesis it was necessary to show that at the same time that Joanne Hayes was having sex with Jeremiah Locke, she was also having sex with at least one other man – Tom Flynn or someone else – and became pregnant with twins, one foetus fertilised by him, and one by Jeremiah Locke. Not only would this man have to be of blood group A, but he would have to have had sex with Joanne within 48 hours of her having had sex with Jeremiah Locke. This was the careful strategy of asking the previous witnesses about Tom Flynn, in order to suggest that there was another man in Joanne's life. With Tralee being depicted as a highly promiscuous society in which all sorts of strange events took place, it would not therefore be unlikely for a woman like Joanne Hayes to have had sex with, and conceived twins by, two different men.

To sustain the claim of superfecundation, the gardaí had to explain how it was that a small, slight-framed woman such as Joanne, who was only 4ft 9in would have been able to carry twins weighing 11 lb. 6 oz during her pregnancy without people recognising that she was very pregnant. This is what Dr Creedon, the gynaecologist in St Catherine's in Tralee said:

> She would certainly have looked very large indeed. She would be grossly distended. I would think that she would suffer from problems of carrying, the mechanical problems of having her central gravity placed forward, and she would have to compensate by leaning back and her attitude would be very military, in fact her spine would be extended backwards in order to maintain her centre of gravity. She would have considerable difficulty getting around with the pregnancy, with both infants, plus two placentas. (TT, 32/2)

In other words, being so small and petite, if Joanne Hayes had been pregnant with twins, she would have been very extended, bloated and off balance given her diminutive frame. Yet the gardaí insisted that pregnancy was in the eye of the beholder. Det. Sgt O'Carroll told the Tribunal:

> There are some women as we know that carry pregnancy and nobody knows they are pregnant. There are other women and I have this curious thing that . . . these Dublin women look hugely pregnant always; while I have noticed a lot of country women, they just don't look pregnant at all. (TT, 41/9)

However, more important than looks, for the superfecundation thesis to stand up, it was necessary to find some evidence that Joanne Hayes had had sexual relations with another man. In the early days of the Tribunal, there had been, as we saw above, an attempt to link Joanne Hayes with a Tom Flynn. It transpired that this was a name which had been written on the side of Joanne's mattress. But on the 33rd day of the Tribunal, Joseph Kelleher who worked in McElligots Furniture Store in Castleisland, testified that Tom Flynn worked in the store from September 1968 to June 1969. Although he could not confirm it, it appeared that Bridie Fuller had bought the mattress and that Tom Flynn's name was written on the side, indicating either that he had sold it or was to deliver it to the family farmhouse at Abbeydorney. Tom Flynn had emigrated to the United States, married and settled there.

The elimination of Tom Flynn did not deter Det. Sgt O'Carroll from believing that Joanne Hayes could have had sex with some other man.

> I believe My Lord that there are many – I don't mean to be facetious or to be hurtful, but I am sure there are many children being reared in the homes all over Ireland where the father or the husband of that union would not be the father of that child. We live in a promiscuous society and there has been umpteen cases that I know myself of neighbours who have got pregnant by their next door neighbours. It is happening. It has happened. I base it on that. (TT, 41/12)

During his cross-examination of Ned Hayes, Martin Kennedy asked about a neighbour who was married with children who sometimes went to the Sports Centre and gave Joanne a lift. He was interrupted by Mr Justice Lynch who asked him if every neighbour who drove Joanne Hayes home from the Centre was to be suspected with having been the father of the Cahirciveen baby. Martin Kennedy admitted that they were. The implication here was that Joanne Hayes not only invited men in the neighbourhood to have sex with her, but they willingly accepted, that one of them was blood group A, and that she had had sex with him within 48 hours of having had sex with Jeremiah Locke (TT, 19/37).

In his cross-examination by Martin Kennedy, Dr Fennelly, the Chief Psychiatrist at Limerick Psychiatric Hospital, repeated constantly that Joanne was madly in love with Jeremiah Locke (TT, 18/10). Yet Kennedy continued to probe Dr Fennelly on this issue: 'In your considered professional opinion did she love this man or did she love what this man or what some other man was prepared to do with her?' (TT, 18/46). Kennedy admitted that he was anxious to show that Joanne Hayes was interested in sexual activity and not in the love of a particular man.

Similarly, Superintendent John Courtney was reluctant, despite the lack of any evidence of any other boyfriend, to dismiss the superfecundation theory. He said that it was unlikely that any man would voluntarily come forward and say that he had association with a woman of loose morals. For Courtney, the fact that she had had sex with her first boyfriend was evidence of her having loose morals.

> She must have been of loose morals because I heard Jeremiah Locke giving evidence here that she had association, that she was intimate with other men, some other man at least, before he had intimate relations with her. (TT, 75/21)

The gardaí's case also depended on Joanne Hayes's depiction as someone who always got what she wanted, who was the dominant force in all her relationships including that with Jeremiah. She had power over other people, was able to get them to do what she wanted, even against their will and, most importantly, used sex as means towards an end. To promote this characterisation, it was suggested that Joanne had sex with Jeremiah, that she had became pregnant and had his children, not because she loved him, but as a means of getting him to leave his wife and to go and live with her.

A sociopath among natural-born liars

In order to make the case that Joanne Hayes had twins, it was necessary to establish that she and her family, but especially Joanne, were liars. If the gardaí could show that she was a liar, then it would be easier to make the case that she was lying about having given birth to only one baby. The gardaí set about showing how she had lied to her family, friends and colleagues about her pregnancy. Lying about sex and being pregnant was not, however, unusual; it was often demanded that pregnant unmarried woman hide themselves from society or at least conceal their pregnancy. It was necessary to go beyond Joanne Hayes lying about her pregnancy and show that lying was a flaw in her character. Above all, if the gardaí could show that the Hayes were liars, then it would be easy to show that their claims of physical and verbal abuse and intimidation, which the Hayes family had said were the reason for their false confessions, were a pack of lies. In other words, if it could be demonstrated that someone had told a lie, that person could be designated a liar. Once a liar, always a liar.

Dr John Fennelly earlier examined Joanne when she was on remand for murder, and had also been asked to examine Bridie Fuller, Ned and Mike Hayes, and to re-examine Joanne. In his cross-examination, Anthony Kennedy asked Fennelly a series of questions taken from a text on abnormal psychology to establish whether Joanne was a sociopath. Fennelly affirmed that she had 'superficial charm and average or superior intelligence', 'no sense of responsibility in matters of little and great importance', 'no sense of shame', 'a cavalier attitude about telling the truth', a 'callousness, insincerity and incapacity for love and attachment' and, an 'unrestrained and unconventional sex life' (TT, 54/64–86).

Later in the Tribunal, the gardaí brought in Brian McCaffery, a consultant psychiatrist with the Eastern Health Board. He had not interviewed or examined Joanne Hayes. Relying on Dr Fennelly's notes and Joanne's statements, he concluded:

> She has a personality disorder, she is inclined to tell lies to people in authority. She is expert at having attention drawn on herself, from what I have read and seen she catches a lot of public sympathy for a while. The relationship with her boyfriend and her wishes – as I think the question was put – to go off and live with him in dreamland. I think it is really fantasy that is typical of histrionic individuals. (TT, 68/82)

He said that Joanne suffered from *pseudologica fantastica*, a term used for individuals who repetitively told major untruths, which they themselves believed in. He would give her nine out of ten as a histrionic individual (TT, 68/83).

It was also important for them to characterise the rest of the family as liars. Anthony Kennedy suggested to Dr Fennelly that when Ned had been previously stopped by the gardaí, he had told them he had taken no drink at all, that 'he told the blackest lies' and asked 'would I be correct in saying that [lying about not having had a drink] typifies lying becoming part of his mental set up, that is his actual working equipment?'

The first explanation put forward by the gardaí was, then, that Joanne Hayes and her family had been lying. Joanne had given birth to two babies that night, one alone in the field, the other later in her bedroom. This explanation had been given an important boost with the testimonies of Mike Hayes and Bridie Fuller, even though they were both mentally weak, and – in the case of Bridie – physically weak.

The superfecundation thesis

The gardaí had to show that not only could Joanne Hayes have had sex with two men of blood group A and O, but that there was scientific evidence that she could then have conceived of twins of different blood groups. The first time the possibility of superfecundation was discussed was in the cross-examination of the state Pathologist Dr John Harbison. He said that experts with whom he had spoken had told him that it was a rare possibility (TT, 5/27). However, Martin Kennedy claimed there was scientific evidence of superfecundation and referred to an article in *International Journal of Fertility* in 1981. Two days later John Creedon, the consultant obstetrician and gynaecologist in St Catherine's in Tralee said that he had never come across any case which remotely suggested superfecundation (TT, 7/67). During cross-examination Martin Kennedy went on to say:

> We have some information from hospitals similar to yours in West Germany where the incidence of child birth in the hospital is between 1,000 and 1,500 per year. In the past 10 years they do both blood testing on parents and on all infants and in the past 10 years they have in the case of multiple births twin births, they found 25 examples where the father, the supposed father could not have been the father of one of the twins (TT, 8/36).

At first sight this appears convincing: 25 cases of the supposed father not being father of one of the twins seems to be a significant proportion. But if there were 1,250 births each year, over the ten years this would give 12,500 births, and 25 births would amount to only 0.2 per cent of all births. Furthermore, there could be a number of social, political and economic reasons for a woman naming a man as father of one twin. Unfortunately, Martin Kennedy did not give any reference for his source so that the information could be checked.

A miraculous journey

In order to sustain their twins theory, the gardaí needed to show that the fertiliser bag containing the Cahirciveen baby's body travelled from Slea Head across Dingle Bay, around Doulus Head and into White Strand. A number of scientific and technical experts were called to give evidence that this was not only possible, but the most likely outcome. Sgt John Reidy, based in Cahirciveen, testified that that it was well known that objects found on White Strand could come from Dingle (TT, 26/86; 27/50).

The first technical expert to give evidence on the likelihood of such a journey was Dr John Barry, Professor of Oceanography at University College Galway. He had examined the winds, tides and currents of Dingle between 12 and 14 April 1984. He accepted that objects thrown from Slea Head could end up in Cahirciveen. He came to the conclusion that for the body in the fertiliser bag to have reached White Strand, it would have to have been submerged between two and eight metres down, and for a northerly wind to be blowing. However, given the conditions prevailing at the time, he thought that there was only a 'remote possibility' of the fertiliser bag and body ending up in White Strand (TT, 27/6; 16).

Nicholas O'Connor, a local boat builder and fisherman, was asked for his opinion. He disagreed with Professor Barry. His view was that the current in Dingle Bay overrode the wind (TT, 29/33). Det. Sgt Gerry O'Carroll said he would prefer to follow O'Connor's evidence, even though, as Mr Justice Lynch pointed out, there was no evidence that objects thrown off Slea Head had ever ended up on White Strand. To prove that they could, the gardaí brought in Dr Peter McCabe, a marine engineer specialising in harbours. He evaluated the currents in Dingle Bay and carried out tests in North Dublin to examine the behaviour of weighted bags in sea-water. McCabe's evidence lasted over a day and a half. Much of his evidence dealt with scientific theory and research regarding the interaction of currents, tides and winds. He gave detailed results of a float test which he had carried out around Dingle Bay in 1966 to measure the velocity of the currents. The results were recorded in full. McCabe also gave detailed results of tests he carried out in the Estuary between Malahide and Donabate in County Dublin with a fertiliser bag and stones of six, seven, nine and eleven pounds weight tied tightly one third of the way from the top.

It is important to remember that McCabe's evidence was intended to support the case that a baby's body thrown into the sea from Slea Head in fertiliser bag could have ended up in White Strand. The strategy of the gardaí was to show that given the existing currents and tides, combined with the winds on the days in question, it was possible for the body to end up in White Strand. But it is also important to remember that the days of scientific evidence given on winds, tides and currents were only relevant if the superfecundation thesis was accepted as plausible.

The death of superfecundation

On the 72nd day of the Tribunal, Dr Patrick Lincoln, a senior lecturer in blood group serology at the University of London, gave his evidence. He carried out paternity testing for the British Home Office and was one of the expert witnesses originally called by the gardaí to testify on their behalf. However, the legal team for the Tribunal considered his evidence to be so crucial that once he had arrived in Ireland, he was ordered by the Tribunal to give evidence. He had examined Joanne Hayes's blood and he said there was no evidence that Joanne gave birth to a blood group A baby. If she had given birth to a blood group A baby there would have been traces of it in Joanne Hayes's blood, even six months after the birth.

> [I]f there had been a very high concentration of anti-A in Joanne Hayes's serum, this would have shown that she had been subject to a stimulus to the A blood group. Such a stimulus could occur through incompatible blood transfusion, which is very unlikely, or to her carrying a Group A foetus. But from my results this morning there is no indication at all that the anti-A is higher than in a normal individual. There is no evidence of Joanne Hayes having had a Group A foetus. (TT, 72/56)

He said that the chances of superfecundation were 'so exceedingly rare that one rules it out'. After this there was little further mention of superfecundation from the gardaí.

Contamination

Apart from the superfecundation theory, the next explanation the gardaí had to support their twins theory was that the blood sample taken by the State Pathologist from the lung tissue of the Cahirciveen baby had become contaminated to such an extent that what showed in the forensic examination as blood group A was in fact blood group O. When this possibility was first suggested to Louise McKenna, the state's forensic scientist, she rejected it. She said that this had been known to occur only when the tissue was very badly decomposed and when bodies had been in the sea for quite a long time, for weeks rather than days (TT, 6/74).

However, the gardaí brought in Dr Declan Gilsenan, a medical pathologist and histopathologist. As in many criminal cases, one expert disagreed with the opinion of another. In this instance, Dr Gilsenan found from his examination of the histology section that Dr Harbison gave him 'very considerable bacterial contamination of those lung sections' (TT, 50/11). He said that a certain bacterial action could have taken place in the boot of Harbison's car which could have produced different types of blood. His examination put considerable doubt in his mind as to the validity or reliability of the blood grouping of the Cahirciveen baby (TT, 50/17). He said that he was not disturbed that his conclusions differed not only from Dr McKenna but from that of two of her colleagues. He claimed that they were testing for agglutination and did not seek to eliminate the possibility of contamination being responsible for the A blood group (TT, 51/38).

The contamination thesis remained a possibility until Louise McKenna came back on the 73rd day and said that Mr Joseph Corr, Chief Paternity Tester in Northern Ireland, had found that '[g]ene products (blood group characteristics) which could not have been inherited from Jeremiah Locke are present in the blood of infant two (Cahirciveen)' (TT, 73/41). This meant that the Cahirciveen baby had genetic characteristics that it could not have received from Jeremiah Locke. This would have been the case whether the Cahirciveen baby were O or A, regardless of contamination. This, in turn, meant that for Joanne Hayes to be the mother of the Cahirciveen baby, she would have had to have had sex with another man; it would have had to be a case of super-fecundation. However, the evidence given by Dr Lincoln the previous day had effectively ruled out superfecundation as there was not the necessary high level of A antigen in her blood.

When Mr Corr came to give his evidence to the Tribunal, he said that bacterial contamination did not render the type of tests carried out unreliable (TT, 77/9). On the same day, Dr Albert Hopkinson agreed with Mr Corr's findings. He stated that the blood groups identified through the EAP system were satisfactory beyond a reasonable doubt. He went along with Mr Corr and said that the findings argued against contamination, but that they did not exclude it (TT, 77/66).

Another explanation given for the twins was that there was a recessive gene in Jeremiah Locke's blood, the Bombay Gene, which caused blood group A to be misread on analysis as blood group O. The argument of the gardaí was that since Louise McKenna did not test for the Bombay gene factor, 'no one can in fact say 100% if Joanne Hayes or Jeremiah Locke could or could not have been the parent of the Cahirciveen baby' (TT, 6/4). Louise McKenna was emphatic, however, that while she did not test specifically for the Bombay gene, it was so rare that her tests would have shown it if it had been there. The Bombay gene thesis was not pursued with any rigour after this.

The Azores baby

The final explanation within the twins theory was the thesis that Joanne was not the mother of the Cahirciveen baby. Nevertheless she gave birth to twins, both of which were probably blood group O with Jeremiah Locke being the father. The second baby was born in the bedroom and had been stabbed to death as described in the different confessions of members of the Hayes family. As with the Cahirciveen baby, this dead baby was placed in the same series of bags, taken over the Kerry mountains as described in the confessions, and thrown into the sea. But the bags or the body of this baby have never been found. This became known as the 'Azores baby' theory.

This theory was first put forward in the Garda Report. The Azores theory was put to various gardaí who gave evidence throughout the Tribunal. None of them had any doubts about the fact that Joanne Hayes had twins. They all admitted difficulty in dealing with the forensic evidence, but they had no doubts whatsoever about the veracity of the confessions. For example, Daniel O'Sullivan, Superintendent at Tralee and one of the first gardaí to give evidence on the thirtieth day of Tribunal, said that it came down to either the Azores baby or contamination.

> I do have doubts as to whether the body found on the beach in Cahirciveen is Joanna Hayes's baby or not, at this stage, in view of the blood group findings, but I have not changed my mind in relation to all the other matters, the birth of the baby in the field, the birth of the baby in the house, because I have no reason to doubt the contents of the statement taken by the Gardaí.

Det. Garda P. J. Browne, who was the main author of the Garda File and Report, had the same difficulty as Superintendent O'Sullivan. He admitted that it was highly unlikely that there were

> two babies floating around Dingle Bay at the same time, both stabbed, both wrapped in feritiliser bags, 0-7-30 fertiliser bags, each containing a brown bag inside and a clear plastic bag inside that again. (TT, 44/25)

But he refused to exclude it as a possibility. More significantly, he refused to accept that the statements given by the Hayes family were untrue.

By the time Superintendent John Courtney, who headed the investigation, was called, the evidence of Dr Lincoln and the other scientific experts had been completed. He was taken through the relevant possibilities. He agreed that following the forensic evidence given to the Tribunal, the theories of the contaminated blood samples, of Jeremiah Locke as the father of the Cahirciveen baby, of Joanne Hayes giving birth to a baby of blood group A, or of the existence of an Azores baby could all be safely discounted (TT, 75/19). But he still firmly believed that she had had twins, and that the confessions had been spontaneous, voluntary and independent. He was also sure that these beliefs were shared by all gardaí involved in the case.

Other weaknesses

The scientific evidence was not the only difficulty for the gardaí in presenting their case; there were numerous others. The first of these was the stabbing. The Cahirciveen baby had been stabbed 28 times, four on the right side, twelve on the front of the neck, and twelve on the chest.

The problem with the evidence given about the stabbing was that while Dr Harbison's evidence was that the stabbing had been done in a frenzy, his view was that the object which caused the wounds was 'a more stiletto like object'. The shape and the width of the wounds would not fit wounds caused by the Hayes family carving knife used in a frenzy (TT, 5/37). When Dr Gilsenan, another pathologist, was called to challenge Harbison's evidence, he concluded that the injuries to the heart could have been caused by the carving knife (TT, 50/4). However, he admitted that the other injuries suggested that they were from a shorter-bladed knife and that if the carving knife had been used, 'you would have to more or less delicately pick at them' (TT, 50/24). This did not correspond with the baby's being killed in a frenzy.

Joanne Hayes stated in her confession that: 'The baby cried when I hit it and I stabbed it with the carving knife on the chest and all over the body. I turned the body over and I also stabbed him in the back.' The problem was that the Cahirciveen baby had not been stabbed in the back. What is crucial here is that Garda Liam Moloney told the Tribunal that he had heard Superintendent Courtney tell the garda conference on the 30 April that the baby had been stabbed in the back (TT, 36/72). If Garda Moloney was right, this incongruity would imply that more than just suggestions were being made to Joanne Hayes. The addition of the stabbing in the back might seem like an attempt to obtain congruence between Joanne Hayes's statement and the facts of the Cahirciveen baby's death.

The carving knife seems to have appeared on the scene when Ned Hayes confessed that the baby had been born in the house and that it had been stabbed with a carving knife (TT, 56/74). Garda Michael Smith told the Tribunal that when he was out interviewing Mary Hayes on the farm on the 1 May, Garda Coote arrived ten minutes after her first statement had been completed.

> I got up and went to the back door and Detective Garda Coote told me that Ned had said that his mother went up to call him around 2.30 a.m. on the morning of the 13th, that Joanne had had a baby and it had been stabbed with a carving knife. (TT, 61/47)

Garda Smith told the Tribunal that Mrs Hayes had taken him and Garda Coote down to the bedroom, had described the scene to them, and they said that there was a white bath brush lying on the bed beside Joanne. Smith said that Coote asked her if there were any stab marks and Mrs Hayes had replied that there were not. He then said that Garda Coote asked her about a carving knife and Mrs Hayes had shown him the one they usually used for cutting the meat. The carving knife, bath brush and a turf bag (which Mrs Hayes said was similar to the one used to take away and dispose of the body) were brought back into Tralee. It was when these were presented to Joanne along with her mother's confession that she became hysterical and later confessed to having stabbed her baby.

Considerable discussion took place during the Tribunal about whether the bath brush had been used to hit the Tralee baby. Harbison was very doubtful that the brush had hit the baby's head. A much more likely possibility was that it had hit the left side of the neck (TT, 66/74). He considered that the brush was so heavy that if wielded with any force it would have crushed the baby's head (TT, 5/38). The problem for the gardaí was that while there might have been some doubt about the brush being used on the Tralee baby, there was little evidence of its having being used on the Cahirciveen baby. This was impor-tant, because to sustain the gardaí's twins theory, any wounds caused in the house would have had to have been on the Cahirciveen and not the Tralee baby.

Another problem with the twins theory related to the plastic bags. In his confession, Ned stated that he and Mike put the dead baby into a brown plastic shopping bag, and that this was then put into 0-7-30 grey fertiliser bag. He said that these were similar to the two bags shown to him by Detective Dillon which had been retrieved from White Strand. In his confession, Mike also said that the turf bag used to transport the body was an 0-7-30 one similar to that shown to him by Det. Garda John O'Sullivan. However, in their confessions, Joanne and Kathleen Hayes said that the turf bag identified by their mother and taken back to the garda station was the one used to transport the body to Slea Head. As Mr Justice Lynch said in his Report, this fertiliser bag bore no resemblance whatsoever to the 0-7-30 fertiliser bag found on White Strand. In other words, not only were there completely conflicting confessions from the Hayes brothers and their mother and sisters about the about the kind of turf bag used, there were also two different types of turf bags in Tralee Garda Station on 1 May 1984. When the Tribunal went to visit the farm during the hearings, Mr Justice Lynch noted that while there were many different types of fertiliser bags lying around, there were no 0-7-30 bags (TR, p. 132).

The next difficulty for the twins theory was that the umbilical cord of the Cahirciveen baby had been cut almost flush with the body, which would have been against all medical practice. The testimony of Bridie Fuller (a nurse for over twenty years), which the gardaí cited in support of the twins theory, was that she cut it over a foot from the body (TT, 24/9). If the gardaí accepted Bridie Fuller's evidence that the second twin was born in the bedroom, they had to say why they would not accept her evidence that she cut the umbilical cord long.

The umbilical cord of the Tralee baby had been cut over a foot long. The crucial evidence of Harbison was that beyond reasonable doubt the umbilical cord of the Tralee baby had been cut either with a knife or scissors or some other sharp instrument (TT, 66/76). In other words, if the twins theory were to be supported, it was necessary that Joanne Hayes gave birth alone in the field, which meant that she tore and broke the umbilical cord herself. Harbison's evidence that cord had been cut not only undermined Joanne's claim that she gave birth alone and broke the cord with her hands, it also undermined the gardaí's theory of twins.

A further problem with the twins theory was that the vivid descriptions by Kathleen, Ned and Mike of the journey out to Slea Head were full of contra-dictions about which of them did what, and when and where. The gardaí were adamant that such inconsistencies were normal in confessions and rightly pointed out that if the accounts had been the same, they would have been less credible. But the confessions had contradictions rather than inconsistencies:

1. The bags: *Kathleen said* that Mike went to the kitchen and fetched a turf bag, and that she went to get a white plastic bag from a drawer under the television. *Ned said* he and Mike went outside and fetched a fertiliser bag from the gable end of the house. They emptied the sand out of it. He said that he went back into the house and found a brown plastic bag of clothes beside the wardrobe which he emptied and used. *Mike said* that he and Ned found a fertiliser bag outside and that he dug up a big stone to put into the bag. He stayed outside and Ned and Kathleen came back out with the baby wrapped in newspaper, and a clear plastic bag and a brown plastic bag.

2. Who went to Slea Head? *Kathleen said* that Ned put the bag in the boot of the car and that she, Ned and Mike drove out together. *Ned said* that the three of them made the journey, but he put the body on the floor of the car behind the driver's seat. *Mike said* Ned put the bag in the boot, but made no mention of Kathleen travelling with them.

3. The dumping of the bag: *Kathleen said* that they stopped about six miles from Dingle at a place where the road runs beside the sea. She said Ned threw the bag into the sea and they saw that the bag sink, resurface and then float on the water. *Ned, who was more specific, said* that he was familiar with Ventry and Slea Head and that he had stopped two miles past Ventry. He crossed a stone ditch, and walked about 20 yards to the edge of a cliff 10 feet high. He saw the bag drop directly onto the water. *Mike said* they stopped about seven miles from Dingle and that Ned took the bag, crossed over a field, and he saw him throwing the bag into the sea.

3. The time: *Kathleen said* that they left the farm at 3.50 a.m., that it was 5.30 a.m. when Ned threw the bag into the sea, and that they arrived home at 7.00 a.m. But if that was the case then they could not have seen the patrol car in Dingle. *Her mother, Mary Hayes, said* that Mike and Ned left the farm at 5.00 a.m. and returned at 7.00 a.m. Not only would this have meant that they covered a four-hour trip across the Kerry mountains to Dingle in two hours, but that they could not have seen the patrol car in Dingle. *Ned said* they arrived home at 10.00 a.m. *Mike said* they left at 4.30 a.m. which, if it was a five hour round trip would have them back at 9.30 a.m.

4. Encounters: Although it was not in his statement, one of the key items of Mike's verbal statement was that he had seen a garda patrol car as they drove

home through Dingle. This was regarded as a crucial piece of evidence as there had, quite unusually, been a police car out on patrol early that morning. It was insisted by the gardaí that this evidence was offered voluntarily by Mike and definitely tied himself, Ned and Kathleen into making a journey to Slea Head. Neither Ned nor Kathleen mentioned the garda patrol car. Nor did they mention stopping off at Horan's garage on the way home to get petrol. Ned said that when he was being questioned, the gardaí were anxious to know where they got petrol; he mentioned Horan's garage since he knew that it opened early. However, the stop off in Horan's garage ended up in Mike's rather than Ned's confession (TT, 19/58; 20/73).

Leaving aside these contradictions, Kathleen, Ned and Mike seemed to be in agreement about the general area – about seven miles from Dingle – where the body had been thrown into the sea. Evidence was produced, however, which showed that there was nowhere along that road where there was a similar field and cliff and where you could see the sea from the road. In his evidence, Superintendent O'Sullivan of Tralee agreed with Nicholas O'Connor's evidence that there was nowhere around Slea Head that matched the description of the journey through the field (TT, 31/19). This was confirmed by Sgt O'Donnell (TT, 48/18).

The confessions

Of all the problems which the gardaí had in sustaining the twins theory, the biggest was maintaining the validity of the confessions despite all the scientific evidence which showed beyond reasonable doubt that the Hayes family had had nothing to do with the death of the Cahirciveen baby. Throughout the Tribunal, all the gardaí followed a united, steadfast line that the confessions had been given voluntarily, spontaneously and independently. They insisted that they fully believed that Joanne Hayes had given birth to twins. There was no dissenting voice, either during the conferences after the discovery of the Tralee baby, or during the Tribunal. This was most evident during the testimony of Superintendent Courtney who, by the time he gave his evidence towards the end of the Tribunal, had heard the weight of scientific evidence against the twins theory. The intriguing question, of course, is why there were no dissenting voices among the gardaí. Was there any dissenting opinion about the twins theory, or about the confessions being voluntary, spontaneous and independent? If there had been, and if they were not voiced, that would imply a good deal about the way the state exercises power, the mechanisms through which gardaí investigate crimes, and produce arguments, evidence and truth. It would suggest that an elite had become an unquestioned, established authority in a social field. That, in turn, would say a good deal about the problems of creating and maintaining a mature, democratic, civil, society. On the other hand, perhaps there was no dissenting opinion. Maybe the twins theory and the nature of the confessions were never openly discussed. Maybe the twins theory was a spontaneous collective belief that arose among the gardaí in the same way that people gathered at a grotto can believe they saw a statue move – a classic example of collective pseudologica fantastica.

CHAPTER SIX

Blaming the Hayes family

The Tribunal Report was published in October 1985. It was unusual in being almost completely free from legal jargon. It some respects, particularly during the first two parts, the Report reads like a good detective story. There is a narrative flow from chapter to chapter. The titles of the chapters are tantalising: 'The Hayes Family', 'The Affaire' (Mr Justice Lynch used the French spelling as if extra-marital affairs were foreign to Ireland), 'The Birth and Death', 'What will we do?', 'Cover-up', 'The Cahirciveen Baby found', 'Family Under Suspicion', 'The Command Structure', 'Visitation by the Gardaí', 'Family Charged'.

But the Report dealt with real events and in this respect it could be classified as an innovative piece of ethnographic research. It provided an insight into the culture and everyday life of a small Irish community, how a family dealt with a crisis pregnancy and birth, and the way the gardaí operated and responded to this crisis and the unfolding events.

One might have expected that the Report would begin with the gardaí. The Tribunal was, in effect, set up to discover how it was that members of a family confessed to involvement in a crime that state forensic evidence indicated they could not have committed. Instead Mr Justice Lynch began the Report with the Hayes family.

Love and death

The first paragraph of the first substantial chapter of the Tribunal Report, *The Hayes Family*, announced that Mrs Hayes was married on the 12 May 1954. 'The Tribunal is satisfied that this is the correct date of her marriage' (TR, p. 13). On first reading, this seems an extraordinary sentence. Perhaps the aim was to prepare the reader for Mr Justice Lynch's conclusion that Mrs Hayes lied about so many things that he wanted to signal that she might even have lied about the date of her marriage.

In the following chapter, Mr Justice Lynch described the love affair between Joanne and Jeremiah. Joanne had 'encouraged herself to develop an over-riding infatuation with him' (TR, p. 15). More important, he stated that she did not have sexual intercourse at the time with any man other than Jeremiah (TR, p. 15). At this early stage in the Report, he announced that he was throwing out the superfecundation thesis. He considered that 'Joanne Hayes was the main or dominant force in the liaison between herself and Jeremiah Locke' (TR, p. 15). He said that Jeremiah Locke pretended to Joanne that he might leave his wife and child, and presumably accepted gladly the sexual favours and pleasures which came his way on the basis of this pretence.

But here we can find another difficulty in Mr Justice Lynch's construction of the truth. He portrays Jeremiah Locke as calculating and instrumental in his approach to Joanne Hayes, yet when Locke was asked during the Tribunal whether he loved Joanne, he replied: 'I did, I suppose, yes' (TT, 3/75). This might seem to lack conviction, but how many Irish men are forthright in declaring their love and affection? One occasion provided a test of his affection. Joanne and Jeremiah had been meeting secretly for months. Regularly on the way home from work or from in the pub, they stopped the car to make love. On the occasion in question, the two lovers were ambushed by Jeremiah's wife, mother and other members of his family. They pulled in front of Jeremiah's mini, walked back, pulled open the doors, dragged them both out, and took the keys of the car. There was an almighty row. Joanne was attacked for breaking up Jeremiah's marriage. They threatened to go and tell Joanne's mother what was happening. Joanne started to walk away. But instead of staying with his wife and mother, Jeremiah Locke went after her, and together they walked to the house of a friend of his some miles away. This does not seem like the action of a instrumental, calculating and selfish man.

The birth of the Tralee baby

Relying primarily on the testimony given by Bridie Fuller, Mr Justice Lynch concluded that Joanne gave birth in her bedroom in the early hours of Friday 13 April. Bridie assisted her at the birth and cut the umbilical cord. The baby, said Mr Justice Lynch, was chesty and unable to clear its lungs, but nobody thought of or mentioned getting medical assistance. He immediately associated this with Mrs Hayes's annoyance 'at the prospect of having to rear another child for Jeremiah Locke'. (R. 19) At this stage, 'Joanne got into a panic and as the baby cried again she put her hands around its neck and stopped it crying by choking it (TT, 22/662 to 665) and the baby did not breathe again' (TT, 40/144 to 156; TR, p. 19). This is an elaboration of what Joanne reportedly said in her letter to her Aunt Joan 'I put my hand on the baby's neck to stop it from crying' (TT, 22/41). Mr Justice Lynch went on to state: 'At some stage during the course of these events, Joanne Hayes used the bath brush from the bathroom to hit the baby to make sure that it was dead.' Joanne Hayes thus choked the baby and then either she or another member of the family went to the bathroom, fetched the bath brush, and she hit the baby with it. In this way, Mr Justice Lynch incorporated the bath brush into the death of the Tralee baby. The state pathologist, however, testified that he was very doubtful that the bath brush had been used to hit the baby on the head, since if it had been, the head would have been crushed. Dr Harbison said it could only have been used lightly. But Mr Justice Lynch was certain beyond reasonable doubt that Joanne had the bath brush and had managed to control herself and not hit the baby on the head. Harbison felt that it was much more likely that if the bathbrush had been used, it had hit the baby on the neck (TT, 66/74). It hardly seems credible that if Joanne Hayes wanted to make sure that the baby was dead that she would just hit it on the neck. The implication of what Mr Justice Lynch claimed is that Joanne Hayes, wanting to make sure the baby was dead, hit it on the neck, and left it at that.

There is one other important consideration. When Mr Justice Lynch said that the baby did not breathe again, his evidence came mainly from the testimony given to the Tribunal by Det. Sgt Gerry O'Carroll, one of the Murder Squad detectives, who told the Tribunal what Joanne Hayes had said to him. Mr Justice Lynch therefore accepted what O'Carroll told the Tribunal. O'Carroll insisted that Joanne Hayes's confession 'was a free and voluntary statement and it was a spontaneous statement. I don't think I asked a question' (TT, 40/35). O'Carroll went on to say that when Joanne Hayes said at the end of her statement, 'When the body of the baby was found at Cahirciveen I knew deep down that it was my baby', he was convinced that they had solved the Cahirciveen murder (TT, 40/37).

The significance of this is that Mr Justice Lynch concluded later in his Report that the Cahirciveen comment was effectively stitched into Joanne's statement.

When Detective-Sergeant O'Carroll and Detective-Garda Browne had obtained the long statement from Joanne Hayes (Appendix K, No. 2) they knew that there still could be difficulty in positively proving that she was the mother of the Cahirciveen Baby, because up to that stage she had not actually mentioned that baby nor made any mention of Cahirciveen. Thus, it was vital for them to get a mention by her of the Cahirciveen Baby as being her own baby. The Tribunal is satisfied that this is the origin of a suggestion by the Detectives to Joanne Hayes that deep down she must have known all along that the Cahirciveen Baby was her baby to which she probably mumbled a 'yes' or and 'uh' or and 'ah' and this assent to this suggestion went in at the end of her statement Appendix K, No. 2., as a statement by her upon which much reliance was put throughout the Tribunal hearings by the Gardaí 'when the body of the baby was found in Cahirciveen I knew deep down it was my baby'. (TR, p. 91)

It is not so much the mention of the Cahirciveen baby being effectively stitched into Joanne's statement that is important here, but rather that it was done by O'Carroll and Browne. O'Carroll, however, insisted to the Tribunal that her statement was completely free, voluntary and spontaneous. Mr Justice Lynch therefore decided that O'Carroll was not perhaps lying so much as bending the truth. Yet when it came to finding out what happened in Joanne's bedroom that night, insofar as he did not quote any other source, Mr Justice Lynch seemed to rely mainly on O'Carroll's testimony to the Tribunal. This would perhaps be acceptable if Mr Justice Lynch had not stated categorically that everything in the Report was based on fact. What it really shows, and this is something which resonates throughout Mr Justice Lynch's Report, is that he was not a scientist asserting empirical facts, but a diviner of truth.

What will we do?

Of all the chapters in the Tribunal Report, chapter 7, 'What Will We Do?' is probably the most contentious. The chapter is based on facts 'found by inference from other facts', or 'by inference from evidence not directly supporting such facts' (TR, p. 21). Mr Justice Lynch concluded that after the birth and death of the baby in Joanne's bedroom, there was agreement that the body should be disposed of quietly, with some suggesting that it be buried on the land, and Mrs Hayes and Bridie Fuller saying that it should be taken away. His evidence for this came from the confessions Mrs Hayes and Bridie Fuller made on 1 May 1984. He said: '[v]arious places were suggested, but the most favoured was the Dingle Peninsula' (TR, p. 21) since Ned knew the area from having made deliveries there. He concluded that this was where the mention of Dingle came from in the confessions of Ned, Mike and Kathleen on 1 May 1984.

Mr Justice Lynch went on to say that once the decision was made to go to Dingle there was a further discussion about getting petrol. Ned had already bought £10 of petrol locally the previous night. A repeat purchase would, he claimed, probably have provoked unwelcome questions. Consequently, Mr Justice Lynch concluded that they had decided to purchase petrol in Horan's Garage in Tralee which opened early in the morning. This, he said, was the origin of the mention of Horan's garage in Ned's verbal statement, and Mike's written confession (TR, p. 22).

However, Mr Justice Lynch claimed that the planned journey was cancelled because Ned refused to have anything to do with disposing of the baby's body, and because, having been charged earlier that year with drinking and driving, he feared being stopped by the gardaí. Mr Justice Lynch said that Mike was similarly fearful and this resulted in his saying that he saw a patrol car in Dingle. Given Ned and Mike's reluctance, it was decided, according to Mr Justice Lynch, that Joanne would temporarily hide the baby on the farm. At a later date, she would arrange with Jeremiah Locke to remove the baby from the land. If the body were discovered Joanne was to say that she had had the baby out in the field without the knowledge of the rest of the family and that none of her family knew she was pregnant. Consequently, he claimed, Joanne got up a few hours after giving birth, took the body from the house and put it some old hay in a field down on the farm. She then took the afterbirth, which was in bucket in her bedroom, and threw it on the grass near her house. Later that morning, according to Mr Justice Lynch, she went out and tried to retrieve the afterbirth with fire tongs, but failed. She also checked that the baby was still in the hay. Although Mr Justice Lynch did not say so, he must have concluded that at some later stage, Joanne went down to where the baby was hidden, put it in an O'Carroll's Chemist bag, and hid it in the briars near the pond, where it was eventually found on 2 May.

It might have been better if Mr Justice Lynch had said that he had a theory about what happened after the birth of Joanne's child. The explanatory power of a theory is defined by the range of facts it is able to explain. In this case, the explanatory power of Mr Justice Lynch's theory is its ability to explain what was said and what was not said, by whom it was said, and why it was said. Mr Justice Lynch obviously doubted this theory. Later in his Report, he said that the Tribunal had given much thought as to whether a journey to Tralee could have been undertaken and abandoned; finally, he came to the conclusion that no such journey had been undertaken (TR, pp. 112–13). In other words, for some time, Mr Justice Lynch pondered whether Ned, Mike and Kathleen had driven into Tralee town in the middle of the night, gone through the town and out on to the Dingle road. They then would have driven out along the north side of the Dingle peninsula before climbing up into the Kerry mountains, over the Conor Pass, and down into Dingle town. Having already been driving for about an hour, they would have driven through the town before going out along the south side of the Dingle peninsula for another half hour before arriving at Slea Head. According to Mr Justice Lynch, the journey was carefully planned and discussed in detail, but never undertaken. It would seem then that this detailed discussion explains the rich detail about the journey in Ned's, Mike's and Kathleen's statements.

The strength of Mr Justice Lynch's theory about the journey at least being talked about and planned is that it helps to explain certain incongruities. First, the references to Horan's Garage made by Mike and Ned Hayes to the gardaí: Mr Justice Lynch argued that the planning of the journey to Dingle was so meticulous that they realised that on the return journey they would have to stop off at Horan's Garage to get petrol. The problem is that it does not explain why they would even have considered getting petrol in Tralee at 7.30 a.m., thus attracting possible attention, especially when they were only a few miles from home. Why in thinking up a journey that was never undertaken did they plan to stop in Tralee? Would they not have imagined keeping their heads down and going home?

Certainly Mr Justice Lynch's theory about Joanne Hayes putting the baby in some old hay the first time round helps to explain the presence of hay on the baby's body. This is important as hay on the body might be seen as evidence of Joanne's claim that she gave birth alone in the field. Mr Justice Lynch said that Joanne left the baby out in the hay until either late on the Friday night or early Saturday morning, when she returned, put the baby into a brown bag and then into the O'Carroll's Chemist bag. Because she had not finished hiding the baby, she was reluctant to go straight into Tralee Hospital which had been urged by Dr Daly after he had examined her in his surgery on the Friday night. Again this is quite a strong theory. The only problem is that it means that Joanne carried the naked and dead baby out from her bedroom the first time without wrapping it in anything. If she had given birth alone in the field, it would seem plausible not to have gone in search of anything in which to conceal the baby.

However, it is more difficult to believe that she would have brought the body of the baby out into the field without first covering it with something.

Another problem emerges in these two chapters. Three times Mr Justice Lynch mentions that it was decided that Joanne Hayes would arrange with Jeremiah Locke to remove the body from the farm (TR, pp. 22, 25). However, he could not cite any evidence given at the Tribunal to support his assertion. Again, as a speculative theory it deserves attention. But Mr Justice Lynch was adamant that it was more fact than speculation.

After the events of Thursday night and Friday morning, Mr Justice Lynch was certain that nothing was said in the Hayes family about the terrible events that had taken place. Like the body of the baby, the issue was dead and buried. An uneasy silence returned, similar to that which reigned during the pregnancy. Nobody talked about what had happened, even when they read and heard about the Cahirciveen baby. They suspected, Mr Justice Lynch claimed, that the Cahirciveen baby might be Joanne's and that 'she had stabbed it after death in a frenzy' (TR, p. 25).

In the next five chapters, Mr Justice Lynch described how the Cahirciveen baby was found, the initial investigation, the emergence of the Hayes family as the primary suspects, the command structure of the gardaí involved in the case, and the process by which the Hayes family were questioned and subsequently charged.

Little is contentious in this description of events. He said that once the body of the Cahirciveen baby had been found, and the post-mortem completed, it was the duty of the gardaí to investigate that death, 'to find the culprit and to bring him, or more likely her, to justice' (TR, p. 27). But Mr Justice Lynch glossed over an important issue. Would the investigation of the Cahiciveen baby have been so intensive and would the Murder Squad have been brought in – to the extent of seven men coming down from Dublin – if Superintendent John Courtney and his two chief deputies had not been from Kerry, and if Courtney had not been on holiday when the baby was found? Perhaps they thought it represented not just a breakdown in law in their native county, but a breakdown of moral order.

There were no details about the background to previous Murder Squad investigations, the controversies concerning what had happened to suspects in Cahir, County Tipperary and Shercock, County Cavan, and, more important, how so many cases involving the Murder Squad had been solved and convictions attained on the basis of confessions made by the culprits.

Mr Justice Lynch went on to describe the blood tests carried out on the Cahirciveen baby which was found to be Group A and on Joanne Hayes and Jeremiah Locke, who were both O. Again he rejected the superfecundation theory and said that the blood tests confirmed that Joanne Hayes was not the mother of the Cahirciveen baby (TR, p. 45).

Liars and allegations of intimidation and abuse

The substantive part of Mr Justice Lynch's Report begins in Part IV. He argues that the strength of the allegations made by Hayes family against the gardaí had to be assessed in terms of the Hayes family's credibility. It seems that by showing how they lied about other matters, their credibility in relation to their allegations of intimidation and abuse could be undermined.

He started with Mrs Hayes. He said that she had 'committed blatant perjury' in her evidence. He claimed that she deliberately changed the evidence she gave on 5 February 1985 (that she knew nothing about what happened on the night in question) to the evidence she gave on 11 February that she had heard Joanne go out to the field. She did so in order to contradict the evidence of her son Mike and sister Bridie who had told the Tribunal that the baby was born in Joanne's bedroom (TR, p. 52). Mrs Hayes had lied when she said that the only reason the family had called in their local GP, Dr Chute, prior to the Tribunal was to get her sister Bridie to take her tablets. Mr Justice Lynch determined that the sole reason for bringing in Dr Chute was to persuade him to certify Bridie as being unfit to give evidence to the Tribunal. Mr Justice Lynch's final example of perjury by Mrs Hayes, related to her claim that neither Sgt Coote nor Det. Garda Smith read over her two statements to her. Mr Justice Lynch said: 'On this occasion she fell into the trap that so many untruthful witnesses who are unfamiliar with Court procedure fall into. She told a totally unnecessary, totally useless and totally obvious lie' (TR, p. 53). However, Mr Justice Lynch could provide no evidence for this lie. He just declared: 'Whatever the Gardaí might do, they would not be so ridiculously stupid as not to read over a statement before getting the interviewee to sign it. A failure to read it over could render the statement inadmissible in evidence and thus make all their work useless' (TR, p. 54).

Mr Justice Lynch said that it was the authority and influence of Mrs Hayes as head of the family which was central to the development of the story that Joanne had the baby alone in the field. This led to Joanne lying about breaking her umbilical cord. The forensic evidence given by Dr Harbison was clear on this issue (TT, 66/76), and it corresponded with her third statement on 1 May when she said that when her waters broke she called her Aunt Bridie and that she had gone to find the scissors and had cut the umbilical cord.

Mr Justice Lynch stated that Kathleen had lied about not visiting her aunt when she was taken to Tralee Garda Station on 1 May. The reason she lied was that she was afraid that someone might have overheard her conversation. She lied about the detectives bringing in a phone to the garda station in Abbeydorney, and making or pretending to make phone calls. He said 'there was not and never was in Abbeydorney Garda Station, a telephone with various plug points in and around the Station and attached dwelling house and from which the telephone might be moved' (TR, p. 57).

Mr Justice Lynch determined that Ned Hayes perjured himself when he said that he had never been in a garda station prior to 1 May 1984 other than for signing on for the dole. Ned later admitted that he had been in Tralee Garda Station six weeks previously in relation to the charge of drunken driving. Mr Justice Lynch also pointed out that Mike Hayes had told lies to the Tribunal until he changed his story and said the baby was born in Joanne's bedroom.

As a result of this analysis, Mr Justice Lynch concluded that if the charges made by the Hayes family against the gardaí had been brought before a jury, they would have been rejected. However, he said that this did not mean that the Hayes family lied about everything. The reason they lied was, he said, to bolster the story about Joanne giving birth alone in the field. And the main reason they lied about this was to protect the good name of the family.

> The purpose of discrediting the statements made to the Gardaí is in order that the neighbours and the public in general may believe the family story that Joanne Hayes had the baby outside in the field; that it was stillborn; that she panicked and hid it; that her conduct was, therefore, not all that blameworthy; and that no other member of the Hayes family nor Bridie Fuller was involved in any way whatever and they are all completely innocent. (TR, p. 58)

The evidence of lying and perjury which Mr Justice Lynch chose might not be the most convincing, particularly in relation to minor issues such as Kathleen lying about the phones in Abbeydorney Garda Station and Ned lying about never being in a garda station previously other than to sign on for the dole. Although a telephone engineer testified to the Tribunal that the phone sockets in Abbeydorney were fixed, it is very easy to disconnect one, carry it in, pretend to make phone calls, and then reconnect it. What Mr Justice Lynch does not address is why Kathleen would have lied about this. As for Ned saying that he had never been in a garda station previously, again there was no major gain to made from lying about this. Perhaps the experience of 1 May was so dramatically different from his previous visit that he did not connect them. But it might have more to do with experience or lack of it in giving evidence, and the amount of skill, care and attention necessary to bring to this task. The process of giving evidence centres not just on telling the truth, but bending it to one's needs and interests, and while doing so maintaining a logically consistent line, free of errors, inconsistencies and contradictions. The Hayes family had no such skill, and did not have the ability to give it proper care and attention. This is not to deny, however, that there were major contradictions in Mrs Hayes's evidence about her recollection of the events of the night in question, and in Joanne's evidence of having broken the umbilical cord on her own.

Even if we accept that the Tralee baby was born in the house, Mr Justice Lynch's analysis fails in relation to his reasoning as to why members of the Hayes family gave false statements to the gardaí. He considered that they did so to maintain their honour and respect in the neighbourhood. There might have been another reason. If the birth had taken place in the house, Joanne, Ned, Kathleen and Mrs Hayes might have held firm to the story about the birth in the field because it distanced them from the false confessions they had made about having been involved in the Cahirciveen baby's death. If the state had been instrumental in getting them to confess to something that they had not done, they would have had reason to persist with the birth in the field story. To suggest, as Mr Justice Lynch did, that it was purely a question of honour, is perhaps simplistic.

The credibility of the gardaí

Having effectively branded the Hayes family as liars, Mr Justice Lynch moved on to discuss the credibility of the gardaí. If he deemed that the gardaí had also been lying, then it would be difficult to decide who was telling the truth about what happened in Tralee Garda Station on 1 May 1984 and how it came about that the Hayes family had confessed to a murder they did not commit. Mr Justice Lynch began by tackling the issue head on. He declared that a garda in the course of his work becomes well used to giving evidence under oath.

For persons who take the Witness Oath relatively frequently, there is the danger that the Oath may become for them largely a matter of form. This does not mean that such a person is likely to tell completely groundless lies on Oath. Where 'familiarity breeds contempt' has affected a witness, it will most often manifest itself in the elevation of honest beliefs or suspicions into positive facts. (TR, p. 59)

This is a very sympathetic understanding of what happens, not just to gardaí, but to anyone who gives evidence frequently. Yet Mr Justice Lynch could have argued the opposite. He could have said that those who are familiar with court procedures, who give evidence on many occasions, know how important it is to tell the truth, the whole truth and nothing but the truth. The way Mr Justice Lynch described it, such people are not at an advantage but at a disadvantage. Close familiarity with giving evidence can breed contempt for the process. This does not lead these people to lie or bend the truth, but in a strange case of osmosis, contempt for court procedures results in gardaí seeing as a positive fact what they suspect or believe might have happened.

This explanation seems to expect us to be sympathetic towards the gardaí as they are overcome by the process of elevating belief and suspicion to fact. But there are two other issues which need to be addressed. The first is that while this malaise might be expected to manifest itself in one or two gardaí, it is strange that it affected all of them without exception. According to Mr Justice Lynch, all the gardaí simultaneously and coincidentally transformed their individual beliefs into a collectively held belief which then became a positive fact. Such a process is dangerous. In the past, people honestly believed that there were witches and that they performed evil magic. These beliefs became positive 'facts', with horrendous consequences. Secondly, in stark contrast to the way in which he drew attention to instances in which he claimed the Hayes family lied, Mr Justice Lynch did not produce any analysis of inconsistencies or discrepancies in the evidence of the gardaí which might have indicated that they too could have been lying.

As an example of honest beliefs and suspicions coming to be seen as positive fact, Mr Justice Lynch referred to how so many gardaí insisted in their evidence that when they were questioning the Hayes family it was not really in relation to the Cahirciveen baby, but to find out what had happened to Joanne's baby. Mr Justice Lynch says that this was 'manifestly a line of defence agreed beforehand among the Gardaí' (TR, p. 59). The question which Mr Justice Lynch does not address is the relationship between an instrumental defence strategy, honest belief and lying. Mr Justice Lynch admitted that '[t]his line of defence required every Garda witness to say that he, or she, still firmly believed that Joanne Hayes was the mother of the Cahirciveen Baby' (TR, p. 60). He went on to note that despite the lack of scientific evidence to support their claim, 'there was a procession of Gardaí swearing that they were still completely convinced that Joanne Hayes had had twins and was the mother of the Cahirciveen Baby'. Yet he did not see this as lying. It was simultaneously an instrumental defence strategy and an outbreak of honestly held collective belief being elevated to positive fact. Mr Justice Lynch said that, in contrast to the members of the Hayes family, the contradictions in the statements of the gardaí were not barefaced lies. '[T]hey are an exaggeration over and above the true position, or a gilding of the lily, or wishful thinking elevated to the status of hard fact' (TR, p. 61).

Conflicts in the gardaí's evidence

The examples that Mr Justice Lynch chose to include in his Report might indeed suggest gilding the lily. There were other examples which he could have chosen, however, in which the conflict of evidence suggested that someone was lying. One of these was in relation to Garda Liam Moloney, who remembered hearing Superintendent Courtney say that the Cahirciveen baby had been stabbed in the back. Courtney emphatically denied this (TT, 74/72). Another example was when, during his evidence, Det. Sgt Dillon said that he told Courtney in the afternoon of 1 May 1984 that Ned, whom Dillon had been interviewing, had said that the baby had been stabbed with a carving knife. Courtney said that he could not remember Dillon telling him this, which was a crucial breakthrough in the investigation (TT, 74/46). A third example of conflicting evidence again relates to Garda Moloney. He testified that he had a conversation with Garda Michael Smith about Mrs Hayes's statement while it was being prepared. Garda Smith disputed that this conversation ever took place (TT, 62/56). So strong was his rebuttal that Mr Justice Lynch intervened and put it to Garda Smith that his evidence directly contradicted that of Garda Moloney (TT, 62/64). Yet when he came to writing his Report, Mr Justice Lynch did not include this as showing a lack of trustworthiness on the gardaí's part.

There were other examples. Det. Sgt Dillon swore to the Tribunal that he and Detective Mahony asked Ned if he knew what kind of plastic bag he and Mike had taken to the bedroom. Ned had replied voluntarily and spontaneously 'it was a grey fertiliser bag 0-7-30'. Mahony said that while he knew there was a fertiliser bag in the station – which had been found in White Strand – 'I did not know of the number on the bag until Ned Hayes told me' (TT, 52/65). However, in his Report Mr Justice Lynch said: 'The Tribunal does not accept that Ned Hayes had earlier spontaneously mentioned an 0-7-30 fertiliser bag during the afternoon of the 1 May 1984' (TR, p. 101). But what does this say about Det. Sgt Dillon's credibility?

Another conflict of evidence occurred in relation to Jeremiah Locke. Locke claimed that Sgt Mossie O'Donnell had repeatedly accused him of taking the body to Cahirciveen. He also claimed that Sgt O'Donnell had shouted at him. O'Donnell emphatically denied that he had done this (TT, 47/87). Similarly, Sgt Paul Downey denied he persistently accused Locke of being involved in the disposal of the Cahirciveen baby, and that he suggested to Locke that Locke had driven the car to Cahirciveen. But the question is why Locke would have lied to the Tribunal.

There was a more important conflict in evidence. Sgt Downey told the Internal Inquiry that since the gardaí suspected Locke of having been involved in the disposal of the body, they took possession of his car for examination. At the Tribunal he confirmed that he and Sgt O'Donnell had locked Locke's car and taken the keys. Later, however, under cross-examination, he claimed that Locke had locked the car himself and had the keys in his possession all the time (TT, 67/47).

Finally, there is Mr Justice Lynch's claim that the gardaí were surprised when Ned mentioned Dingle because they all thought that the baby had been dumped in the sea near Cahirciveen (TR, p. 100). Garda Tim Collins told the Tribunal that it was only on 2 May, after the charges had been brought against the Hayes family, that the gardaí thought of checking winds and tides. At this stage during the Tribunal, Mr Justice Lynch said that Collins's evidence was very important since it suggested that if they did not check the tides until 2 May, it would suggest that they were not trying to fabricate the Dingle connection (TT, 60/65). This was confirmed by Superintendent O'Sullivan who told the Tribunal that prior to the questioning of the Hayes family 'nobody ever mentioned Dingle or Slea Head' (TT, 31/16). However, in his testimony, Jeremiah Locke said that when he was being questioned about his involvement in transporting the body to Cahirciveen, one of the gardaí mentioned Dingle (TT, 3/52). It must be remembered that Locke was one of the first to be interviewed that day. Moreover, Superintendent John Sullivan told the Tribunal that when the investigation began, the easiest place to look, after having made no progress in the Cahirciveen area, was across the bay to the Dingle Peninsula. Finally, Dónal Browne, the County Solicitor, emphatically told the Tribunal that it was his clear recollection that when the case for formally charging Joanne with murder was being put to him on 1 May 1984, Superintendent O'Sullivan told him that there would be evidence for the winds and tides washing the body from Slea Head to White Strand (TT, 76/50). How could the gardaí have accumulated such evidence if Dingle and Slea Head were not in their minds until mentioned by Ned Hayes that afternoon?

The more important issue is whether, as Mr Justice Lynch claimed, the description of the journey to Dingle from members of the Hayes family was voluntary and spontaneous, solely because they actually planned such a journey. If that were the case, it would exonerate the gardaí from involvement in constructing all the fantastic details, corresponding with each other across three voluntary and spontaneous confessions, about a journey that had never been made. Mr Justice Lynch rejected any notion that the idea and the details of the journey to Slea Head came from the gardaí. He did not countenance the theory that once the Hayes family had become primary suspects over the weekend of 28 April 1984, somebody should have thought of alternative explanations of how the body of the Cahirciveen baby could have travelled from Abbeydorney to White Strand other than being driven there. Such a theory would not, though, tie in with the very strong belief that the baby had been washed ashore. If the baby had been washed ashore, then it could easily have occurred to the gardaí that the most likely spot connecting White Strand to Abbeydorney was Slea Head.

Allegations of assault

It was crucial, then, for Mr Justice Lynch to establish the gardaí's credibility, since in later chapters of the Report he set about systematically dismantling the claims made by members of the Hayes family that they had had been assaulted, abused and intimidated when being questioned in Tralee Garda Station. Having established on the one hand the trustworthiness of the gardaí and, on the other, that members of the Hayes family told groundless, barefaced lies, Mr Justice Lynch then moved to examine the claims of assault. He opened this section of the Report by stating that if the gardaí had been prosecuted before a jury, it 'would have no hesitation in throwing out all such charges because of the unreliability so far as truthfulness is concerned of the Hayes family' (TR, p. 63).

Consequently, he decided that when it came to Joanne Hayes's allegation that Superintendent Courtney had shoved his pointed finger into her shoulder that this was untrue. He accepted Det. Garda Browne's evidence which contradicted Joanne's claims that he had twice slapped her hard across the face and that he had sat her on his lap. He claimed that while Joanne Hayes swore on oath about these assaults, in his closing submission her counsel backtracked on these allegations. In the final analysis, and in the absence of independent witnesses, Mr Justice Lynch was by and large forced into accepting the word of the gardaí or the word of the Hayes, and he had already established that most of the Hayes family were liars.

He dismissed Kathleen's claim that she had been slapped on the back of the head by Sgt Mossie O'Donnell. He also dismissed her claim that she had told Garda Liam Maloney about this the day after, on 2 May 1984, when she went with him across the farm to locate the Tralee baby. Again Mr Justice Lynch accepted the word of the gardaí. Moreover, he suggested that elements of Joanne's and Kathleen's allegations of harassment became transposed and this was linked to 'consultations which the sisters had between themselves when preparing their statements of complaint' (TR, p. 66).

He was satisfied that there was no truth whatsoever in Ned Hayes's allegations of assault. Ned had claimed that Det. Sgt Dillon had punched him on four occasions for about two minutes, that he had been turned upside down for three minutes, and that while this was happening Det. Garda Mahony tried to catch him by the private parts. Finally, he claimed that Det. Garda Mahony knocked him off his chair, put him face down on the ground, and kneed him in the back. In relation to Ned's allegation that Dillon or Mahony had 'lifted him upside-down', he decided that since Ned was well over 12 stone and despite the fact that Dillon and Mahony were hefty men, he was satisfied that 'they would not be able to perform this feat of strength' (TR, p. 69). There are two problems here. First, even though Mr Justice Lynch claimed that Ned was prone to colourful, dramatic and absurd descriptions (TR, p. 102), it is odd that he would dream up this form of assault. Second, it is not such a remarkable feat of strength to push a man to the ground, grab his legs around the knees and hoist him up while leaning against a door or wall. The question, of course, is whether this form of assault was known or practised elsewhere, or whether Ned Hayes just dreamt it up.[1]

Finally, Mr Justice Lynch dismissed Mike Hayes's claims that Det. Sgt Skelly grabbed him by the collar of his jacket and pulled him towards him, and on another occasion punched him in the stomach while walking around the room.

Specifically, Mr Justice Lynch said he was satisfied that Mike's claim about being caught and pulled by his jacket collar was false as he was not wearing a donkey jacket on the day in question and that this allegation was 'a fabrication concocted for him by his sisters and sworn by him on their orders' (TR, p. 72). But as Gene Kerrigan pointed out, Mike, in his statement of complaint made no mention of a jacket, just that he was caught by the collar.[2] On the allegation of punching, Mr Justice Lynch said a reading of Mike's responses to questions that he was asked during the Tribunal shows that he watered down his allegation of having been punched to Det. Sgt Skelly making 'pretence of phantom punches' (TR, p. 73). Moreover, he argued that, given that Mike was being questioned in the billiards room in Tralee Garda Station, it would have been difficult to walk around this room and punch him at the same time.

Having decided that the allegations of physical assaults were groundless and had been fabricated, Mr Justice Lynch moved on to analyse why they had been made. He said that finding the Tralee baby on 2 May and dropping of the murder charges on 10 October helped convince everyone in Abbeydorney that the Hayes family had had nothing to do with the murder of the Cahirciveen baby. However, when extracts of the family's confessions were published in the *Sunday Independent* on 14 October, the family's reputation was once more seriously damaged. They therefore had to come up with a reason for confessing so readily to a crime they had not committed, and so they alleged grossly improper conduct by the gardaí; allegations of mere verbal abuse, he argued, would not have done (TR, p. 75). In Mr Justice Lynch's view, when they made the allegations first on the media, particularly during a special programme broadcast by *Today Tonight*, the family had no realisation of the serious nature of such false allegations. He said 'the Hayes family considered these allegations as an everyday event, as indeed they are'. The failure to appreciate the seriousness of their allegations was contributed 'by imbalance in media reporting of such cases' (TR, p. 75). He pointed out that there were 11,400 gardaí in the country. If 114 were unsuitable to be gardaí, this was only 'a tiny proportion of the Force and yet their misconduct can bring the whole Force into disrepute'. (TR, p. 75) He said that the media fell down because they did not give equal publicity to cases in which allegations of assault were found to be false, or were abandoned.

Mr Justice Lynch said that while the allegations of assault by the Hayes family reached a climax and took on a new seriousness during their interviews with the media, the allegations had begun on 2 May 1984, the day after they had been questioned. This was when Sr Aquinas, Mrs Hayes's sister, visited from Ballybunion. Mr Justice Lynch claimed that, for the reputation of the

Hayes family to be preserved in the eyes of Sr Aquinas, they, particularly Ned, had to come up with some explanation for their confessions. The only one they could come up with was that they had been obtained by physical duress. Mr Justice Lynch said that the lies told to Sr Aquinas that day, to protect the family reputation, followed on from the lies she had been told when she called at the house on the Saturday 14 April. On encountering Joanne being taken to the hospital, she said she was told that it was for a check-up on her blood.

Mr Justice Lynch's final difficulty in accepting allegations of assault was whether or not these allegations were made by the Hayes family to their solicitor Patrick Mann, and if so in what detail. Mr Justice Lynch said that any evidence of such allegations was extremely unsatisfactory (TR, p. 78). He said that although Mr Mann stated in evidence to the Tribunal that complaints had been made to him by members of the Hayes family in May 1984, a written record of the allegations would have been expected, but there was none. He pointed out that 'not one scrap of paper with a contemporary record exists to corroborate that such complaints were made to Mr Mann before the RTÉ "To-Day To-Night" programme transmitted on the 16th October, 1984' (TR, p. 78). While one could understand him not taking detailed instructions from his clients about a criminal case until the Book of Evidence were produced, this was, nominally at least, a murder case (TR, p. 79). Moreover, Mr Justice Lynch said he was satisfied that Mann told the Internal Inquiry held by the gardaí in October 1984, that while he had not taken full instructions from the Hayes family, they had not made any complaint of assault. Mr Justice Lynch could not determine whether any complaints had been made by the Hayes family in May 1984, but concluded that if there had been, they 'were made for the purpose of protecting the family reputation in Mr Mann's eyes' (TR, p. 79). Again there could be a different explanation. Members of the Hayes family could have made allegations of assault, but Mr Mann deliberately made no written notes because of the seriousness of the allegations. It would have opened up a can of worms to take on the Murder Squad on this issue. Perhaps he hoped that the charges would be dropped sooner rather than later. The problem with this strategy was that once the allegations had been made, he had no written verification of them.

Leaving aside the veracity of the allegations of assault and, for the moment, accepting Mr Justice Lynch's view that they were false, two issues still remain that need to be addressed in relation to his analysis. He argued repeatedly in his Report that the reason members of the Hayes family said they had been physically abused was to protect the family's reputation. In other words, the allegations of assault provided a rational explanation for their confessing to a crime they had not committed. Without the allegations, Mr Justice Lynch argued, it would have appeared that members of the Hayes family readily and willingly confessed. But it is unsatisfactory to say that this was just a question of honour, for this, once again, puts all the blame on the Hayes family. It is very difficult to describe how terrifying it is to be interrogated by skilled practitioners for nearly twelve hours. Those who have not been rigorously interrogated know little of the strategies and tactics which members of the gardaí use to extract the truth from those who they suspect are telling lies. In other words, if the allegations of assault were false, it had less to do with protecting honour and more to do with trying to explain the experience of terror.

Mr Justice Lynch is himself guilty of gilding the lily when he said that even if there were 114 members of the gardaí who were unsuitable for the job, this would have been only a tiny proportion of the 11,400 force. He does not address is the whole tradition of the gardaí's reliance on confessions to solve crimes, and of the courts' acceptance of these confessions. He does not address this culture of securing convictions through confessions which had become established in the criminal justice system. Finally, his suggestion that there were 114 unsuitable gardaí is not relevant; it glosses over the question of whether a sizeable proportion was deliberately or coincidentally gathered in one area or unit.

Allegations of intimidation

In opening his discussion of the alleged pressure and intimidation to which the Hayes were subjected, Mr Justice Lynch decided not to deal with 'trivial' allegations such as whether or not Detective O'Carroll told Joanne that her baby would haunt her for the rest of her life. He noted caustically: 'It was not a tea-party they were at' (TR, p. 80). He said that if such a threat had been made to Joanne, it would have to be decided if it was a temporal threat or a moral one. This is an important distinction as temporal threats or promises such as 'you will never walk the streets of Abbeydorney again' would, if issued, render any statement or confession invalid. However, a moral threat such as 'you will end up in Hell for all eternity' is permissible. Mr Justice Lynch made it clear that he did not see 'how the giving of such a warning or threat could be regarded as a matter of urgent public importance leading to the establishment of a Public Tribunal of Inquiry' (TR, p. 81).

He cast doubt on the veracity of the allegations of verbal abuse and insults by saying that the allegations made to the Internal Inquiry 'were all prepared by the Hayes family concurrently in their own home in consultation with each other' (TR, p. 81). He said that the statements of allegations were 'masterminded by Joanne Hayes and Kathleen Hayes' and that there was definite evidence of cross-seeding between the statements. To demonstrate this, Mr Justice Lynch showed how the allegation by Joanne Hayes that Detective O'Carroll had said to her – 'It is unknown how many people yourself and herself have killed between the two of you' – was very similar to the allegation made by Mrs Hayes that Detective Smith had shouted at her – 'It is unknown how many you have killed out there'. Of course, what is interesting here is that while Mr Justice Lynch readily accuses members of the Hayes family of cross-seeding their written complaints, he does not accuse the gardaí of doing the same in relation to the vivid descriptions of a journey to Slea Head which he eventually decided never took place.

Mr Justice Lynch concluded that there were indeed stern warnings and admonitions to tell the truth issued to members of the Hayes family. He noted, however, that Joanne was never refused permission to go the toilet, nor was she told that if she wanted to be sick she should do so on a newspaper on the floor. Ned Hayes's cigarettes were not taken away from him and that he was free to smoke whenever he wished to do so. Having discussed the issue of verbal abuse and pressure, and having suggested that many of the allegations were doubtful since there had been considerable cross-seeding in statements from members of the Hayes family, Mr Justice Lynch determined that he was not going to consider the matter any further and that it would be much more fruitful to investigate why the Hayes family made false confessions. In this way the matter of verbal abuse and pressure, central to the whole purpose of the Tribunal, is bypassed.

> The Tribunal has come to the conclusion that it is not practicable to make individual findings on the large number of complaints about things allegedly said to the Hayes family and which range from things of some consequence to things of little consequence. The Tribunal considers it will be more practicable and useful to determine the circumstances which led the Hayes family and Bridie Fuller to make the various Statements to the Gardaí which they did make. (TR, pp. 82–3)

CHAPTER SEVEN

Explaining the false confessions

After dismissing the allegations of assault and intimidation, Mr Justice Lynch then began his careful analysis of each of the statements made by the Hayes family and Bridie Fuller on 1 May 1984. Leaving aside Joanne Hayes, his view of the background to these statements was that the rest of her family thought or suspected that Joanne was the mother of the Cahirciveen baby and responsible for its death.

He noted that Joanne claimed at the beginning of her interrogation that she had had a miscarriage. When she realised that the gardaí were associating her with the Cahirciveen baby, she changed her strategy and told the story of giving birth in the field alone. He pointed out that shortly after 2.00 p.m., Joanne stood up and told Detectives O'Carroll and Browne 'I am a murderess. I killed my baby.' She told them that she had given birth in the field, that the baby had cried after birth, and that she put her hand around its neck until it stopped crying. She gave explicit directions to the pond on the farm where she had hidden the body. Mr Justice Lynch said that when the search proved unsuccessful, Superintendent Courtney refused to take her to the farm because 'he did not want the pressure that was then built up on her to be broken', and he 'was almost 100% certain' that she was the mother and murderer of the Cahirciveen baby (TR, p. 87). The judge dismissed Courtney's claim that he was going to take Joanne to the farm, but had changed his mind after hearing Mrs Hayes's confession. Mr Justice Lynch considered there was nothing new in Mrs Hayes's statement to add to what Courtney already knew from the statements of Ned and Mike.

When the second search proved unsuccessful, Mr Justice Lynch said that Joanne Hayes had thought that the body's disappearance might have been attributable to foxes or vermin. She had felt the net was closing in around her. When Detectives Smith and Coote told her that her mother had confessed that the baby was born in the bedroom, and showed her the turf bag, bath brush and carving knife, 'she shouted out that she was insane, a murderess, had killed her baby and that she had stabbed the baby with the knife, she had beaten the baby with the bath brush, and the baby was taken away in a bag similar to that produced' (TR, pp. 88–9). Mr Justice Lynch determined that at this point Joanne Hayes had become 'at least half convinced that the Cahirciveen baby was her baby' (TR, p. 89).

> Although Joanne Hayes is not the mother of the Cahirciveen Baby and had nothing to do with it, she was nevertheless persuaded into believing that she was its mother and had killed it. (TR, p. 89)

Although Joanne Hayes could have heard about the Cahirciveen baby, Mr Justice Lynch did not explain how she could have known that it had been stabbed. He claimed that when Joanne heard that her brother Ned and her mother had said that the baby was born in the bedroom and had abandoned the agreed story about giving birth alone in the field, she became vulnerable, confused and very suggestible. For over seven hours she told the story of giving birth in the field. It was disregarded and never written down. However, Lynch said that as soon as she implicated herself in the case of the Cahirciveen baby, her statement was 'written down as soon as she proffered it'.

Mr Justice Lynch's insistence that it was internal pressure which led Joanne to confess is of crucial importance here. Whether it was said or not, the implication was clear to her – 'a person of quick mind and very considerable intelligence' – that if she refused to give them the statement which she clearly understood them to be seeking, the consequences would include prison for herself and all the family, Yvonne would be put in an orphanage, and there would be nobody to milk the cows (TR, p. 90). Mr Justice Lynch again glossed over an important issue here. It makes a considerable difference whether Joanne concocted this image of 'total gloom and disaster for the whole family' or whether it was concocted for her. He decided that it was because of her guilty conscience about the Tralee baby that 'she became convinced, or half-convinced, that she had done away with her baby in the manner suggested by the Detectives' (TR, p. 91). The key phrase here is 'in the manner suggested by the Detectives'.

Mr Justice Lynch was having it both ways. He said that the detectives wrote down Joanne's statement implicating herself in the Cahirciveen baby's death as soon as she proffered it. This gives the impression of a voluntary, spontaneous confession. He went on to say, however, that her confession was at least partly the result of suggestions made to her by the detectives. Mr Justice Lynch avoided the key issue of whether Joanne when she made her second statement freely and spontaneously (see pp. 31–2), or whether it was said for her and she simply agreed.

It is extraordinary that Mr Justice Lynch, whose primary task was to discover how and why innocent people confessed to a crime they had not committed, did not analyse how Joanne Hayes came to describe in detail an event he determined had not taken place, despite analysing in depth so many other aspects of the case. It is not that he did not believe that some or indeed a good part of her statement was said for her, but rather that he did not attempt to analyse in what manner and to what extent. For example, he agreed that the detectives interviewing her realised after her statement had been completed that there was no specific mention of Cahirciveen (see p. 87 above). If the gardaí knew that the statement had been suggested or 'mouthed' for Joanne Hayes, then they were doing more than gilding the lily when they insisted that all of her confession was voluntary and spontaneous.

Concocting stories for the gardaí

According to the Report, Kathleen Hayes saw the Tralee baby at about 10.00 a.m. on Friday 13 April, under some hay near the gate with the bedstead. But Mr Justice Lynch claimed that

> When the finding of the Cahirciveen Baby was publicised, including a short description of its injuries, Kathleen Hayes had an uneasy feeling that the baby might be Joanne Hayes's baby transported by Jeremiah Locke to Cahirciveen although the presence of the wounds as described in 'The Kerryman' of the 20th April, 1984, was somewhat puzzling. (TR, p. 92)

Kathleen Hayes then became suspicious or aware during the night of 1 May 1984 that other members of the family had departed from the birth in the field story. She realised that she would not be able to leave the station that night unless she gave the gardaí the story they were looking for, namely that which linked the family to the murder of the Cahirciveen baby. She then began her long written confession. She was able to do this, Mr Justice Lynch said, because 'she herself half believed' that the story about the family being involved in the Cahirciveen murder was true (TR, p. 96). This was because of

> her guilty knowledge of what had happened to the Tralee Baby in the bedroom, the disappearance of the Tralee Baby from under the hay, the total silence as to

what had become of that baby, and the coincidental finding of the Cahirciveen Baby and the publicity about such finding and its injuries. (TR, p. 96)

He insisted that Kathleen was not 'terrorised nor was she overborne' (TR, p. 96). He pointed to her testimony to the Tribunal. 'She herself says that she made up large sections of the story and not that they were put to her by the Garda Officers in such a way that she had merely to assent to have them written down as though they were stated by her' (TR, p. 96). She made a conscious decision to give the gardaí what they were looking for, and that 'although Joanne Hayes may have her way most of the time with the family', Kathleen 'is the tougher personality and she ultimately influences the decision as to what must be done' (TR, p. 96).

So Mr Justice Lynch constructed the truth as follows: Kathleen was a tenacious and tough person. She adhered to the line of the baby being born in the field. Then, realising that other family members were telling a different story, she decided to tell the gardaí what they wanted to hear. Little or none of this was suggested to her. She made up most of it.

This closely corresponded with Garda Moloney's testimony about Kathleen giving a vivid demonstration of how Joanne stabbed the baby. Moloney had told the Tribunal that he was taken aback by Kathleen's confession. He realised at the time that she was rattling off 'a terrible incriminating statement without prompting, without anything being put to her'. He said that she was relaxed and composed, that she smiled while she was giving her statement and was humorous (TT, 55/62).

Mr Justice Lynch accepted this testimony as an accurate account of how Kathleen's statement was made. The main problem, and it is a very significant one, is that not only was Kathleen Hayes's confession false, but it also tied in very closely with the confessions of Ned, Mike and Joanne. Given that Mr Justice Lynch accepted the credibility of the gardaí and that the statements taken by them had been freely and spontaneously given, he failed to explain the similarity in the fictitious details about the stabbing, putting the body into bags, and the journey to Dingle. Even if a trip to Dingle had been talked about in great detail, this would not explain the close correspondence in the accounts of the stabbing and the bags.

Explaining the knife and the journey

The analysis of Ned Hayes's statement is perhaps the most critical to Mr Justice Lynch's explanation of events because Ned was the first to make a detailed false confession about the baby being stabbed to death with the carving knife. After the birth of the Tralee baby, 'all efforts to persuade Ned Hayes to get rid of the body in the sea off the Dingle Peninsula failed'. Mr Justice Lynch was reiterating here his claim that there were detailed discussions among the Hayes family about disposing the body off the Dingle peninsula. He claimed that Ned was 'as pliable as putty that the Cahirciveen Baby was his sister's baby seeing that this was what he, himself, really believed' (TR, p. 98). Ned believed that the Tralee baby had been removed by Joanne from the lands with the assistance of Jeremiah Locke and that it had been disposed of safely and permanently.

As Mr Justice Lynch described it, Ned Hayes broke with the story of the birth in the field after just over an hour of being questioned, and declared that 'whatever happened, happened in the house'. Ned then announced that he had been asleep in the cottage and was awakened by his mother who told him that Joanne had had a baby which she had stabbed to death with a carving knife (TR, p. 100). This, Mr Justice Lynch claimed, was made up. It was part of Ned's vivid imagination, fed by reading history and his involvement in amateur dramatics, made up from what he had read in *The Kerryman*. Mr Justice Lynch never discussed the possibility that the stabbing and the carving knife came from the gardaí even though they were the only ones present who knew that the Cahirciveen baby had been stabbed. He concluded that Ned knew that the detectives wanted to solve the Cahirciveen murder and deliberately gave them a story that fitted in with it. Indeed, not only were the gardaí surprised at the mention of the carving knife and stabbing, they were also surprised when Ned mentioned going to Dingle as 'they thought all along that the baby had been dumped into the sea somewhere in the Cahirciveen area'. Mr Justice Lynch seemed to forget that the gardaí believed that the body had been washed ashore, and if that had been the case and if the body had come from Abbeydorney, then it would not have taken much thought to locate Slea Head on the Dingle peninsula as the most obvious intermediate dumping spot.

Mr Justice Lynch did not accept that everything in Ned Hayes's confession was spontaneous, in particular Ned's statement that the bag they used for the body of the baby was a grey 0-7-30 fertiliser bag. Mr Justice Lynch concluded that it was more likely that Ned Hayes mentioned the bag when it was shown to him for identification while he was making his statement

(TR, p. 102). This does not explain how the turf bags emerged in Mike's and Mrs Hayes's statements.

When it came to discussing Mike Hayes's confession, Mr Justice Lynch was ambivalent. He pointed to the 'suggestibility of Mike Hayes in accepting something as true because he, himself, either half or fully believes it to be true, but does not positively know it to be so' (TR, p. 106). On the other hand, he later said that while Mike might be slow, he was nobody's fool. He agreed with Detective Shelly's description of Mike possessing 'a degree of native cunning', and insisted that a good proportion of Mike's confession was true, particularly the section in which he described the scene he discovered in the bedroom after the baby was born. (TR, p. 105)

> On the Tuesday night of the week before Easter week myself Johanna and Bridie, my Aunt went to bed at about 11.30 p.m. to three different rooms. Shortly after going to bed I went to sleep. I was awakened at about 2 am to 2.30 am by a person roaring and shouting. I got up and I heard that the shouting and roaring was coming from Johanna's room. I went into her room, my Aunt was there before me standing near the top of Johanna's bed. Siobhan was in a cot beside the side of the bed. There was a new born baby on the bed beside Johanna and she had her arm around it. The bedspread was wrapped around the baby. The baby was alive and crying. I got a fright when I [Michael Hayes] saw another baby there again even though I knew she was expecting. I was frightened all the time, when she wasn't married or anything. I stayed for a few minutes in the room, I didn't say anything. My Aunt was saying something, I don't know what she said. I left my Aunt in the room and went out to the kitchen. (TR, p. 214)

Mr Justice Lynch claimed that the reason Mike was able to tell this part of the story to the detectives was because it was true. The only problem is that in this section Mike used the term 'Johanna' to describe Joanne, which, as Joanne Hayes pointed out, would suggest an important anomaly if Mike's statement had been freely and spontaneously given. Referring to Superintendent Courtney's testimony to the Tribunal she noted:

> Most revealing was his persistence over three days in calling me Johanna. My brother Mike calls me Joanne but his statement on 1 May is full of Johanna and Detective Superintendent Courtney spent more than two hours with Mike that day. (TR, p. 153)

When Mr Justice Lynch insisted that the passage identified in Mike Hayes's statement was true, it suggests that large sections of the rest of his confession were not true. Mr Justice Lynch seemed to accept that these were the result of the leading questions put to him, yet in a clever twist, he blamed Mike for them: they resulted from a mixture of guilt and desire to help the detectives solve the Cahirciveen murder.

> Mike Hayes was well aware that the Detectives were convinced that Joanne Hayes was the mother of the Cahirciveen Baby and in view of what had happened to Joanne Hayes's baby, which he himself had seen, he believed that the Cahirciveen Baby might indeed be Joanne Hayes' baby. The knife, the bags and the journey were suggested to him in leading questions by the Detectives and were accepted by him, but they were so accepted, not because of any unfair questioning or pressure, but because of his own belief that Joanne Hayes' baby had ended up in Cahirciveen. (TR, p. 108)

The problem, which Mr Justice Lynch did not address, is that this questions the gardaí's trustworthiness. Lynch was constantly ready to take the gardaí's version of events, particularly in relation to what happened during the interrogation, yet he did not tie this in with the gardaí's insistence that the confessions were voluntary, spontaneous and independent. In the above passage he in effect rejected the gardaí's claims about the voluntary and spontaneous nature of Mike's statement. This perhaps leads to the most important question. How, if the statements were completely voluntary and spontaneous, were there such rich details of a stabbing that never happened, fertiliser bags that did not exist, and a journey that never took place? This was how Ned described the journey to Slea Head.

> I emptied out a brown plastic shopping bag of clothes which I found beside the wardrobe in the room. We caught a leg each of the infant and put it head first into the brown shopping bag. As we lifted the dead infant I could see blood on its chest. It was stabbed in the chest. I couldn't say how many wounds were in the chest. When we [E.H.] had placed the dead infant in the brown plastic bag, Joanne asked to be left alone in the room with the child for a few minutes. Both of us went back to the kitchen and left her alone for about 10 minutes. We layed the bag containing the infant on the floor beside the bed. When we returned to the room, she was on the bed turned towards the wall. The brown bag had been rolled closed so that the infant was not visible. We opened the grey fertilizer

bag, which was an 0-7-30, wider and each caught an end of the brown bag and put it into the grey bag. I have on this date been shown a grey fertilizer bag 0-7-30 and a brown shopping bag by Det. Sgt. Dillon and they are similar to the ones we used that morning. When we had placed the brown bag with the infant into the grey bag, my sister Joanne asked to be left alone again with the infant. We again placed it on the floor and left for about 2 minutes. When we returned she was in a similar position facing the wall and the top of the grey bag was tied with a string. I caught hold of the top of the bag and Michael caught the bottom of the bag. We took it through the kitchen. My sister Kathleen had the door of the car open as I had already asked her. Kathleen had the keys of the car and she handed me the keys of the car afterwards. I placed the bag on the floor of the car behind the drivers seat. Our car is a Ford Fiesta, blue colour registered number 822–ZX. The car is the property of my Auntie Bridie but both Michael and myself are insured to drive it. I went back into the house and brought a road map with me. I went back into the kitchen and told my mother and Aunt that we were leaving. My sister Kathleen had gone down into Joannes room where she was sleeping on a mattress. I drove the car and my brother accompanied us in the front passenger seat of the car which is a two door. We brought a shovel with us in case we might get a quite place to bury it. We had fully intended when we left the house that we would go to the sea with the bag and the further away the better. I drove the car into Tralee onto Blennerville, out the Dingle Road. At Camp Cross I stopped and took out the map to decide which road we would go. We decided to go by Conor Pass as we thought it would be the quietest. Going up Conor Pass we stopped for about 3 minutes and looked at the map again to decide which way we would go. We didn't pick out any place on the map to dispose of the body and we decided to drive on for another bit. We went on into Dingle and went out the Ventry Road. We stopped this side of Ventry and looked at the map again. It was then we decided to go to Slea Head. We drove on until we came to a spot about 2 miles on the Ventry side of Slea Head. I am familiar with Ventry and Slea Head as I have been there on a number of occasions. When I got to this spot which I though was the most suitable place I got out of the car and took out the bag containing the body. I walked around the back of the car with the bag and opened the door for my brother. I asked my brother to keep a watch out and I went in over a stone ditch, walked about 20 yards to the edge of the cliff. I flung the bag from the cliff and into the sea. I would say there was a drop of about 10 feet and I watched the bag drop directly into the water. I returned to the car, turned the car about on the roadway and drove back the same way as we had come. We arrived back home in Abbeydorney about 10 a.m. (TR, pp. 212–13)

Even if this was mostly due to Ned Hayes's vivid imagination, how did Kathleen and Mike both give equally vivid descriptions of a non-existent journey?

The patrol car in Dingle

Although the Dingle patrol car was not mentioned in Mike's statement, it was significant in persuading the County Solicitor, Dónal Browne, to go ahead with the charge of murder, and was therefore vitally important to the case. Browne told the Tribunal that it had been checked whether the Hayes brothers could have passed a patrol car, and one had been out early that morning (TT, 76/11). It was claimed that Mike had said freely and spontaneously during his interrogation that they had passed a patrol car as they were coming back through Dingle after dumping the body. During the Tribunal, Garda Tim Collins told the Tribunal that Mike was asked 'Did you meet or see anything on the way to Dingle on the morning in question, between your home and Dingle'? An entry in Collins's notebook read: 'said he saw a Garda car outside Dingle on the way back home' (TT, 60/62). Collins told the Tribunal that he drove back to Dingle the following day and that he talked to another local guard who could not explain how a patrol car would have been out at that hour of the morning, since garda patrol cars do not normally leave until 9.00. However, when they went back and checked the station log, they discovered that most unusually a car had been out at 7.30 a.m. on Friday 13 April. This provided crucial corroborating evidence that a journey had in fact been made. Given that, as Garda Collins insisted, Mike Hayes's claim to have seen a patrol car had not been suggested to him, but was voluntary and spontaneous, how did he manage to see the patrol car unless he had actually been there? Mr Justice Lynch explained this by returning to the detailed discussions he claimed were held in the farmhouse after the baby was born.

> Mike Hayes was also reluctant to get involved in such a journey and was very worried as to what they would do or say if they met a Garda Patrol car as feared by Ned Hayes. This is the origin of Mike Hayes' reference to meeting a Garda patrol car when asked by Garda Tim Collins if he had met anybody or anything on the journey. (TR, p. 22)

Mr Justice Lynch was therefore again blaming the Hayes family. It was a pure coincidence that Mike was worried about meeting a car along the route of a journey that was never undertaken, and that there was a car on patrol in Dingle that morning.

The importance of the bath brush

In his analysis of Mrs Hayes's statement, Lynch emphasised how she had lied to Detectives Smith and Coote at the beginning of her interview about what had happened that night. When Detective Callaghan arrived at the farmhouse, he told Smith and Coote about Ned's confession: how the baby had been born in the bedroom, stabbed with a carving knife, and taken away. Smith and Coote had gone inside and told Mrs Hayes what they had learned from Callaghan about Ned's confession. (TR, p. 111) This does not tally with Det. Garda Smith's evidence to the Tribunal. Smith said he did not in fact put to Mrs Hayes what Ned had said, when he took her second statement. (TT, 63/13)

Sgt. Coote told the Tribunal that while making her statement Mrs Hayes had said freely and spontaneously that Joanne had used the bath brush to beat the baby. He had then gone to the bathroom and returned with three or four different brushes from which Mrs Hayes selected the loofah or bath brush. Sgt Coote then asked Mrs Hayes if there were any stab marks on the baby, to which Mrs Hayes said 'No, just marks'. (TT, 63/46) He asked Mrs Hayes if she had a carving knife. Smith and Coote told the Tribunal that at this stage, Mrs Hayes got up, went to the kitchen drawer, brought back the knife and said 'this is the knife we normally carve the meat with'. This is the explanation for the sudden mention of a carving knife at the end of Mrs Hayes's statement when there had been no mention of any stabbing earlier in her statement.

There are two points of importance here. First, Mr Justice Lynch does not analyse the inclusion of the carving knife statement at the end of Mrs Hayes's confession. He noted: 'Mrs Hayes never said that Joanne Hayes stabbed the baby, or broke its neck. When the carving knife was produced, she merely identified it as a carving knife for the meat.' But there is a direct implication that the carving knife had something to do with the death of the baby. The inclusion of the carving knife in the statement seemed to provide important corroborating evidence for what Ned Hayes had confessed. Moreover, Garda Moloney, in his testimony to the Internal Inquiry, said that Smith and Coote had told him that Mrs Hayes had made a statement that Joanne Hayes had stabbed the baby. During the Tribunal, Maloney said he could not be certain about this (TT, 36/62). Mr Justice Lynch pointed out the importance of remembering that Mrs Hayes's statement was made in the comfort of her own home, that Smith and Coote knew nothing of the case until they had been dragooned into it that afternoon and that, consequently, 'they were in no position to put anything of significance into Mrs Hayes's mouth' (TR, pp. 109, 114). But if Mrs Hayes was not under any pressure, and her statement was purely voluntary, where did the reference to the carving knife come from?

Secondly, Mr Justice Lynch was certain that Joanne beat the baby with the bath brush in the presence of her mother and sister. It was this beating, he said, which caused the family to panic. If the baby had been stillborn or had died naturally after birth, it would have been reported to the proper authorities. This, he said, might even have been the case if 'the baby had been helped on its way by being momentarily choked by Joanne Hayes to stop it crying (as it was)' (TR, p. 112). Once the baby had been beaten with the bath brush, Mr Justice Lynch said that the whole idea of concealment and the story of Joanne giving birth alone had been concocted. The fact that Joanne had beaten the baby with the bath brush 'made it easier for the other members of the family to believe, suspect, or fear that she had stabbed it after death and broken its neck in a frenzy, when they read in "The Kerryman" of the 20th April, 1984 of the finding of the Cahirciveen Baby and a short description of its injuries'. (TR, p. 113) Much of what Mr Justice Lynch claimed is plausible. Whether it is beyond reasonable doubt is another question.

The bath brush, then, was a significant part of the unfolding scenario. Mr Justice Lynch claimed that when the turf bag, carving knife and bath brush were shown to Joanne Hayes on the evening of 1 May 1984, she became hysterical and confessed to having stabbed and beaten the baby. It was only after the carving knife had been produced, however, that Joanne Hayes suddenly realised that they were linking her to the Cahirciveen baby. This, combined with the realisation that her mother had made reference to the bath brush, which Mr Justice Lynch determined she had used to ensure that her baby was dead, was what made Joanne Hayes hysterical (TR, pp. 88, 91, 112).

In trying to identify how the bath brush came into Mrs Hayes's statement, it is important to remember that there was no clear forensic evidence to confirm that the Tralee baby was ever hit with it. This is not to deny that the emergence of the bath brush is peculiar. What made the murder of the Cahirciveen baby so gruesome was that it had been stabbed to death. It is, as Mr Justice Lynch recognised, quite easy to help newborn babies to their death without having to stab or beat them with a bath brush. But if the Tralee baby had not been beaten with the bath brush, and if it had not been mentioned to Mrs Hayes, how then did it come into her statement? It seems strange that, as Mr Justice Lynch argued, three of the family watched Joanne beat the baby with the bath brush, the baby died, and they then put the bath brush back in the bathroom to go on using it as if nothing had happened.

Mr Justice Lynch's insistence that the main thing to remember about Mrs Hayes' confession was that it was made in the comfort of her own home still left him with the problem, as with all of the Hayes family statements, of divining when she was telling the truth in her second statement. He took it that Mrs Hayes was telling the truth when she said that Joanne had used the bath brush to beat the baby. He insisted that Mrs Hayes witnessed Joanne beating the baby. Later in her statement Mrs Hayes said that Ned and Mike fetched a turf bag, put the baby in it and drove off at 5 a.m., returning at 7 a.m. But Lynch decided that this was not the truth. The baby was not put in a turf bag and no journey was made. Where then did the turf bag and the journey come from? Were they suggested or did Mrs Hayes mention them spontaneously. Once again, we enter the domain of what was suggested and what was made up. Finally, given that Mr Justice Lynch placed so much weight on Bridie Fuller's statement, it is strange that in her statement and evidence to the Tribunal she made no reference to the baby being beaten. Moreover, after her false confession, Joanne Hayes admitted in a letter to her Aunt Joan that she put her hand on the baby's neck to stop it from crying, but never mentioned beating it with a bath brush.

A botched investigation?

In the final part of his Report, Mr Justice Lynch turned to some important issues. He discounted the notion that once the Tralee baby had been found, the twins theory had been invented to cover up a botched investigation. Yet surely, although a reading of the confessions could lead one to suspect two births – one in the field and one in the bedroom – it was wrong to assume that Joanne had had twins and not reappraise the whole case. Such a reappraisal was all the more necessary when the blood groups of the two babies were shown to be different. The twins theory was more than just a defect; it was central to the whole case and the whole Tribunal. Mr Justice Lynch never explained adequately why all the gardaí, without exception, held so rigidly to the twins theory. Why were no doubts raised or expressed and no critical reflection made of the interrogation? He did not put forward the notion that the reason the gardaí were so adamant to maintain the twins theory was that to accept that only one baby had been born that night (the Tralee baby) would be to acknowledge that the Hayes family had confessed to a crime they had not committed. Perhaps the gardaí could not accept such an appalling scenario. Perhaps something was said, or perhaps the vista was so awful that nothing needed to be said.

Mr Justice Lynch acknowledged that, despite the presence of seven detectives from the Murder Squad, the investigation had been carried out in a slipshod manner. He attributed this to the gardaí's not expecting the case to result in a full court hearing or be anything more than a quickly completed investigation (TR, p. 131). He mentions some defects in the investigation. For example, the turf bag and the two other plastic bags discovered on White Strand went missing because they had not been properly identified and labelled. There could be another plausible explanation. The turf bag brought into Tralee Station by Garda Smith and Sgt. Coote was the one which Mrs Hayes identified, again supposedly freely and spontaneously, as being of the same kind as the one her two sons had used to transport the body of the baby from the farm. This bag was shown to Joanne and Kathleen and in their confessions they confirmed that it was similar to the one used that night. However, Ned and Mike were shown the 0-7-30 bag found on White Strand and confirmed that this was the type of bag they had used. Is it not reasonable at least to speculate that the conflict of evidence about the two bags was noticed and that it was not a coincidence that the bag which remained in the station was the one found on the farm?

In a strange twist, Mr Justice Lynch used the slipshod nature of the investigation and its many defects to sustain his argument of lack of communication rather than it being a concerted attempt by the gardaí to pressure members of the Hayes family into making confessions.

> The Tribunal is, of course, well aware that the Gardaí might get the same ideas and quite independently of each other put to different interviewees the same sort of things by coincidence, or on the other hand, they might talk together and agree on a line of attack on the various members of the family. (TR, p. 82)

While Mr Justice Lynch seemed to agree that the interrogation was a type of war played by other means, he rejected any notion of members of the Hayes family being subject to pressure. And while he admitted that suggestions were made to members of the Hayes family, he vacillated on the important issue of the extent to which the statements were given voluntarily, spontaneously and independently. He concluded that the notion that there was a conspiracy on the part of the gardaí to frame the Hayes family for the murder of the Cahirciveen baby was 'ridiculous – or if it were true, monstrous' (TR, p. 135). But while there might have been no overt, direct attempt to frame the Hayes family for the Cahirciveen murder, there could be a thin line between framing people and pressurising them to the point where they make false confessions.

PART II

CHAPTER EIGHT

The context

The first part of the book provided a detailed examination of the Kerry babies case. The aim was to try to uncover the truth about what happened, to retell the past as it really was. However, as we have seen, it was not a simple and straightforward case. There are still distinct, contradictory explanations of what occurred. The gardaí still insist that Joanne Hayes had twins and that the confessions made by her and other members of her family were voluntary, spontaneous and independent of each other. Joanne Hayes refuses to speak to anyone, including to me. She still, presumably, claims that she gave birth to the Tralee baby alone in the field at the back of the house. And she and members of her family still, presumably, claim that they were intimidated in confessing to a crime they did not commit. Mr Justice Lynch has retired as a Supreme Court judge. He, presumably, still holds to the findings of his Report that although the gardaí were sloppy in their investigation they were honest, unlike members of the Hayes family who were mostly liars.

Trying to tell the past as it really was is, then, quite difficult. There are still many conflicting versions of what happened in that small part of Kerry in April 1984. Even the Tribunal Report, which claimed to declare what were the facts of the case beyond reasonable doubt, left many things unexplained, particularly how the false confessions were made. We may never know what exactly happened. There is after all a price to telling the truth.

In the second part of the book, I draw back from the specific details of the case and explore what the case tells us about Irish society at that time. To what extent can we gain an insight into the structure of Irish society from one fragment of Irish life? To what extent can the analysis of the particular illuminate the whole? In doing this, we might not discover the exact truth about what happened, but we might find out, or understand better, why things happened the way they did. To begin the illumination, it is necessary to start shining a light on the wider context of what else was happening in Irish society at the time.

Rising violence

In December 1983, a businessman, Don Tidey, had been kidnapped. He was eventually rescued, but in the process two members of the security forces were killed. The Government promised a major review of security. In January 1984, the Minister for Justice, Michael Noonan, introduced a new Criminal Justice Bill to deal with the rise in crime. It was proposed to limit suspects' right to remain silent. The Association of Garda Sergeants and Inspectors were against any curtailment of the Bill.[1] By June, the number of serious crimes had risen to an all time high.[2]

In August, Garda Frank Hand was murdered during a raid on a Post Office in County Meath.[3] This brought the number of gardaí murdered since 1970 to 11. Before 1970, no garda had been murdered since 1942. In December, gardaí launched a concerted effort to halt the escalating number of attacks on elderly people in their homes in the west and north-west of the country. This followed an attack on two elderly sisters in County Roscommon, one of whom was murdered.[4]

In June, Tim Callaghan and Con Sullivan, two detectives who had been involved in the Kerry babies case, were accused during a murder trial of beating a suspect, sticking a poker in his mouth, and pulling a towel around his neck. The presiding judge was Kevin Lynch.[5] In October, Det. Garda Thomas Jordan denied in court unlawfully killing Peter Matthews in Shercock Garda Station in April 1982. Matthews had died from a heart attack which the state patho-logist testified had been precipitated by injuries to his head, arms, back and pancreas. Jordan testified that the station sergeant, Peter Diviney, had beaten Matthews. But Diviney had already been acquitted in a previous trial.[6] In December, three gardaí at the centre of the case were dismissed.[7] In November, two detectives were deemed to have been fully vindicated in the High Court following a defamation case in which their superior had claimed that a finger-print on a workman's helmet was that of a known IRA suspect and that he was willing to testify to this in court. It transpired that the fingerprint belonged to one of the detectives who had carried out the testing.[8] In December, in the Dáil, Michael Woods referred to the case of Amanda McShane from Tallaght, County Dublin, who it appeared was told to sign a statement that had been written out by gardaí. In another case, Michael Ward, a 21-year-old itinerant, was supposed to have committed 26 burglaries. When the case was investigated, it was found that he was in Mountjoy Prison when some of the alleged offences had been committed and, in others instances, no burglaries had been reported by the householders.[9] The previous March, John Ellis (Fianna Fáil) alleged in the Dáil that a small section of the gardaí were going beyond their proper role and that it looked as though the 'heavy gang', which had operated between 1973 and 1977, had been 'born again'.[10]

It is difficult to assess what impact the conflict in Northern Ireland had on the state, society and everyday life of the Republic.[11] This conflict, together with the general rise in crime that had been affecting Western Europe since the 1960s, had led to increasing violence and brutality and this, in turn, led to changes in the way the police, judiciary and politicians saw, read, and understood the world. Fear and suspicion were rampant, and a general feeling prevailed that the fundamental basis of society was under attack, in a way similar to that experienced after the terrorist attacks in America on 11 September 2001. This resulted in a determination to root out terrorists and those who attacked the basic values of society. It is therefore necessary to understand the mindset of members of the Murder Squad who became the first line of the state's defence against suspected hardened criminals and terrorists. Gardaí in a town like Tralee had of course developed methods for dealing with such suspects, but these methods were anathema to the way a guard such as Liam Moloney operated in Abbeydorney. The story of the Kerry babies is about what happened when two opposite types of policing had to work together.

Economic recession

By 1984, the economic boom of the 1970s was imploding. The incoming tide of economic growth, which was supposed to lift all boats, began to recede rapidly. The signs were everywhere. Investment fell to its lowest level in 15 years. At the beginning of the year, unemployment had risen to an all-time high of 15 per cent.[12] By the end of the year it had reached 17 per cent, the worst in Europe.[13] Inflation was at 10 per cent.[14] In August, an EEC report showed that one in three Irish people were receiving some form of social welfare benefit.[15] Emigration was on the rise; 11,000 had left in the previous two years.[16] House prices had fallen 15 per cent in the previous 18 months.[17] The public debt was rising rapidly, from 21 per cent in 1974 to 41 per cent in 1983.[18] The Irish pound was worth less than a dollar.[19] Car sales were down 40 per cent on the previous year.[20] In April, the Government realised that revenues from taxation were falling short of its target, and cuts in health spending were planned.[21] In August, it introduced a mini budget, part of which was to cut food subsidies in half.[22] In October, it launched a new austerity plan, *Building on Reality*.[23]

The economic recession that had begun in the early 1980s was deepening in 1984. It came after a long period of sustained economic expansion from the early 1960s and was enhanced by the entry of Ireland into European Economic Community in 1973. Slowly but surely the effects of the recession began to be felt at local level. Chances and choices in the labour and consumer market began to dwindle. The recession impacted on people's social, family and personal lives, but it is not exactly clear who was most affected. The links between economic recession and people feeling pessimistic and depressed are rarely direct and necessary. Do people, particularly the socially weak and vulnerable, become less self-confident, more reclusive, less rational and more emotionally unstable? Do they start looking for signs, 'hoping against hope', seeing and believing in things that are not really there?

At the same time, in a recession it is likely that the balance between freedom and control shifts to greater control, with traditional authorities more likely to assert themselves, and the majority more likely to insist on having its morality put into practice. The social elites and established are more likely to get their way. Not only do the outsiders and marginalised in society acquiesce, they are also more likely to support and identify with the elites. There is less sympathy for minorities and less tolerance of behaviour that deviates from prescribed norms.[24]

Sexual morality

In September 1983, the Irish people passed an amendment to the Constitution by a two-thirds majority, which held that the 'State acknowledges the right to life of the unborn, and, with due regard to the equal right to life of the mother, guarantees in its laws to protect, defend and vindicate that right'.[25] In January 1984, the Society for the Protection of the Unborn Child (SPUC) began a drive against abortion information and referral services being offered in Ireland. Open Door Counselling said that it was approached by 20 to 25 clients each week, the majority of whom went to Britain for abortions.[26] In July of that year, it emerged that 3,700 Irish women had had abortions in Britain the previous year, three quarters of whom had not been using any form of contraception.[27]

In January 1984, the Coalition Government sought all-party agreement to amend the family planning law, but this was rejected by Fianna Fáil. The Government proposed to make condoms available to all over 16 year olds, although sales would be from chemists and to those with a doctor's prescription.[28] The Bishop of Kerry, Kevin McNamara, said that making contraceptives freely available to unmarried people 'would produce seriously harmful consequences': contraceptive legislation had led to the moral corruption of youth, the alarming increase in abortion, the spread of pornography and venereal disease, the increase in marital infidelity and the instability of marriage, the corrosion of moral standards, the acceptance of pre-marital intercourse as an integral part of the social system, the spread of knowledge and use of contraceptives to young people of ever-lower age groups.[29]

Later in January, in a written submission to the New Ireland forum, the Catholic Church's Irish Hierarchy said they were completely against divorce, and that the family had an existence prior to and independent of the state.[30] In the same month, the Supreme Court ruled that a child born out of wedlock had no succession rights under the 1965 Succession Act.[31]

In August, a new pressure group 'Family Solidarity' was formed to defend family values. Fr Leonard Coughlan, a member of the group's national committee, wrote:

> Our society is sick financially, socially and spiritually. One way of getting the country back on its feet is through the basic unit of society, the family, which itself is being attacked from all quarters: by divorce, contraception, abortion, euthanasia and the encroachment of the civil authorities on the rightful duties of parents in areas such as sex education.[32]

In May, a motion put forward at the National Priests' Council of Ireland claimed that current affairs and entertainment programmes on radio and television 'consistently showed a marked bias in presentation, comment and general policy, inimical to the doctrines and moral principles of Catholicism'.[33] In October, a Wexford man was jailed for one month for running naked up and down a beach with a pair of sunglasses over his genitals. The judge said it was an 'outlandish crime' of gross indecency.[34]

In February, Germaine Greer had a promotional tour for her new book *Sex and Destiny* which was reported in the newspapers. She declared that 'recreational sex is the norm – we shouldn't have intercourse for children, power or prestige, only for fun. This, I claim, is masturbatory and infantile.' She said that people were subject to a barrage of temptation in the media. 'They believe sex is a social duty. They don't even know if they want it or not, but everybody is doing it, so they do it too.'[35]

Two opposing social movements had been gathering in Ireland during the previous two decades and, rather like when a large depression encounters a large anticyclone, gave rise to a violent emotional storm, particularly among young people. On the one side was traditional, conservative, Catholic teaching emphasising purity, chastity and self-denial. On the other was modern, liberal, individualism emphasising self-expression, eroticism and sexual experience. When these two movements collided, as they did over Kerry in April 1984, lightning struck and people were badly injured.[36] What happened in Kerry was not unique: ten weeks earlier a similar tragedy occurred involving a single mother and the death of her newborn baby.

Ann Lovett

On 30 January 1984, Ann Lovett went to Our Lady of Lourdes' Grotto in a secluded area of St Mary's Church grounds overlooking the town of Granard in County Longford. She was about to give birth and took with her a pair of scissors. She lay down in the trees in the pouring rain. Three hours later her cries attracted the attention of a young boy on the way home from school. She had lost a lot of blood; beside her, wrapped in her overcoat, was her baby. Two hours later they were both dead. Ann was 15 years old, the third youngest child and eldest girl in a family of nine. Her parents were described as very respectable people who kept themselves to themselves. It was said that neither her parents nor the authorities at her local Convent of Mercy school were aware of her condition. The Superior of the Convent of Mercy said, 'Ann was an intelligent girl and very happy in school and this can be borne out by her classmates. If she was having any problems they had not come to my attention nor to the attention of the school principal, Sister Maria.'[37] It emerged later that Ann had told a school friend about her condition shortly after Christmas, but had sworn her to secrecy. Nuala Fennell, Minister of State for Women's Affairs, commented 'There is little indication that a caring society has emerged fully in the wake of the three year pro-life debate we have just gone through.'[38] As one woman recalled to Gay Byrne on his morning radio show:

> When I learned that the thing that happened between men and women, as it was locally known, had happened to me, I slowly realised that I might also be going to have a baby . . . In terror and panic, I tried to find out from newspapers any snippets of information. I learned that babies like the one I might have were usually placed in brown paper bags and left in a toilet and I resolved to do this . . . For that reason, I started to carry around the one penny I would need to

get into the toilet to have the baby . . . I kept the brown paper bag in my schoolbag and kept the bag under my bed at night . . . Since I spent most of my time in the chapel praying, the nuns told me I had a vocation.[39]

In February, less than a month after Ann Lovett's tragic death, a baby was found abandoned in a shopping trolley in Ballymun in North Dublin.[40] Not long after this, there was an inquest into the death of an eight-day-old baby girl who had been found dead in a cattle trough on her family farm.[41]

In 1985, just after the Tribunal had begun, the Minister for Education, Gemma Hussey, said that her department and the government had a responsibility to introduce sex education in schools where it was lacking, or when parents felt the need for it.[42] However, it was not until 1994 that another Minister for Education, Niamh Breathnach, set about organising a comprehensive relationships and sexuality programme for Irish schools. The impetus for this initiative was the discovery of the body of a dead baby girl on the banks of the River Feale in County Kerry.

Single mothers

As Mr Justice Lynch pointed out in his Tribunal Report, the number of births to single mothers in the Irish Republic rose from 5.2 per cent in 1981 to 7.8 per cent in 1984, an increase of 44 per cent. Applying this increase to County Kerry, he estimated that the level of illegitimacy there rose from 3.4 per cent to 4.9 per cent. He concluded that this meant there were '103 illegitimate registered births in County Kerry in the year 1984, or in other words, two illegitimate registered births per week'. Little did Mr Justice Lynch realise that what he was describing was the beginning of an enormous social change. By the end of the century the number of births outside marriage had risen to one in three – a 323 per cent increase.[43]

Signs of this sea change taking place were already evident in 1984. In June, a study showed that the number of single mothers who were keeping their babies had increased.[44] Yet single mothers were still struggling. There were continual reports during the second half of 1984 of the efforts of the County Manager of Westmeath to evict a 19-year-old single mother from a house in which she was living in Athlone.[45] In January 1985, just before the Tribunal began, a single mother was evicted from her flat in Dun Laoghaire in County Dublin.[46] The most famous case was that of Eileen Flynn.

In February 1984, an Employment Appeals Tribunal upheld the right of an Order of Nuns to sack a single teacher, Eileen Flynn, who was living with and had become pregnant by a married man. Sr Anna Power complained bitterly about Eileen Flynn's behaviour in school during the Tribunal. 'She just flaunted it and did not try to hide it or to redeem herself'. The Tribunal upheld the dismissal mainly on the grounds that Eileen's lifestyle had become repugnant to the nuns' values.[47] In July, the judgement was appealed to the High Court, but again the dismissal was upheld. In giving his judgement, Justice Noel Ryan said: 'In other places women are condemned to death for this sort of offence. They are not Christians in the Far East. I do not agree with this, of course. Here people take a very serious view of this, and it is idle to shut one's eyes to it.'[48]

Moving statues

During the week beginning 11 February 1985, while the Tribunal was in session, 36 children in Asdee, a village about 20 miles from Tralee, claimed they saw movements in the statues of the Sacred Heart and the Virgin Mary in the local church. One of the children said she saw the figure of Jesus moving. 'His hand moved and called me. Then I saw the eyes of the Blessed Virgin move.'[49] She called over the other children. All 36 said they saw the statues move in various ways. On the following Sunday two thousand people turned up in the village. Adults as well as children began to see movements in both statues, hands being lifted, eyes moving, spots appearing on the Blessed Virgin's neck. One man who touched the Blessed Virgin statue said that his finger and thumb were held in the statue's grasp for several seconds as he tried to release them.[50]

The story of the moving statues reveals something else about Ireland at that time. It tells how much a magical-devotional habitus was central to being Catholic in Ireland at that time.[51] At the heart of this habitus – this ongoing, predisposed, but flexible way of interpreting the world – is a belief that the circumstances in this world can be transformed through divine intervention. This can be linked to a mentality characterised by a belief that the only way by which circumstances can be changed in some cases is through prayer and penitential practices. This, in turn, can be associated with a surrender of self-control – 'it is in God's hands'. One reason for the Catholic Church becoming and remaining so dominant in Irish society and elsewhere is that, unlike Protestant churches, it is able to combine this magical-devotional habitus with the rationalisation of everyday life.

Eamonn Casey

Eamonn Casey had been Bishop of Kerry during the 1970s. It was then that he developed a passionate love affair with Annie Murphy, an American who came to Ireland after her marriage failed. She became pregnant, gave birth to a son and, after living for some time in Dublin, returned with her child to United States. It was not until 1992 that the story broke in the national media. In the meantime Eamonn Casey had become Bishop of Galway. It emerged that he appropriated funds from parishioners in his diocese, using them to support his son growing up in America. After the story broke, Annie Murphy wrote a book about her affair, describing in detail when, where, and how they had made love, their passions and pleasures, and their trials and tribulations in avoiding being discovered.

While there are many differences between the affair of Bishop Casey and Annie Murphy and that of Jeremiah Locke and Joanne Hayes, there are some similarities. Although both couples were very much in love, and enjoyed their sexual relationships, their affairs were very Catholic. They engaged in unprotected sex. They realised that what they were doing was immoral and illicit according to the teachings of the Church but, even had they been able to obtain them, they refused to use contraceptives. This demonstrates the effect of a deeply imbued Catholic habitus which on encountering sex becomes not only unsettled, but also caught up in a massive cultural contradiction:[52] it is wrong to have sex outside marriage; it is also wrong to use contraceptives. And as the adage goes 'two wrongs do not make a right'. There are two possible explanations for following this line of reasoning. One is that using contraceptives is the greater evil of the two. The second is that using contraceptives demeans the completely voluntary and spontaneous giving of the self to the other which is at the heart of the Catholic Church's teaching. The use of contraceptives means premeditated sex, and this is seen to demean the sacred character of the love. The danger of unprotected sex is that it leads to pregnancy, which in sexual relationships outside marriage often ends in tragedy.

What is remarkable about the Annie Murphy story is the way in which she was cast as the witch who had led the innocent bishop astray. Once she put her eye on him he was ruined. She was, as Fintan O'Toole described, the Catholic Church's worst nightmare come true, 'a figure from the medieval witch-hunter's manuals: wild and indiscreet, loose-tongued and lusty'.[53] As I shall argue, the picture painted of Joanne Hayes was often not very different. She, too, became an infamous Irish woman who had the intimate details of her sex life picked through in public. The difference, of course, was that Joanne Hayes's story was extracted during a long and painful public tribunal.

CHAPTER NINE

Long-term processes of change

To understand what happened in Kerry in 1984, it is necessary to understand how people are caught in time, circumstances and relationships rarely of their own choosing and making. They become embedded in social structures that exist before them, in families, communities, nations, states and churches. They are enmeshed in relations of gender, age, class, race and ethnicity. They are caught up in long-term processes of social change, in becoming more rational, civilised, sexual, secular and informal. It is in the process of living their lives that they constitute themselves as individuals and, at the same time, reshape the structures, forces and processes within which they have been shaped.[1] To understand how people come to be the way they are, how history works through them, we have to have an understanding of these processes of change. This does not mean that people are not free to choose what they do, that they do not have free will, but rather that the choices they make are limited. As moral actors, people struggle to be happy, to take pleasure and enjoy themselves, to be responsible, honest, fair, loyal and caring. But the ideas and rules as to how the good life can be achieved vary over time and place. By looking back at the Kerry babies we can see how people were caught in time. The problem, of course, is that Irish people are still are caught up in the legacies of that time. It is still part of the present; it is not yet history.

In this chapter I want to draw attention to long-term processes of social change that took place in Ireland during the second half of the twentieth century. Processes of change throughout Western society were beginning to reach into the hearts, minds and bodies of Irish people. Economic relations between people were becoming more commodified, based more on the market and less on community practices of swapping, bartering, and exchanging gifts and favours. Social life was becoming more rationalised, as were bureaucracies in the formulation of policies, rules and regulations. At the same time increasing equality between men and women, children and adults, and different social classes was becoming apparent, and social life was undergoing a general democratisation. The state, the Catholic Church and other social institutions were becoming more accountable for their actions. These processes of change were linked to individualisation and a shift from self-denial to self-indulgence, the sexualisation of love, the informalisation of social relations, and to a change in the balance of power in social relations between men and women.

The secularisation of Catholic Ireland

Throughout the second half of the twentieth century there were notable changes in the nature and level of religious adherence among Irish Catholics, in the power of the institutional Church and its influence on everyday life. Popular devotional religion has declined steadily with fewer people making pilgrimages, participating in novenas, putting up religious icons in their homes and villages, saying the rosary and venerating saints. Orthodoxy – sometimes termed 'simple faith' – has become less prevalent. At the centre of this was a decline in the legalistic adherence to Church teachings, rules and regulations. Instead, there was a move to an *à la carte* Catholicism in which an increasing number of Irish Catholics chose the teachings, practices and beliefs to which they wished to adhere.[2] A shift took place from orthodoxy to heterodoxy, from dogmatism to debate and discussion, from authoritarianism to liberalism, and from a rigid adherence to rules and regulations to Catholics choosing certain teachings and practices and disregarding others. These changes can be seen as the protestantisation of Irish Catholicism, and as part of a longer process of secularisation.[3]

During the long nineteenth century of Irish Catholicism, when the Catholic Church held a monopoly over Irish morality, the power of the Church was reflected in its ability to limit and control what people did and said, how they viewed and understood themselves and the world in which they lived. The power was maintained through the control and influence that the Church had in education, health and social welfare. The Church presided over family, community and social life, setting parameters and boundaries to what could be said and done. Church teachings and practices structured the Irish Catholic habitus – the automatic predisposed way that Catholics read and interpreted events in everyday life as good or bad, right or wrong.

During the second half of the twentieth century, there was a gradual change in position of the priest in Irish society, from being an authority to be obeyed to being an authority struggling to be respected. People were no longer as dependent on his blessing or good word. He no longer symbolically dominated families and parishes. The decline in the influence of the priest can be measured by the decline in the number of priests and the decline in the numbers attending Confession.[4] To understand what happened in Ireland in 1984, we have to realise that the grip which the Church and its priests had over the moral life of the laity was markedly loosening. Young women like Joanne Hayes might have had a high level of adherence to the beliefs and practices of the Church, but they were no longer afraid of his power to shame, demean and demoralise those who failed to adhere to the Church's laws regarding sex and birth outside marriage.

In 1984, those who distanced themselves or rejected the advice of the priest and the teaching of the Catholic Church were left in a state of anomie or moral limbo. They had rejected traditional Catholic moral values, but they had not replaced them with new ones. They had become used to bending, adapting or disobeying Church rules, rather than developing their own. This state of anomie was often associated with a deep sense of isolation and meaninglessness. The Catechism, ten commandments, church pronouncements, and the dictates of the priest were no longer seen as adequate guidebooks to the moral twists and turns that took place in pubs, discos, back alleys and the back seats of cars. It was not to be until the 1990s that the state stepped into the breach and offered an educational programme that would teach young people how to bypass the Catholic Church and become self-directed, ethically responsible individuals.[5]

These transitions and tensions can be seen in the Hayes household. Being a good Catholic was based on an unquestioned orthodoxy, an automatic way of reading, understanding and interpreting life. It was founded on regular, ritualistic, practice that became part of the calendar and routine of everyday life. This was how Joanne Hayes described her religious practices and beliefs.

> Religion was an important but unobtrusive factor in our everyday lives. Almost from the time that we could talk we would be helped by Mom and Aunt Bridie to say a prayer before going to bed and of course as we got older our night prayers were extended. Each evening after tea we would all kneel to say the Rosary and Mom would announce the mysteries and lead the prayers afterwards. We still say the Rosary each evening. Like most Irish families we would never dream of missing mass on Sundays and holy days and on the night before there would be arrangements about who would go to first mass and who would wait for second. This was to ensure that there would be somebody available early to milk the cows and feed any dry stock that would need attention, especially in

the winter, and those who went to the later mass would do the shopping and get the Sunday papers. On Sundays and holy days only the most essential work, like milking and feeding, would be done as it was considered very important to respect the Sabbath. Most Sundays we would go to a hurling or football match or the beach if the weather was suitable.

To non-Catholics it may appear that in fact religion did intrude in our lives but we regarded such religious duties as an element in life that was as basic as eating and drinking. Likewise, going to confession and holy communion each month was never seen as a nuisance and we have tried to maintain that practice all our lives.[6]

The Hayes family household had many of the usual pictures and statues of Christ, Our Lady and the saints. During the Tribunal, they all relied heavily on the solace, comfort and consolation brought by these. This impressed Mr Justice Lynch.

Each member of the family brought the same little statue and medals into the witness box with them, one after the other, to support them, but the one who worked with them most furiously from hand to hand and in his fingers was Ned Hayes when the pressure of maintaining a false story was greatest. (TR, p. 102)

In July, while Joanne Hayes was waiting for the case of murder to be heard in court, she made a pilgrimage to Knock Shrine where she made an all-night vigil to Our Lady. 'If Our Blessed Mother couldn't help me I was doomed I felt, and I have always believed since that it was her intervention that saved me from being convicted in the wrong.'[7]

Although this Catholic way of life, particularly religious practice, was closely linked with everyday life in the Hayes's family home, the institutional Church, represented by the local priests in the parish, seems to have distanced itself from the Hayes family during their ordeal. Certainly there is little evidence of their moral or spiritual support. None of the local priests assisted at the burial of Joanne Hayes's baby. The Parish Priest, Fr Hickey was apparently ill, and no curate was available; the Hayes family had to rely on a priest from Tralee. Nor was help forthcoming when the family was in need of support during the summer.

Mom asked our local curate Fr Nolan to say mass in our house, but he declined and offered to say mass in Kilflynn church, which is not our local church. We were disappointed but not really surprised. However, in February we did have the privilege of having mass celebrated in our house by a visiting priest and each of us took an active part in the service. Unfortunately we could not invite our neighbours because the priest did not wish our local clergy to hear about it in case they might be offended.[8]

This indicates the way the power of the Catholic Church operated at parish level in 1984. It provided no public – nor, it would seem, private – support for members of the Hayes family. Instead local clergy, in distancing themselves from the family, used a shaming strategy (see chapter 10). The Hayes family wanted to reaffirm their honour in the community through the Church, but were refused. They were publicly shunned by the Church. What is remarkable is that the Hayes family were well known and well established. It is an indication of the power of the local clergy that they could initiate such a strategy without fear of negative repercussions.

The distancing of local clergy from the Hayes family appears to have begun before April 1984 and the birth of the Tralee baby. It possibly started with Joanne Hayes's 'effrontery' in challenging Catholic norms by having a quite open affair with a married man and then having his child. This might help to explain why the local Garda, Liam Moloney, and not one of the local priests, came to speak to Joanne to ask her to give up her affair with Jeremiah Locke.[9]

Changing economic strategies

The institutional strength of the Catholic Church in Ireland and the monopoly that it developed over morality was closely linked to a rural economy based on small-scale agricultural producers.[10] The vision the Catholic Church had of a good, morally healthy society corresponded closely with the way social life was organised in Ireland from 1850 to 1950. Social life was predominantly rural and based around small family farms. In 1922, 58 per cent of male workers were employed in agriculture. In 1926, 57 per cent of farmers had fewer than 30 acres.[11] Farms were not fully commercialised, profit-oriented enterprises. The production and distribution of farm produce was in and through small towns. The duties and responsibilities of farm life and family life were closely connected.

The Catholic Church's teaching, which promoted the virtue of self-denial and attacked the evils of materialism, was linked to an economic policy obsessed more with protecting indigenous industry and agriculture than with economic growth. The strategy of protecting the fragile home market from outside influences was related to the strategy of protecting Catholic souls from the pernicious evils of foreign films and books promoting sex, sensuality and selfishness. Unchecked free trade was seen to lead to the growth of cities, industries and manufactured goods and to the decline in importance of people producing food. The Church held that the natural unit of society was the family. Only through stable, secure families could the evils of state control, industrial life, totalitarianism and communism be overcome. It was within the family that children were taught 'to sacrifice themselves for the welfare of others'.[12] It was through the creation and maintenance of a 'purely rural culture' that farms and families could be maintained. This rural culture had to create a 'distinctive way of life – dress, food and amusement, dwellings'. Only with such a culture could the tide of individualism that was sweeping through Europe and Ireland be stemmed.[13]

To appreciate Joanne Hayes's situation it is important to realise what it was like to grow up in an unsettled, contradictory period in Irish history, when the nature of work, farming and family life were changing, and when young people were caught between identifying with and remaining loyal to the Catholic vision and interpretation of life, and breaking free and creating a new meaning and identity.[14] The Hayes family farm was a typical medium-sized holding of 58 acres in North Kerry.[15] Some of the land was scrub, but the rest had good natural drainage. This made it 'potentially one of the best small farms of its kind in the area'.[16] Although the Hayeses produced crops such as barley, beet and potatoes, the farm was built on milk production. In his time, Joanne's father, Paddy, had built up a good herd of twenty cows.[17]

As on many other small farms in Ireland, the Hayes farm afforded family members a standard of living related to how well it was worked, and to the number of dependent people living off the proceeds. As a way of protecting that standard of living, various conventions, rules and regulations had developed concerning transfer of ownership and control of a farm. If one lesson has been well-learned in Ireland from the nineteenth century, it was that the subdivision of holdings to allow sons and daughters to marry was a recipe for disaster.

After the Famine, marriage increasingly became confined to one son who inherited the family farm and one daughter who was given a dowry to marry locally. The number of marriages declined and, because sons had to wait for their fathers to retire or die before they could marry, the age at which people married increased. Other brothers and sisters could stay on the farm, or migrate or emigrate. But if they stayed on, they could not marry and have children.

They had to remain celibate and deny themselves the sexual pleasures of life. They also had to be protected from being led into temptation. A cultural ring of steel had to be placed between men and women to prevent any occasions which could give rise to irresistible temptations.[18]

Marriage and inheritance strategies were adopted to ensure that farm holding was maintained as a unit. They required a new form of discipline and control to be instituted over sons and daughters. All desires, urges and pleasures, particularly those of a sexual nature, had to be controlled. Unexpected and unwanted pregnancies could lead to unwanted marriages which would upset the new social order. In the new regime of bodily discipline, there was a strict supervision and control of emotion, affection, love and sex within families and in the outside world. Contact between eligible single males and females had to be closely monitored. The notion of forming a relationship with a member of the opposite sex had to be eliminated. The Catholic Church provided the moral teachings and practices necessary for fathers and mothers to instil this rigorous regime in their families.

From the late 1950s, the Irish state began to distance itself from the Catholic vision of Irish society by ceasing its ambivalent, half-hearted engagement with capitalist growth and introducing policies to embrace it fully. It was not until the 1970s, however, with the beginning of an influx of foreign capital into Ireland, that the economy began to develop rapidly. The penetration of foreign capital, entry into the European Economic Community, and the gradual shift towards the semi-periphery of the world capitalist system, were to have a dramatic influence on what happened in Irish cultural life during the second half of the twentieth century.

The 1970s was a time of economic expansion in Ireland. Part of the survival strategy of many small-scale farmers was to hold on to their land, to take up non-farm jobs and to continue farming on a part-time basis.[19] Employment opportunities were increasing in Tralee, the main town in Kerry and about five miles from the family farm. Joanne, like her brother Ned and sister Kathleen, had no difficulty in finding work.[20] But when the bubble of economic expansion burst at the beginning of the 1980s, they were among the first to lose their jobs. Like many others, they became dependent on the unemployment assistance provided by the Irish welfare state.

What were remarkable in these transformations were the economic strategies and tactics by which members of the Hayes family lived their lives. Until the arrival of Yvonne in 1983, six adults lived together in two separate houses, only two of them – Mike and Joanne – were direct income earners. The other four, Mrs Hayes, Aunt Bridie, Kathleen and Ned were all dependent on some form of pension or social welfare assistance. Mr Justice Lynch concluded that this combination of working and social welfare payments brought in a considerable income (TR, p. 14). Thus the expansion of the capitalist economy and the state social welfare services enabled Joanne to make choices which would not have been possible at other times in Irish history.

The increased opportunities for off-farm employment in the 1970s did not alter the traditional Catholic farm and family strategies outlined above. Given that Mike Hayes was running the farm and in line to become the inheriting son, it might have been expected that Ned, Kathleen and Joanne would have left the farm to seek employment and marriage partners elsewhere. The fact that they all stayed on the farm and stayed single was a reflection of the residue of traditional strategic practices to maintain a decent standard of living, as well as of a lack of realistic alternatives. What was interesting, but not unusual, about the Hayes family in 1984 was the number of single people living on the farm. Kathleen, Mike and Ned were single. None was engaged, or appeared to be involved in any serious relationship. Mike, as the son running the farm, might appear to have been the most likely to start a serious relationship. However, not only was he not readily identified as the inheriting son, but it would appear from the Tribunal that he was not 'the marrying kind'. In the 1940s and 1950s, Ireland had one of highest levels of postponed marriage and permanent celibacy in Western societies.[21] The Hayes family reflected a pattern of postponed marriage and permanent celibacy which were dominant features of rural life in Ireland for over a hundred years. In the previous generation, five children were on the farm. Joanne's mother Mary was the only one who married. Her brother Maurice (Joanne's uncle), the inheriting son, did not marry. None of her sisters (Joanne's aunts) married. Kitty became a nun, Bridie a nurse, and Joan a priest's housekeeper.[22] These, then, were the family structure, culture and marrying practices within which Joanne Hayes came of age. If girls like Joanne wanted to have romantic liaisons, to marry and have children, the convention and expectation was that they would leave the farm and make a life for themselves elsewhere. Joanne Hayes did not leave the farm, but she began to make a new life for herself. She resisted and challenged the dominant conventions of sex, marriage and children.

Individualisation: from self-denial to self-indulgence

The decline in the Catholic Church's monopoly over morality – and sexual morality in particular – was associated with changes in the way people perceived, understood and presented themselves. The dominance of the Catholic Church in Irish social and cultural life brought with it a discourse and rhetoric of self-denial. The creation of self-denial and suffering became central to the early Christian notion of the soul controlling the body.[23] The theory and practice of self-mortification became combined with a conception of ethics that was based, not on an overall lifestyle, but on an identification and codification of discrete acts that were seen as right or wrong.[24] This became central to modern Christian conception of sin and to the development of priestly power. Irish monks in the fifth and sixth centuries, through their penitentials, developed a detailed catalogue of sins and appropriate penances and the model of an ascetic life based on self-denial.[25] There are many vestiges and models of asceticism and self-denial in Ireland. Each year on the last Sunday in July, up to 20,000 people, many bare-footed, climb Croagh Patrick, a mountain in the West of Ireland. Thousands also go to St Patrick's Purgatory in Lough Derg. This involves fasting on bread and tea or water for three days, keeping awake for 24 hours, and spending hours praying as one goes around beds of stones and gravel in bare feet.[26] The most recent and perhaps the most venerated Irish model of asceticism was Matt Talbot, a twentieth-century working-class Dubliner who lived a life of celibacy and poverty, slept on planks of wood and wore a hair shirt.[27]

The ascetic regime instituted in Ireland in the nineteenth century was not substantially different from that of Victorian Britain or America.[28] The differences lay in the lack of organised opposition and resistance in Ireland. Three factors were associated with this. First, as Carroll has pointed out, penitential practices have not only been central to Irish religious life since the fifth century, but were also an important part of the first devotional revolution during the Counter Reformation in the sixteenth century.[29] The re-emergence of the Catholic Church brought a new rigorous moral code imparted in seminaries and passed on within schools and homes. It may not have been Jansenistic, but it was certainly Augustinian in its approach. In the long nineteenth century of Irish Catholicism, self-denial became the *doxa* – the rhetoric and order of the day. It became an embodied, unquestioned moral demand.[30] Catholics were taught that there was no greater virtue than self-sacrifice for the greater good of others. This was the heart of Christ's message. It was exactly what the Christian martyrs had done. Those who repressed and denied themselves for the good of others were the virtuous – the pious, the meek, the humble – who were told that they would inherit the earth. The corollary of this was that those who questioned, challenged and resisted Catholic ethos and practice were disloyal sinners and outcasts. They were the ones who expressed rather than denied themselves. Self-expression within the rules and regulations of the Church was encouraged and rewarded, but any other expression of the self led to sins of self-obsession and selfishness.

The moral messages passed on within churches, homes and schools about how to be a good girl, how to talk and present oneself, how to be pure, chaste, and obedient, gave rise to personalities which, in an ideal Catholic world, would be shy, demure, pious, humble, chaste, dedicated, loyal, self-deprecating virgins who, once they were married, would become chaste mothers. These messages were contained in stories about the virgin martyr saints. They were encoded and inculcated in the way the Church talked about women, the way mothers raised their daughters, the way girls were taught in schools, and the way women enforced the message on each other.[31]

In the latter half of the twentieth century, this Catholic meaning and identity, particularly the emphasis on asceticism and self-denial, came under attack. From the 1960s a new philosophy of liberal individualism and self-indulgence began to emerge. This provided a new way of reading and interpreting life and of relating to other people. At the heart of liberal individualism was the notion of freedom of choice. As long as they do not interfere with others or the common good, then individuals should, as much as possible, be allowed live their lives as they see best. Moral absolutes, especially those dictated by an authoritarian institution such as the Catholic Church, were seen as relics of fundamentalist religion.

Liberal individualism was a complete new ethic of self-realisation. What was a marginal and unacceptable philosophy at the beginning of the 1950s was to become the predominant philosophy by the end of the 1990s. But the cultural residue of Church teaching still inhabited the souls of Irish Catholics. Hundreds of years of practising self-deprecation, of surrendering the self to others, of denying pleasure and desire, could not be overturned in one or two generations. Notions and practices of putting oneself down, not considering oneself to be worthy, and denying oneself would not only linger for many years to come, but would re-emerge at times with vigour and certainty. The second half of the twentieth century in Ireland was at best an unsettled time when people tried to reconcile the differences between Catholic fundamentalism and liberal individualism. Sometimes this led to social turmoil, particularly with regard to contraception, abortion and divorce. The struggle between these two ethics sometimes broke out into open social warfare. The battle still continues on many fronts and it was a struggle that affected the lives of most Irish Catholics. Joanne Hayes was one of them.

Liberal individualism accords well with postmodern notions of all values and beliefs being relative – right and wrong for some people might not be right and wrong for others. Moreover, the view that individuals should not only actively pursue happiness and the pleasures of life, but that in some respect they have an ethical obligation to do so, was becoming prevalent. People who did not know how to let go and enjoy themselves were seen not so much as being unethical as leading an unbalanced life.

Instead of denying themselves, individuals were encouraged to discover themselves, to allow their feelings, emotions and passions to surface. They were encouraged to dance, let go, scream and shout. They had to shed their inhibitions. They had to get in touch with themselves and their bodies. They had to understand how pleasure and desire manifested and operated within their minds and bodies. They were encouraged to explore new avenues and paths towards discovering themselves. Young people no longer embraced being obedient, demure, pious, humble and chaste. They wanted to taste the fullness of life, to express themselves, and to experience rather than deny their pleasures and desires. Sex was at the heart of this challenge and resistance.[32]

The shift from the Catholic culture of self-denial to a consumer culture of self-indulgence was not a smooth or even process.[33] It was represented in the shift from the closed, restricted, well monitored and supervised life of a rural village such as Abbeydorney, to the relatively anonymous, unsupervised life of Tralee town. The Sports Centre where Joanne Hayes and Jeremiah Locke worked was an icon to the new sense of self. The idea of caring for oneself, of keeping fit, healthy and good looking, as an end in itself, was new to Ireland in the 1970s. It replaced the idea of penitential practices. The result of Lenten fasting and going on a pilgrimage to Lough Derg might be similar to dieting and going to the gym, but they represent very different conceptions of self.

The media, especially television, were in the vanguard of the ethic of liberal individualism central to stimulating consumption and production. Television brought new images of men and women, new lifestyles, desires, pleasures, needs and interests into Irish homes. The messages of the media slowly, subtly, and effectively counteracted the traditional Catholic fundamentalist message of self-denial. Religion and priests were pushed into the background of social life. The plots and characters in the imported soap operas and serials emphasised the importance of self-expression and self-fulfilment. These changes were to lead to a transformation in the way people in Ireland lived their lives and realised themselves as individuals.

Any attempt to measure the influence of the media on people's attitudes, beliefs and behaviour, for example in relation to violence or its impact on children interpretation and understanding of the world, has been fraught with difficulties. At one level we can try to estimate the impact of different portrayals and images of women on television, particularly within foreign soaps and serials. We can say definitely that the image of women represented in these soaps and serials was very different from that promoted by the Catholic Church. Women became icons of beauty and sexuality. They were romantic, passionate, wilful women engaging in highly competitive sexual liaisons with men, inside and outside marriage. The impact of television on life in rural Ireland has not been adequately described or analysed. But it seems to have had a dramatic impact in the Hayes household.

> As we grew up and learned to play cards there was many a hectic game of 110 in the kitchen before we went to bed. Mom loves a game of cards and she taught us all in our turns but since the arrival of television the cards are rarely produced and 'Dallas' and 'Dynasty' have taken their place. Nowadays the television is switched on whether we are watching or not; it has become a way of life.[34]

Much of the hidden message of television programmes is connected with individuals struggling to realise their interests and pleasures in life. The female characters in serials such as *Dallas* and *Dynasty* were constantly plotting and struggling against each other and the male characters to get their own way and to achieve pleasure, fame and fortune. This is the message of liberal individualism. If you do not look after yourself, if you do not look out for number one, you will be trampled on. This is a very different message from the Church's teaching of self-denial.[35]

Lessening inequality, greater equality between the sexes

From the end of the nineteenth century, in Western society respectable women began to move out from the confines of the home, domesticity, and the role of being 'good' wives and mothers. Throughout the twentieth century women began to demand and achieve greater social, political and economic freedom.

They began to stay on in education, take on occupations that were traditionally the preserve of males, play male sports, go to pubs, wear male clothes and take on roles in most facets of social and cultural life that were traditionally male.[36] Given the dominance of the Catholic Church in Irish society and its view of women, the process of greater integration and equality between the sexes was slower in coming into Ireland. It was not until 1974 that women could continue to work as civil servants after they married.[37] In the early 1980s some men still challenged, resisted and resented women's struggle for equality. While we can trace this in social legislation and policies, and in the rules and regulations of organisations and clubs, it is also important to see how it was translated into everyday social life and the emotional struggles between men and women at work, home and at leisure. At the heart of the Kerry babies case is a clash between women and men, particularly between older, conservative men and younger, liberal women, as to what is appropriate, right and fitting for women to do and say.

When Joanne went to work in the Sports Centre she came to know other single young women who were working there. She began to join them when they went for drinks after work. The other women were from the town and were much more lively and adventurous. They had a steady income and money to spend, and the social and moral climate of Tralee had changed since the 1960s. It had not been long since women had been first allowed into pubs in Ireland. These young women were not afraid to go to the pub unaccompanied by men and openly enjoy themselves. After the pub, there were discos and dances, and fast-food restaurants to go to. They had economic resources and they were rewriting the conventions about appropriate behaviour for women. Joanne was quiet and self-restrained. The others encouraged her to break out and express herself. They gave her presents of new, fashionable clothes. Gradually she began to become more self-confident.

The development of women's self-awareness and confidence was something that was happening all over Ireland in the 1970s and 1980s. Irish women were struggling to break free from the language of Catholic Church teaching with its emphasis on motherhood and self-denial and to find a new language and way of thinking, writing and talking about themselves. Women began to form groups, to counsel and advise themselves, and to set up their own education courses. They were beginning to reflect critically about themselves, and the families, communities and society in which they lived.

In this respect, the struggle for self-development and women's education in Ireland can be seen as part of a larger feminist struggle to reconstitute the way

Irish women knew and understood their world.[38] Part of this process involved women coming together and validating the importance of their feelings, experiences, desires and pleasures. They knew intuitively how years of domination, marginalisation and oppression had been written into the bodies and minds of Irish women. They listened, and told stories, to each other. They asserted the right to do this together, on their own, in pubs throughout the country. The women with whom Joanne worked and played became an informal women's support group. They had jobs. They were independent. They distanced themselves from how traditional males expected them to behave. They worked hard and felt that they had earned the right to enjoy themselves as they wanted to. It took courage and support to go out and stay out, to have another drink if they wanted to. The banter, joking, messing, and teasing added to the sense of freedom. There was a new romantic headiness that came from the drink and the company. People could say what they wanted. Those who had the courage could do what they wanted. They could show their feelings. They could break free from the shackles of convention and the age-old restrictions on love, passion and sex.

The informalisation process

What Wouters has described as a process of informalisation took place during the twentieth century. It involved a relaxation of the formal social codes of behaviour which had emerged in the course of the civilising process that had spread throughout Western society from about the early sixteenth century.[39] Between then and the late nineteenth or early twentieth century, social behaviour had become subject to stricter, more formalised and more detailed rules, norms and manners. In the steering of individuals' behaviour, the balance tilted from external controls – the constraints placed upon people by other people's disapproval and other sanctions – towards more even, more all-round, more automatic and habitual self-constraint. Then, during the twentieth century, manners became less hierarchical, formal and rigid, reflecting the trend towards relatively less unequal power – and increasingly more equal interdependence – between the rungs of the old hierarchies, including between men and women. Yet while the trend towards more formalised rules of behaviour was reversed, Wouters has sought to demonstrate that the process of informalisation actually brings with it still *more* demanding standards of self-constraint and emotion management. As social interdependency increased, manners developed more nuances. People were expected to be more flexible and sensitive when it came to assessing good or required social behaviour. 'From a set of rules manners turned into guidelines, differentiated according to the demands of the situation and relationship.'[40] No longer were greeting or speaking to people in a certain way inhibited by the old demands. There was greater freedom in dress, dancing, music, hairstyles – and sexuality. This process of informalisation was reflected in the way people dealt with social hierarchies. The gaps between men and women, parents and children, teachers and pupils, priests and laity, upper and lower social classes, all narrowed and became less formal. Social superiors or those with more power were not automatically deemed to be better people. At the same time, identification with and sympathy for the underdog was increasing. The priest, the politician and the policeman were not automatically seen as being in the right. Again this process helps to explain the increase in sympathy for the unmarried mother and the greater disdain for priests and policeman who treated those at the margins of society too rigidly and without sympathy.

But as with the move from self-denial to self-indulgence, the move to greater informality, flexibility and promiscuity in social relations did not occur evenly or smoothly. Some in positions of authority associated the demise of formality with a lack of respect. Others felt that increased promiscuity and the tilting of the balance from external to internal forms of self-constraint was leading to a breakdown in moral and social order. Some in positions of authority were willing to forgo formal deference and respect, but others resented the change. Women who showed lack of deference and respect to men in high social positions were in danger of being castigated and labelled not only as socially inferior, but also as a threat to social and moral order.

At school, Joanne was a quiet, reserved girl. She does not appear to have had any teenage romances. At the school debutante's dance, she was one of those who came without a male partner.[41] In the beginning, Joanne's life was still strongly centred on village life in Abbeydorney. Her colleagues saw her as a quiet, shy and very retiring girl. She kept to herself. She would often sit silently in the company of others without feeling any obligation to take part in conversation.[42] When her female colleagues came in to work with stories of the previous night's escapades, Joanne would have little or nothing to say. In the beginning her evenings were taken up with watching television and reading her favourite *True Romance* magazine.[43] Her new job brought her in contact with a wide range of people. Her leisure time activities began to centre on Tralee. Her confidence increased. She learnt to deal with people. She was experiencing quite a different lifestyle. She had a reasonable income and she was able to enjoy new pleasures such as going to the pub for a few drinks after work with some of her colleagues. There was a new freedom and anonymity, and no longer the supervisory eye of her family, village friends and neighbours. She became self-assured. Her colleagues began to buy her new clothes. She began to dress fashionably. But as she grew accustomed to the people she knew at work, and who came into the Sports Centre, the demure, shy, awkward girl gradually became a confident, outgoing woman with a disposable income, who was able to indulge in the pleasures of buying clothes, going to films, dances and discos, and the pub. Having a job not only brought her money, it also brought her status and recognition in her home and in the village of Abberydorney – where her sister Kathleen and brother Ned soon became unemployed.

This is how Nell McCafferty described the transition from shy country girl to confident, outgoing, urban woman.

> Sometimes when spirits were high, she'd roll down the window of whatever car they found themselves in and yell out to pedestrians. There were pubs and discos and bright lights and fast-food places for their entertainment.[44]

Joanne began to discover herself socially and sexually. She began to express herself in secret in an urban society in which she was not so well known. At night she went home to a family and a traditional way of life in which notions of self, desire and pleasure had a long history of denial and repression.

As we saw in chapter 5, Det. Sgt Gerry O'Carroll believed that there were 'umpteen' cases in Ireland where women had become pregnant by their next-door neighbour. In the Tribunal Report, Mr Justice Lynch noted that the level of illegitimacy in Ireland and County Kerry was such that there was nothing extraordinary in two unmarried mothers doing away with their babies in the same week (TT, 41/12; TR, p. 148). This reflected a common way of thinking about unmarried mothers over the previous fifty years. In February 1930, M. J. Kennedy, TD, asserted in the Dáil that the vast majority of mothers of illegitimate children 'observe no moral code whatever'.[45]

The romanticisation of love

The trend from a culture of self-denial to a culture of self-indulgence was combined with changes in the relations and intimacies between men and women. The control of marriage within the Irish modernisation project necessitated the physical separation of boys and girls, men and women in social and cultural life. Men and women learnt to keep to themselves. There were strict controls and supervision of the contacts between men and women. The number of occasions on which they could be together on their own became limited. The history of Irish courting has yet to be written, but myth and folklore would suggest that much of the intimate contact between men and women was confined to the private spaces of fields, hedgerows and back lanes.[46] Marriage was portrayed more as a means of ensuring labour for the land and an heir for the family than as the natural conclusion of a romantic courtship.[47] It became devalued and seen as an obligation to be avoided as long as possible,[48] not as an opportunity for love and intimacy. The lack of intimate contact between men and women can be linked to unease, awkwardness and embarrassment in each other's company. This is often associated with communicative incompetence between lovers about their fears, thoughts and feelings. This incompetence often carried through to married life.[49] In other words, it would seem that for most of twentieth-century Ireland the romanticisation of love was the hidden exception rather than general rule. Where do we find in twentieth-century Irish literature the level and type of romanticism that characterised much of French novels during the second half of the nineteenth century? (A cursory examination of twentieth-century Irish literature would suggest, that with certain exceptions, romance and sex preside in their absence. The greatest writer, James Joyce, would suggest that in the case of Ireland the exception proves the rule.)[50] In the absence of historical ethnographic research, we have to turn to literary sources to discover the type of intimacies that took place between men and women in the hundred years after the Famine. Perhaps the rigour with which Catholic sexual morality was enforced led to a spatial and emotional distance between Irish men and women that were reflected in their courting habits as well as in their marriages. This leads to the conclusion that the romanticisation of love did not arrive in Ireland until the second half of the twentieth century. More significantly, it did not have a long incubation period before it became conflated with the sexualisation of love. To put it simply, in the history of Irish love there was not much of a gap between Irish men and women practising being lovebirds and becoming sexual lovers.[51]

In the absence of reliable ethnographic research, we have to depend on cultural commentators and analysts to decipher when, how and to what extent a romanticisation of love took place in Ireland. In the 1960s, Dorine Rohan quoted Ethna Viney's claim that farmers' wives were starved of love and affection.[52] At around the same time, Bishop Birch of Ossory said that in many families no one showed any emotion until somebody died. 'The young were growing up without any real knowledge of love in their lives, and their characters were often deformed for that reason.'[53] The absence of romance and intimacy was often linked to poor sexual relations in marriage. Rohan said that one of the most frequent complaints she heard from Irish wives was that their husbands were completely insensitive to them as lovers. On the other hand, she said that many husbands complained that Irish girls were frigid and not interested in the sexual side of marriage. In many instances it appears that the couple developed a mental block about their sex life and never discussed or referred to it at any time.[54] Throughout the twentieth century, visiting anthropologists suggested that the relationship between husband and wife in rural Ireland was cold and formal rather than warm and intimate, and that relationships between mothers and sons were closer than those between husbands and wives.[55] Hugh Brody depicted men and women as living in different social worlds, with different life experiences, identities and aspirations.[56] As O'Donoghue points out, following Masters and Johnson's research, it is not the Catholic Church *per se* which is the source of Irish sexual inhibition, but rather that the Catholic Church was another example of a number of strict orthodox religious regimes which produced sexual dysfunction; this happened equally, for example, among Jews, Presbyterians or Hindus.[57] Of course the issue is not one of dysfunction from some eternally normal way of being sexual, but rather that being sexual has always being closely linked with being religious. Ireland was different in that its way of being sexual, of thinking about sex, of being with members of the opposite sex, was primarily constituted within the institutional outlook, teachings, rules and regulations of the Catholic Church. What was exceptional was how deeply the institutional teachings of the Church penetrated the bodies and minds of so many Irish people, and that this penetration lasted until the 1990s. If we take discussion about important personal issues as an indicator of intimacy, then the results of a survey in 1982 suggest that Irish husbands and wives were not close, certainly when it came to sex and fertility control. Three quarters of the women interviewed said that they had little or no discussion with their husbands about family planning.[58]

When Joanne Hayes fell in love with Jeremiah Locke, she was not the first woman in Ireland to fall in love with a married man. But the decline in the Catholic Church's monopoly over morality, the individualisation of social life and the move towards self-indulgence, the breakdown in the formal social codes that had restrained social contact between single women and married men, and the romanticisation of intimacy all increased the likelihood that she and

Jeremiah would respond physically to the emotional bonds that emerged between them. Joanne Hayes was caught in the middle of a process of social change which saw the balance of social control tilt from external forms of authority towards more individualised and internalised forms of self-constraint. In 1980s Ireland, romantic liaisons could develop between colleagues at work, between a single woman and a married man. But, as Joanne Hayes noted herself, the absence of the external constraint of patriarchal rule in her home in Abbeydorney had a major influence over her behaviour.

> My father's death in 1975 was a terrible shock to me because we had always been very close. I resented his being taken away from us and when I think back now I have no doubt that if he and Uncle Maurice had lived just a few years longer I would never have found myself in the trouble that blighted all our lives.[59]

The sexualisation of love

During the second half of the twentieth century in Ireland, love began to change from having a romantic and spiritual meaning to being seen as inseparable from the erotic longings and pleasures of sex. This was a process that had emerged in America during the early decades of the twentieth century, but because of the Catholic Church's monopoly over morality, and because of the culture of self-denial, did not emerge in Ireland until the end of the century.[60]

From the end of the 1960s, sex began to move outside the confines of Catholic Church discourse. Censorship was lifted in 1967 and people began to talk, write and portray sex in different terms. Debate and discussion about sex was less hidden and problematic.[61] It moved from the confessional to radio and television. It was displayed rather than hidden. It moved from being a sin to being a pleasure. People became less shameful and embarrassed about their sexuality. It was not an even process, and the Catholic Church fought to prevent the sexualisation of Irish social life.[62]

In the 1970s, a new Principal was appointed to the Mercy Convent in Tralee where Joanne Hayes went to school. Sister Kathy had worked in the United States and had come in contact with a new Catholic liberalism that followed on from Vatican II. She often appeared in public in ordinary lay clothes and once attended a dinner dance in a Tralee hotel wearing a dress. She changed the nature of the annual retreats in the school, introducing sessions for debate and discussion. In Joanne Hayes's final year, pupils were given a detailed lesson in sexual intercourse by the school's career guidance officer who was accompanied by his pregnant wife. The girls were divided up into small groups and the nature of sexual intercourse was explained with the aid of diagrams. Sister Kathy left the school in 1982 and took up a post in London.[63] Despite Sister Kathy's attempt to break the mould of sexuality education, the concentration appears to have been on the biological dimension rather than sexuality and relationships. Joanne Hayes, however, felt that she was well educated about sex:

> In my teenage years I used to join in the chat about boys and who we liked. Coming from a farm, I didn't have a lot to learn about the basic facts of life: at some time or another you see it all enacted among the animals. Girls weren't obsessed with sex in the same way that boys appear to have been. I never heard a girl say that she had had sex or that she would be prepared to do so with any fellow in particular, whereas I have since discovered that boys would boast proudly of such a 'distinction' and even lie about it to impress friends.[64]

The weakening of central authority – the process of internal reform, and the move to adapt the Church's teaching on sexuality to the changing realities of Irish social life – can be seen as part of the slow decline of the Catholic Church's monopoly over Irish morality in general, and sexual morality in particular. This process was also evident in people, especially young people, making up their own minds about what was right and wrong when it came to sex. Their attitudes to pre-marital sexual intercourse, the use of artificial contraceptives, birth outside marriage and homosexuality, were changing. Again, it was not a smooth or even process. Catholic Ireland was in turmoil, and church leaders were regularly in heated debate with politicians who wanted to liberalise the laws on contraception. The illegality of abortion had been cemented by being made unconstitutional the previous year. Divorce would remain unconstitutional until 1996. Homosexuality was illegal.

Irish people were becoming free from a traditional, conservative approach to sex, but they were still bound up in the chains of Catholic thought and teaching. This led to contradictions in the struggle to combine sexual activity with remaining a good Catholic.

The Sports Centre in Tralee, where Joanne went to work in 1978, epitomised the new ethical regime of health and fitness, sexualisation and the aesthetics of the body. Leading a good life began to shift from the penitential body of self to looking after oneself, and keeping fit and healthy. Bodily self-discipline and control were in vogue. Men and women were beginning to jog, run and work out. Community halls and sports centres were being built around Ireland, particularly outside large towns like Tralee. 'In a sense, the sports centre symbolised the vigour, enthusiasm, and unabashed sexuality of youth which was now a potent and vibrant force in Ireland.'[65]

Since there was no bus service to Abbeydorney, which was four miles outside Tralee, and since Joanne did not drive, getting home from work was always a problem. Generally one of the family drove into town and collected her. On 26 October 1981, for the first time, Jeremiah offered her a lift home. They stopped on the roadside on the way and made love in the back seat of his car.[66]

A number of resources and facilities became available to Joanne and Jeremiah in the early 1980s in Tralee – work, leisure, pubs and a car – which had previously been the preserve of the more well-to-do urban middle classes. Their intimate romance might have imitated the stories that Joanne had seen in *Dallas* and *Dynasty*, and read in *True Romance*, and so a knowledge and a competence in returning looks, smiles, greetings, words of affection, touches and embraces might already have been acquired. They knew how to play the game of romance. But the game of sex was quite different. Joanne Hayes might have been sexually experienced when she met Jeremiah Locke, but it needed a skilful player to be able to handle men and deal with drink, desire, love and affection. Playing the game of love and sex in Tralee in the early 1980s meant having to deal with and perhaps engage in sudden, passionate, lustful sex without the language to discuss birth control, or having access to contraception. Sex outside marriage between consenting adults was not illegal, but it was illicit in the eyes of the Catholic Church, and the state was reluctant to alter the rules of the game by enabling young people to learn about sex and sexuality or to have access to contraception. There was not a contraceptive mentality. Love and sex were conflated. They were seen in the Catholic sense of the complete giving or surrender of the self to the other. To use contraception would be to reduce sex to an instrumental means of satisfying one's desires. One's partner would become a means towards an end. This would demean the relationship. Sex had to be seen as the complete giving of the self to the other, regardless of the consequences. It might have been wrong for unmarried people to make love, but it would be worse to introduce any artificial barrier to making love.

I have been asked many times why we weren't using contraception in view of our precarious situation. The truth is that we never considered it. I was deeply in love and to use contraception merely to have sex would have been placing a barrier where emotionally I felt none. My commitment was total and unlimited. Contraceptive facilities were available but we didn't consider using them and it is ludicrous to suggest that the Catholic church's opposition to contraception had anything to do with it. By falling in love with a married man I had broken one of the church's cardinal rules anyway.[67]

When Joanne Hayes met Jeremiah Locke, the game of love and sex had two sets of rules, one devised by liberal individualism, the other by the Catholic Church. Joanne had learnt to express herself, to become self-confident, to challenge convention and to follow her heart. She also knew fully that by having sex with a married man she was breaking a fundamental rule of the Church and an established social norm. Her interpretation of what happened was a mixture of liberal individual reasoning (she was madly in love) and a legacy of Catholic morality (she believed contraceptives undermined the complete giving of the self to the other). For sex to be moral it had to be done with an overall intention of creating life, and so when she had sex with Jeremiah it was not out of lust, or just for pleasure alone. Yet Joanne seems to have wanted a demonstration of his love, to conceive and have his children.

Although illicit sex can be seen as a game played by two players, the rules and results have always been very different for men. The rules were never explicit. Since there was no education in relationships and sexuality, they had to be picked up along the way, through what was read in magazines, or heard from friends. The first cardinal rule was that while it might take two to tango, men might make the initial advance, but women did the leading. Men had to learn that if they continued to advance when women were not willing, they were on the verge of rape. The second cardinal rule was that if anything happened as a result of playing the game, it was the woman who would bear the burden of the shame, disgrace and, in many cases, the pregnancy.[68] The game of sex in rural Ireland in the early 1980s was played for high stakes. Joanne Hayes might not have received much education in relationships and sexuality, but she was well aware of what happened to single women who became pregnant. There were many stories of girls disappearing from the scene. Some went to Britain to have abortions. Some went to Magdalen homes to have their babies and then give them up for adoption. Some abandoned or killed their baby shortly after birth. These responses were done in secrecy and silence. Some like Joanne defied convention, had their baby, became unmarried mothers, and continued to live in the community.

CHAPTER TEN

Honour and shame

On the 55th day of the Tribunal, Mr Justice Lynch became exasperated.

> They are a very odd family. They knew there was a baby out there on the lands the whole lot of them for two and a half weeks, and they carried on normally, not just put on a face of being normal, but, when I specifically asked were they normal or trying to be normal, I was told they were perfectly normal. (TT 55/61)

If we look at what was considered normal Irish cultural life of the time it should help us to understand the events of Kerry in 1984, especially bearing in mind that they occurred at a time of cultural change, social transgression and personal crisis. It is easy to dismiss the Hayes family as being different – not like us – but because we are all constituted as individuals within the same cultural system, we share a similar way of reading, understanding and interpreting the world. Moreover, we can learn something about ourselves from the people and events in this story, as from a Greek tragedy. To dismiss the Hayes family as completely different or abnormal makes them out to be weird, almost exotic, individuals (other from us) which, in turn, makes them vulnerable to being turned into scapegoats.[1]

As mentioned at the outset of this study, it is difficult for an outsider to enter into and understand the mentality, hearts and minds of the people who lived in Abbeydorney and Tralee in the 1980s.[2] Of course, the corollary is equally true: it could be equally difficult for those who lived and grew up in Kerry to enter into the mindset of urban, middle-class, academics and intellectuals. But unless the latter understand and appreciate the logic of life as lived in Kerry at that time, they will have understood little about what happened, and what it was like to be Irish at that time. To understand social life, it is necessary to theorise about and understand very real but quite abstract social structures and long-term social processes. Unless we understand how these structures and processes are acted out in the lives of individuals in everyday social life, we will have committed the cardinal error of assuming that everyone else reads and understands the world not just in the same way, but also in the way that intellectuals and academics do.[3]

Much of what happened during the Kerry babies case can be seen as a struggle involving honour, pride and shame. Most of the tactics employed by members of the Hayes family leading up to the birth of the Tralee baby and the events surrounding its death were a desperate attempt to maintain the honour and respect of the family in the community. It was a struggle to keep their good name, to avoid being the subject of scandal and gossip.

On the other hand, throughout the winter of 1983–4, Joanne Hayes experienced the shame of being an unmarried mother, of being abandoned by her lover, and of being ignored by her family. She tried to conceal all signs of being pregnant. Everyone knew she was pregnant although, with the exception of some friends, nobody said a word. During her pregnancy with the Tralee baby, Joanne Hayes lived with the stigma of being pregnant but not married. Though it had changed a great deal over the years, it was a stigma as old as the hills in Kerry. She retreated into herself and lived within a regime of silence, denial, and shame. But shame and stigma can lead to tragic results. A continual, unrelenting sense of shame often, suddenly, turns into a rage that is taken out on the source of the shame.

It would be wrong to say, as Mr Justice Lynch suggested, that only the Hayes family, and Mrs Hayes in particular, was obsessed with honour (TR, pp. 58, 77, 113). The case called into question the good name of the gardaí. The reputation of the Murder Squad, the state's elite police unit, was on the line. After years of dedicated, often unrecognised, service, it seemed that they had slipped up on 'a banana skin'. It was tragic and shameful for them that it was not a case involving dangerous criminals or terrorists. Rather it was a case which, for the leaders of the Murder Squad, involved their own people – members of an ordinary, decent Kerry family.

Understanding honour

Honour is about the integration or standing of the individual within society.[4] Because it is something that pertains to individuals and to the society to which they belong, it has both an individual and a social dimension. It is a personal feeling or estimation an individual has about self-worth. But this feeling of self-worth has to be matched against society's evaluation.

Pride, then, can be seen as one's own personal estimation of being a good person; it produces an emotional sense of well-being. Pride is based on feeling good. Honour, on the other hand, is the objective side of the same coin. It is the way one is perceived by others. Unlike pride, honour is not an emotion or sentiment.[5] It is more objective or empirical. It is identifiable when people say good things about or do good things for you, your family, community, people or nation. Receiving honour makes one feel proud. However, if one's objective honour is undermined or attacked, the point of contact is one's pride; one feels ashamed.

There are two sources of honour.[6] *Personal* honour comes from one's behaviour. It is achieved through adhering to conventions, norms and values. You develop a personal record for honourable behaviour. You are seen as truthful, loyal and dependable. It is built on engagement in normative behaviour; staying within the boundaries of accepted social codes, laws, manners and morals. Personal honour leads to the accumulation of what Bourdieu calls symbolic capital.[7]

In rural Kerry in the 1980s, personal honour or distinction might have come from a variety of sources in everyday life, for example the way people greeted each other, the way they spoke, dressed, walked or held themselves. It might have also come from the way they kept their word, returned favours or avoided giving offence. At another level, personal honour might have come from engaging in the rituals and conventions around which daily life is constructed: showing an interest and concern for others, sharing the latest news, telling a story, making a joke, teasing, smiling, laughing. It is through creating and recreating a shared sense of meaning that people develop a sense of identity and belonging. They also come to be liked and respected. This symbolic capital can be seen as a form of points accumulated for good behaviour. Having a good store of points, or having an accumulation of symbolic capital, helps when it comes to getting a favour done, obtaining permission or resources, or getting a job. Thus honour, or symbolic capital, can be traded for social, political and economic capital.[8]

Public honour is the respect that comes from holding other forms of capital, particularly cultural capital. It is accumulated not so much from what you do, but what you have, who and what you are. It comes from occupational position, property, wealth, education, courage, skill and cleverness. It comes from being recognised as superior, whether by virtue of your sex, family and kin, your education, your occupation, your abilities, or your services to the community. This could include the family and kin to which one belonged, the type of farm and how well it was run, the number and type of educational degrees, certificates or diplomas, the amount of wealth. It could come from achievements at sport, or being a good musician, cook or storyteller. Public honour marks a person out not merely as being different, but also as superior.[9]

The overall social position of someone in a rural community such as Abbeydorney is based not just on their occupation – priest, doctor, policeman, publican, teacher, nurse – but on the volume and mix of the different forms of capitals they have accumulated.[10] A person's standing in the community would depend on wealth, occupation, level of knowledge, understanding and education, network of social contacts and, what I have emphasised here, their level of honour. It is important to realise that in a rural community like Abbeydorney, people might be honoured and respected and have high levels of symbolic capital without having much political or economic capital.

Ned Hayes, like his uncle before him, was passionately involved in the local GAA club and was on the selection committee. He may have been unemployed, and he may have worked only as a van driver, but he was well known and respected. He read history and was involved in theatre and drama. His brother Mike did not have much cultural capital. He had left school early. He was not involved much locally. His standing in the community came from owning and running the Hayes family farm. Similarly, the status and respect of Joanne and Kathleen would have come primarily from their family name and home. In comparison with their aunts Bridie and Sr Aquinas, however, they had not accumulated as much position and status in society. Despite their inherited cultural capital, they had not accumulated any significant political or economic capital.

Life in Abbeydorney in 1984 and today, as in many other villages, revolves around regular, face-to-face contacts with people, most of whom, like their ancestors, were born and reared there. An individual's standing in the community comes from the standing of their family. To save the family name and face it is necessary to keep up appearances. It is family honour that produces a sense of acceptance and belonging, a sense of pride and well-being. If one member of the family behaves badly, the honour of the family can be undermined, and this can bring shame on all its members.

Anthropological studies have shown that public honour is often associated with gender and sex; it tends to be a male obsession. These studies show that it is mostly men who become enraged, get into physical confrontations, and end up fighting to defend their own and their women's honour. Most studies also suggest that a woman's honour is closely linked with her modesty, purity and chastity.[11] Pitt-Rivers, for example, argued that a woman was dishonoured when her sexual purity was tainted. When she committed adultery, her husband's manliness was attacked. It brought dishonour not only to him, but also to his family, and 'to all the social groups who are involved reciprocally in his honour'.[12]

The honour of the Hayes family

Joanne Hayes's public honour came from being well educated (having attended the local Mercy convent in Tralee), having a good job (particularly in a time of economic recession) and, most of all, coming from a well-known, well-established family.[13] It was within her family that Joanne Hayes was socialised into laws and practices which formed the shared commonsense view of the world which became the basis for attaining personal honour.[14] The honour of Joanne Hayes came from symbolic capital accumulated in previous generations when her father, Paddy Hayes, married Mary Fuller.[15]

In openly challenging the norms and conventions of married life, Joanne was not just undermining Catholic Church teaching, she was challenging the well-honoured system of family life around which the Hayes farm and household had revolved for generations. She was challenging the reproductive strategy on which the viability of the farm and economic capital had depended. She was undermining the previously unquestioned, naturally accepted notion that men and women only have sex within marriage, that marriage is not simply a matter of individual choice, and that having sex outside marriage is an attack on the reproductive strategy which has been developed over a hundred years. The honour of the Hayes family, the symbolic capital it had accumulated over the years, had been built around the embodiment of these reproductive strategies.

The Fuller family were politically and socially well connected. Ned Fuller had been headmaster in the local school. In the 1980s he was still referred to as 'the Master Fuller'. Maurice Fuller, Joanne Hayes's uncle who had lived with the family, was involved in politics and the local football club. He was President of the local branch of Fianna Fáil, the largest political party in Ireland. He was also the Peace Commissioner for the area. The local guard Liam Moloney was a regular visitor to the Hayes family farm when Maurice Fuller was alive to have him witness documents and give 'his seal of approval'.

Maurice Fuller had four sisters. Mary had married Paddy Hayes, Joanne's father. The other Fuller sisters had high status positions. The eldest, Kitty, trained as a teacher and then became a nun – Sr Aquinas – in the Mercy Order.

The youngest, Joan, also trained as a teacher, but gave up for health reasons. She worked as a priest's housekeeper in Kildare. Bridie, the middle sister who lived at home with the Hayes family, had trained as a nurse, worked in Malaysia after the war for a number of years, returned home and worked in the local hospital. She was the only woman in the village, and one of the few single women in 1950s Ireland, to own a motor car.

Aunt Bridie

When it comes to understanding how honour was won and lost in a village community like Abbeydorney's, the life of Bridie Fuller is particularly revealing. After leaving school she was sent to Cork for a poultry instructors' course. However, she left this within a few months and went to train as a nurse in England. She did very well and passed her exams in 1942. When she finished her training, she joined the British Army and was sent to serve in Malaya in 1945 at the end of the Second World War. She was a diligent, efficient and highly competent worker, well liked and highly respected. She became a theatre and ward sister, was decorated, and promoted to the rank of Major. When she was in Malaya she had an active social life and became romantically involved with an army doctor. Malaya was a completely different climate and social environment with its own lifestyle. Photographs of Bridie in Malaya reveal these differences. In one, she is dressed in a short white blouse and matching skirt that is cut well above the knee. She is standing against a rock with a male and female friend. They are obviously having a good time and were caught joking, laughing and smiling. They have taken up highly contrived poses that are a subversion of the formal camera poses of the time. It portrays an informal, liberal and self-indulgent lifestyle that is confident enough to poke fun at formality. Most important of all there is vibrant sexuality about the photograph: two good-looking women with a handsome, debonair man.

The photographs of Bride Fuller in the farmhouse in Abbeydorney in the last years of her life are in stark contrast to those taken in Malaya. She is literally a pale shadow of her former self. Bridie left all that she had come to know and like about an informal, liberal, self-indulgent lifestyle behind her in Malaya. Once she returned to Abbeydorney, she became enveloped in her family. She stayed to help and mind her mother. But her mother did not live much longer and died in 1949. Bridie then worked in St. Catherine's Hospital in Tralee. Her status and honour in the community were very high: she was a nurse; she had

Bridie Fuller (left) on the beach in Malaya in the 1940s.

travelled abroad. She was also outgoing, self-confident, good looking and very eligible for marriage. She used to go to dances with her close friend Margaret Brown. They even thought of buying a car between them which would have added to her status in the community in the 1950s. But Margaret married and went to live in another village. Whatever romantic liaisons Bridie had, they came to nothing. The language of love, romance and sex in traditional Catholic Ireland in the 1950s and 1960s was very different from what it had been in Malaya.

Bridie became the traditional Irish woman who surrendered herself to the love and care of others. As the Catholic Church taught: family was everything, the self nothing. She lived at home with brother Maurice and her sister Mary. When Mary married Paddy Hayes in 1954, she became enveloped in Mary's life. When she was not working, she was helping Mary rear her four children. She had a good steady job and a relatively good income. She was a proud and efficient worker who was highly regarded in the hospital. When she arrived back from Malaya she became the dominant person in the Fuller family and, later, the Hayes household.

As time went by and the liberal days of Malaya became a memory of a land far away, Bridie began to drink quietly, secretly, on her own, at home. She slowly became an alcoholic. She stayed up late into night and slept during the day. At the same time, she began to lose the symbolic capital – the honour, status and respect – that she had accumulated. She was forced to resign from her job in St Catherine's. There were complaints about her driving. Out of deference to the family and her age and status, the local guard Liam Moloney did not confront her directly. Instead he phoned her sister, Sr Aquinas. It was her sister who told Bridie that she would have to give up driving the car. Bridie withdrew into the family home and into herself. Nell McCafferty tells the story of Bridie turning up at a funeral:

> Not an eyebrow was raised when Bridie turned up once at the funeral of a former nursing colleague, in a state of disarray. She joined the guard of honour wearing her old uniform. She had put the uniform on over her civilian clothes, which hung down below the hem. A tattered cardigan, pulled on over the lot, completed the ensemble.[16]

After the death of Paddy Hayes (Joanne's father) in 1975 and Maurice Fuller (her uncle) in 1979, the Hayes family was vulnerable. There was no grand patriarchal figure to defend the honour of the family. The economic recession of the 1980s brought unemployment. Only Joanne had a steady job outside the family farm. But the family was well established and were still honoured and respected in the community.

Bridie Fuller (left) in the Hayes home with Mary Hayes, Joanne Hayes's daughter Yvonne and a neighbour.

Shame, guilt and pride

Throughout her pregnancy with the Tralee baby, Joanne Hayes lived in shame. She did not tell her family she was pregnant. She withdrew from social life. She did not go to a doctor. Part from a couple of minor exchanges in conversation, she did not talk to any of her friends and colleagues about her condition. There was no appropriate language in which she could express her feelings and sense of shame.[17] She was caught in the transition from traditional to modern Irish society. She had been part and parcel of the new Ireland. With the pregnancy and birth of her daughter Yvonne, she had managed to stand up to the Church and traditional morality, yet during her pregnancy with the Tralee baby the old Ireland regained control. The traditional shame of the Irish unmarried mother began to envelop her.

Shame is the intense pain that comes when self, self-esteem, and sense of belonging have been diminished, or are under attack. It is a fear of social rejection, of being avoided, shunned, or laughed at. Fear of being shamed induces conformity. Those who do not conform feel the conflict of being different, but are able to overcome this. On the other hand, when bonds linking a family, community or village are strong, not conforming is seen not as an act of betrayal or disloyalty, but rather as a threat to the social bond. In this scenario, individual deviancy is tolerated.

In some respects, then, the reaction of Joanne Hayes's family, fellow workers and local community to her becoming a single mother was an indication of the strength of the social bond. She might have felt the conflict of failing to conform, but she did not feel ashamed. She said that her family were 'very upset at first' and wanted her to have the baby adopted. She refused. She told them they could throw her out, but they 'never threatened such extreme action and they accepted her [daughter Yvonne] happily when she was born'.[18] The social bonds in her family, village and workplace were sufficient to prevent any major shaming strategy over what might have been deemed a major sexual transgression at the time.

When Joanne Hayes and Jeremiah Locke began their affair, they did not appear ashamed of themselves. They met openly and frequently around the Sports Centre, talking, laughing and playing during their breaks from work. They went to the pub and sat together. Jeremiah regularly gave Joanne a lift home in his car. They were challenging the notion that it was shameful for a married man and a single woman to be seen regularly together. More significantly, when Joanne became pregnant with her first child, Yvonne, there was no sense of shame. She neither concealed her pregnancy, nor that Jeremiah Locke was the father. She was, in effect, a new genre of Irish women, a proud single mother-to-be. Her pride and self-confidence enabled her to withstand any loss of face or honour that might have come from within her work or her village for becoming pregnant outside marriage by a married man. This lack of shame, this sense of pride, appeared to come from her deep and sincere love for Jeremiah Locke, and a profound belief that he would one day leave his wife and set up home with her. One of the central tenets of the romantic side of liberal individualism is that it is not just right and acceptable, but almost necessary, to be true to oneself, one's feelings and emotions, not to hide or deny them. During the pregnancy, birth and rearing of Yvonne, Joanne demonstrated a strong, independent, self-willed determination to challenge and resist the existing norms and conventions about having children outside marriage. As Mr Justice

Lynch concluded in his Report, perhaps with a certain sense of indignation, 'she made no attempt to conceal the fact that she was pregnant' (TR, p. 16).

In some respects, by unashamedly resisting and challenging the traditional moral conventions of Catholic Ireland, Joanne Hayes, and to a lesser extent Jeremiah Locke, rode the tide of liberal individualism that had been sweeping through Ireland. She was willing to suffer the very real sanctions against such behaviour, sanctions that had maintained social conformity for over a hundred years. A consideration of the dynamics between family, shame, and personality formation will help us to understand what happened..

Families, pride and shame

In traditional, relatively undifferentiated societies, where the balance between individual and group favours the group, the individual is often engulfed in the group.[19] In Ireland, the family has been long regarded as the most important social institution. What the Church perceived as state interference in the family led to the first, and probably only, major conflict between Church and state – the Mother and Child Scheme in 1951.[20] The traditional Irish family tended to engulf everyone. It valued self-denial and abhorred self-indulgence. In modern societies, the balance has shifted from the group towards the individual; the strength of family bonds is being weakened. People have alternatives; they make their own choices. Families are not strong enough to prevent individuals doing what they want. The death of Joanne Hayes's father Paddy, and her uncle Maurice, the two patriarchal figures in her life, weakened the bonds of the family. As she admitted herself, the whole case would not have happened if they had been alive.[21]

Scheff claims that a real sense of pride only comes from the type of strong social bonds that occur in some groups and close-knit families. These families help the development of individuals with strong personalities that enable them to be different but secure. He argues that when family bonds are weak, what appears as a strong personality is often based on a false sense of pride. Individuals may appear to be very proud and have high self-esteem, but in reality they live in fear of being ashamed. They do everything to keep up appearances, to deceive themselves and others. They devise various mechanisms to conceal and hide their shame, but this is often ineffectual and spills over into anger. This suggests that the social bond in the Hayes family was weak. Consequently, the reason for Joanne Hayes being strong and proud about the pregnancy and birth of her daughter Yvonne, and then becoming weak and ashamed of being pregnant with the Tralee baby, was that she did not have a strong personality. It was not based on a strong bond. It was based on a false sense of pride. It was this false sense of pride that so easily turned to shame. And it was this unacknowledged sense of shame, built up over eight months, which so easily turned to rage after her baby was born, leading her to abuse and abandon it.[22]

Honour as a strategic struggle

Honour is not a spontaneous, collective recognition of a person's social worth, but something that emerges from a strategic struggle. It is a game of strategies and tactics with its own institutional logic. It is based on challenge and riposte.[23]

When Joanne Hayes began her affair with Jeremiah Locke and became serially pregnant by him, she was breaking the traditional Catholic principles of purity, chastity and self-denial. In this respect, she was an agent of social change. She might have been following her emotions, she might have been romantically swept off her feet but she nevertheless weighed up the costs of breaking the official norm with the gains from respecting it.[24] Honour is at stake in almost every social encounter. A rude word or gesture or an immodest act at an important moment can seriously undermine one's honour. Bourdieu points out that instead of strict rules of honour, contravention of which would lead to dishonour, people living in any culture become players of the cultural game of honour and shame and develop a sense of what is honourable and shameful.[25] When their honour is challenged, skilful players know what can be said and done in riposte. They have an automatic, intuitive, second-nature understanding of the rules of honour, how they apply to specific contexts, the extent to which they can be stretched and, generally, what is possible and permissible. It is a different matter when the game of honour and respect is moved out from a rural village or town into the judicial field and into a public inquiry. It is no longer viable to use the usual strategies of silence, denial, and lies to protect the family name.

The game of honour as it was played out in Tralee in the early 1980s had its own peculiar rules. By becoming pregnant, giving birth and rearing her daughter Yvonne at home, Joanne Hayes was running the risk of social dishonour. She was insulting the social norms around which most other people based their lives. The game play which she hoped would be successful and which would restore any lost honour, would be if Jeremiah Locke did what he might have promised to do, and left his wife to live with her.[26]

When Joanne became pregnant for the second time, she did not appear have the same ability to challenge the system a second time round. It was as if she understood the underlying attitude and opinion of the community as 'becoming pregnant is a mistake which can be forgiven, becoming pregnant a second time – so soon after the first – was not just careless but unacceptable'. From September 1983 onwards, once she knew that she was pregnant again, there seems to have been a growing sense of shame. Her second pregnancy was completely different. As Mr Justice Lynch pointed out, she attempted to conceal it from everybody. 'She attempted to live her life as though she was not expecting at all' (TR, p. 16). She was, in effect, shamed into silence and living a lie.

The shame of having to live a lie, of trying to pretend that you are not pregnant when, particularly because of your small size, it is obvious to everyone who takes the trouble to look, gradually becomes an enormous crushing weight that not just demoralises but dehumanises the person. Joanne's attempts to conceal her pregnancy by wearing heavy jumpers and remaining seated whenever possible were futile.

It was not simply Joanne that suffered from the shame of being pregnant a second time. It was something that impinged on the whole family. Although Joanne's pregnancy confronted them on a daily basis, it was something that they could not talk about and the family lived in silence and denial about what was happening. Although she had been pregnant before, this second pregnancy was undermining the honour of the family. The sense of shame was so strong that nobody seemed able to talk about the slow, unfolding drama that was taking place and which was bound to end in dramatic circumstances.

We may never know exactly what happened on the night of the 12 April 1984, but we do know that Joanne Hayes gave birth to a baby and that the baby died. When the acute trauma of the birth and death had passed, it was agreed that if anything happened as a result of the events that night, Joanne would take the blame. According to the Tribunal Report, it was left to Joanne to hide the dead body and to tell a story of having given birth alone in the field. This would exonerate the other members of the family from being discredited by anything that had happened.

Mr Justice Lynch argued that honour was the key explanatory factor in the case. In 'Cover Up', chapter 8 of his Report, he gave some of the details of what happened in the days following the birth, describing how 'the whole family embarked on a planned deception of the neighbourhood' (TR, p. 25). He argued that Joanne Hayes deceived people into thinking that she had had a miscarriage. He concluded

> Thus it was hoped to minimise the damage to the family reputation which this further pregnancy of Joanne Hayes had caused. More especially, it was hoped to avoid altogether the damage which would be done to the family reputation if the very unhappy circumstances of the birth and death of the Tralee Baby were ever to become publicly known. (TR, p. 26)

Mr Justice Lynch argued that 'Mrs Hayes was particularly obsessed with protecting and restoring the good name of the family'. He went on to state that the reason the Hayes family stuck to the birth-alone-in-the-field story was that if the neighbours and public in general believed that the baby was stillborn and that Joanne panicked and hid it, her conduct would not be so very blameworthy. There was no question for Mr Justice Lynch of the gardaí's lying about how their statements were made to protect their honour, jobs, promotion prospects and pensions.

In the early days of the Tribunal, Martin Kennedy also argued that Joanne Hayes had lied to people about her pregnancy and the birth of her child. It could be contended that there was a normative expectation in her family, neighbourhood and place of work for Joanne to show her shame by lying about her pregnancy. This was the traditional price unmarried mothers had to pay for their sin. It was a private matter that would not and could not be talked about openly. It was a dark but open secret. Joanne Hayes was forced to live the lie of being pregnant, of knowing that everyone knew she was pregnant and, except for a couple of people at work, of nobody saying a word. In their words, looks and gestures, people expected Joanne Hayes to carry on as normal. To mention her pregnancy, to mention it in conversation with her or a member of her family would have to break a fundamental norm of privacy. Individuals and families in Abbeydorney were allowed to have their secrets. The order and stability of the family and community were maintained by strategies of silence and by people giving Joanne and the family space, by not interfering and distancing themselves, and by allowing the family to keep up their appearances, honour and respect.

The way people related to Joanne and her family during her pregnancy and after the birth sheds light on what had happened to Anne Lovett earlier that year, and what had happened to thousands of women in Ireland who became pregnant outside marriage. As 'fallen' women, the expectation was that they would hide their shame and withdraw from society. Women were expected to go away to another part of the country, perhaps to a Magdalen home, have their child, be forced to give it up for adoption, and then return quietly to the village. Fallen women were made to feel ashamed. Those who did not go away, who resisted and stayed at home, were ignored. If people were ignorant, they were not responsible for what was happening. By becoming involved people would be interfering in a private matter. It is important to remember that after the birth nobody did interfere. The doctors and nurses who examined and treated Joanne might have been very suspicious that she had had a baby, but she was not challenged and was allowed to tell her own story. When Joanne told people at work that she had had a miscarriage or that she had lost the baby in hospital, they let her tell her own story. In a society where sex outside marriage was intrinsically evil, it was inevitable as well as practical for the mother to lose her baby, perhaps in hospital, perhaps in a field.

Honour involves making challenges about someone's character, and responding to these challenges. But in this struggle, there are certain fundamental rules.[27] Bourdieu argued that in the tribe he studied, the struggle for honour generally took place within people of the tribe. Consequently, when Joanne Hayes had an affair with a married man and became pregnant, it does not appear, at least initially, to have impinged on the family honour. There was no public challenge by anyone. It was in the public domain, but it was deemed to be a private matter to be dealt with by the family. Once the state became involved, first through the police, then through the Tribunal, an open, public and very serious challenge was made to the personal honour of Joanne Hayes and the public honour of the family.

Bourdieu noted that among the Kabyle a struggle for honour took place between social equals.[28] The Kerry Babies case was a very unequal struggle. There was very little equality between the Hayes family and the middle-aged, professional policemen and lawyers from Dublin who set about attacking their honour. The Hayes family were simply punished and branded as liars. They were denied any honour, yet the gardaí were defined as honourable. Furthermore, according to Bourdieu, in a conflict of honour it is not permissible to humiliate an opponent. Everyone has to have the chance of responding; it is not permissible to take unfair advantage. In the Kerry Babies case, the original challenge was made by the Hayes family when they challenged the honour of the police by saying that they had been abused and intimidated into making their confessions. The riposte from the state was devastating. Given the depleted forces of the Hayes family and the legal setting in which the conflict took place, it was difficult for them and their legal teams to respond.

Honour is accumulated over time. It is accumulated by individuals, but they can and do share in the collective honour of the family, group, community or people to whom they belong. Although the ties of family and community may not be as strong in modern urban societies, it would be wrong to think that honour in these societies has simply been reduced to personal honour. As a symbolic accumulation, honour is particularly vulnerable to being easily tainted, if not destroyed.[29] Once a challenge is made to one's own honour, or that of one's family, then the stack of symbolic cards that has been carefully constructed over the years could come tumbling down. Of course, it all depends on who makes the challenge. For example, challenges made to one's honour by the Catholic Church in Ireland could, certainly in the past, be socially damning. But its capacity to shame has been reduced considerably. It is a different matter when the challenges come from the state and are made by the police, lawyers, and judges.

Shaming strategies

Shame emerges as a spontaneous feeling in people, but also emerges in power and dependency relationships, particularly as part of an overall strategy of demeaning. Most shaming takes place in personal relationships, particularly within families when parents shame their children.[30] As we saw above, shame also functions to maintain social conformity. We need to broaden the focus here to include larger social groups and identify and describe the different strategies that are used. Shaming strategies can be unconscious, spontaneous, or automatic reflex mechanisms. Other strategies, particularly those employed by the police and their lawyers during the Kerry babies case, can be extremely rational and calculated. The case shows that we need to understand institutionalised ways of shaming. The strategic attempt to shame Joanne Hayes and her family did not come from the local villagers. In effect, it came from institutional representatives of the state.

Shame may be a universal emotion but, like sin, what causes shame and people to blush is culturally and historically constructed. Shame is a result of shaming: who and what are shamed, and how they are shamed, depend on the groups and society and their particular social codes, laws, manners and morals. It results from a transgression of values, norms and conventions. However, it is wrong to think of those who make people feel ashamed as ordinary individuals trying to maintain social conformity.[31] Shamers often belong to institutions and organisations which, because they protect morality, specialise in bringing shame. In Ireland, the power of shaming has rested primarily with policemen, lawyers, judges, priests, teachers and journalists. The traditional power of the priest in Ireland centred on shaming strategies, particularly denouncing people from the altar.[32] Again it would be wrong to think that the priest was acting as a private individual. The institutional church helped devise and implement the shaming strategies for transgressing its moral rules and regulations. Until the 1980s, orders of Irish nuns, particularly the Good Shepherd Sisters, ran Magdalen homes for unmarried mothers. Women who became pregnant outside marriage were encouraged to go to these homes where they performed menial manual work in return for their board and keep. When the baby was born the expectation was that it would be given up for adoption. Some of the women never returned to the community; some stayed in the homes for the rest of their lives. These homes were part of the institutional strategy of shaming and saving honour.

As a disciplinary strategy, shaming can be very subtle. During the police investigation, while the court case was pending, and in course of the Tribunal hearings, there was no public condemnation of Joanne Hayes or members of her family by the Catholic Church. However, when the Tribunal hearings were completed, the family asked the parish priest to say Mass in the farmhouse, thereby symbolically blessing it. He refused. It is important to realise that while this shaming strategy was enacted by the priest, it was instituted by the Catholic Church. The lack of open support and the silence from the local priests were part of a strategy of distancing the Church from the Hayes family. The denial of their request to have a Mass said in their home became common knowledge. It inevitably had the effect of creating public shame for the Hayes family.

Ritual humiliation and shaming were primary tactics used by the police in interrogating the Hayes. In the Tribunal Report, Mr Justice Lynch argued that if insulting or shameful remarks were made to members of the Hayes family, it was 'of no great importance'. The family were helping the police with a murder investigation. 'It was not a tea party they were at' (TR, p. 80). This suggests that ritualised insulting and shaming strategies may have been an accepted part of the process that police used to 'soften' suspects during interrogation. Used repeatedly on a vulnerable family it could lead to false confessions. However, the main shaming strategy used by the police was to claim that Joanne Hayes was a promiscuous woman who, having had sex with two different men within 48 hours, gave birth to twins of different blood groups. Given that only eight such cases are documented in medical history, to sustain this claim they had to argue that, in effect, Joanne Hayes was a sexual freak.

The Tribunal Report was the final stage in the process of shaming Joanne Hayes and her family. Mr Justice Lynch declared that the Hayes family were perjurers and liars. More importantly, he in effect declared that Joanne Hayes was a murderer. Although the state pathologist's report and evidence had indicated that there was no evidence that Joanne Hayes's baby had achieved an independent existence, Mr Justice Lynch ruled that she had killed her baby.

The honour of Catholic Ireland and the state police

The Murder Squad was an elite corps which specialised in investigating serious crime. While infanticide and the abandonment of newborn babies was nothing unusual in Irish society, the murder of the Cahirciveen baby was particularly brutal and grotesque. It could be that the leading members of the Squad were anxious and willing to go to Kerry to help the local police in their inquiries not just because it was a serious crime, but because they were ashamed that it had happened in their home county. The honour of Kerry people and especially Kerry women had been impugned. Once the investigation began to focus on Joanne Hayes, it might have appeared that through her sexual promiscuity she had dishonoured the women of Kerry.

There is another twist to the story. The shame of having obtained false confessions from Joanne Hayes and her family could have provoked the state police into a deep-seated resentment against them.[33] Instead of feeling guilt about what they had done, they redirected the anger from their shame back on the family, thus in effect blaming the victim. This suggests that emotions of shame-rage erupted simultaneously among the police. However, while there were undoubtedly feelings of shame among the police, it is more likely that there was a deliberate plan to protect the honour of the state police in Irish society by blaming Joanne Hayes and her family for what had happened. In this respect, the tactic of making the Hayes family out to be immoral, uncaring liars who were obsessed with saving face was a shaming strategy used in the strategic struggle to protect the honour of the police.

CHAPTER ELEVEN

Telling lies

The art of dissimulation reaches its peak in man. Deception, flattering, lying, deluding, talking behind the back, putting up a false front, living in borrowed splendour, wearing a mask, hiding behind convention, playing a role for others and for oneself – in short, a continuous fluttering around the solitary flame of vanity – is so much the rule and the law among men that there is nothing which is less comprehensible than how an honest and pure drive for truth could have arisen among them. (Friedrich Nietzsche)[1]

They are not barefaced lies on the part of the Gardaí (as regrettably is the case with members of the Hayes family) but they are an exaggeration over and above the true position, or a gilding of the lily, or wishing thinking elevated to the status of hard fact. (Mr Justice Lynch, TR, p. 61)

For persons who take the Witness Oath relatively frequently, there is a danger that the Oath may become for them largely a matter of form. This does not mean that such a person is likely to tell completely groundless lies on Oath. Where 'familiarity breeds contempt' has affected a witness, it will most often manifest itself in the elevation of honest beliefs or suspicions into positive facts. (Mr Justice Lynch, TR, p. 59)

Lying, or deliberately distorting messages, is a complex matter. It is morally detested and yet endemic to social life.[2] In their everyday lives people embellish stories, present false images, deceive each other, bend and distort the truth. They do to others what is done to them. Social life is a complex mixture of deceit, lies and truth. We almost expect politicians and spin-doctors to evade or at least be economical with the truth. It is no longer a surprise when ministers, priests and bishops are found to have been lying. Rooting out liars has become an ongoing public spectacle in Ireland. A striking characteristic of the last two decades of the twentieth century in Ireland was the recurrent exposure of former paragons of virtue as cheats, liars and perverts. Bishops and priests deceived people not only about their affairs with women, but also by becoming fathers. Instead of looking after children in their care, some priests, nuns and brothers physically abused and sexually assaulted them. Politicians, including a former Taoiseach (Prime Minister), lied about payments they had received from businessmen. Bank officials colluded with customers to set up bogus accounts to help them evade paying taxes. As well as these 'big' lies, institutional 'white' lies seem to have become common currency. For example, the gardaí are not allowed to strike, yet in pursuance of a pay claim on two days in May and June 1998, the majority of rank and file gardaí reported in sick and unable to attend for duty. It became known as 'the blue flu'.

This process of rooting out the honourable and powerful as cheats and liars stands in contrast to what previously happened when the weak and vulnerable were the most likely to be found out and punished for their lies. As part of a process of resistance and emancipation, of changes in power relations between social classes and a general development of more egalitarian relations, people have begun to identify more with outsiders and lower classes and to start looking for lies where they did not look as keenly before. At a time when the lower orders were more dependent on their 'betters', more resigned to their dependency and willing to accommodate to it; and when in consequence they identified with the rich, powerful, elegant and seemingly moral, they were more willing to believe that the established were paragons of all virtues including honesty. There seems to be no need for them to tell lies, so why should they? The stronger the identification with the established, the more they are able to lie and get away with it.[3] This is what happened in Ireland in the 1980s when it was thought that the gardaí never lied.

Lying is an everyday activity. We live our lives between truth and lies. Children growing up are told to tell the truth. They learn to value the truth; they also learn to value lies. They learn that people tell lies to impress others, to get their own way, to protect themselves and their interests. They also learn that people tell lies to protect others and are praised and respected for doing so. For example, when children visit relations and are asked if they enjoyed the meal provided, they quickly learn that if they did not like it they are expected to lie and say that it was very good, even though they thought it was dreadful.[4] Children learn that lying is a social skill which depends on context. They have to learn when, where, how and to whom they can lie. They have to be able to make a distinction between telling 'big black lies' and 'small white lies'. Being successful in social life depends on knowing not only when to tell the truth and when to lie but also how to lie and how to tell the truth.

Lying may be a universal feature of human society, but the lies people tell and how they tell them vary considerably between cultures.[5] They can also be evaluated differently: some lies will be recognised as comparatively malevolent and others as comparatively benign. But while all cultures distinguish between big and 'white' lies, there is no historic or cross-cultural uniformity in this process.

As well as these differences between societies, there are also differences *within* societies, for example between social classes, and this has particular importance for the exercise of power. The way those who are dominated lie and the type of lies they tell are very different from the lies of those who dominate.[6] More fundamentally perhaps, as Scheff reminds us, not only is the reading of reality, the world and its events negotiated, but when there is a dispute about events, 'what actually happened' is generally decided by power-holders – professional experts who, through legal procedures, name the world, adjudicate between parties and their accounts, and apportion responsibility.[7]

Lying is culturally conventional. There is, as Nietzsche pointed out, a 'duty to lie according to a fixed convention, to lie with the herd and in a manner binding upon everyone'.[8] There are conventions about lying to family and friends, to colleagues, and to members of the public. There are complex, hidden, but nevertheless strict rules about who can lie to whom, when and where people can lie and, most importantly, about what they can lie. Learning the conventions of lying is at the heart of being a successful social actor. There are some things about which it is not permissible to lie. But there are other things, perhaps connected with one's personal life, about which people are allowed to lie. There is a convention about lying in the game of love and romance. Lovers may deceive, delude, and lie to each other in an attempt to gain affection. It is as if it is accepted that lying is as acceptable in love as it is in war. The conventions of lying change with the context and the people involved. How many married men have lied to single women to obtain sexual favours? How many single women who have become pregnant have been forced to conceal their pregnancy, to live the lie of not being pregnant? How many people have colluded in this lie, pretending not to see the evidence of the advancing pregnancy? In rural Ireland, it was the convention that a single woman in trouble from having sex outside marriage would 'lie' about her condition by hiding or disappearing from public life. The convention was that once they concealed themselves and their condition, they were allowed to live the lie of their condition. From the beginning of the 1980s, an increasing number of unmarried women decided that they were no longer going to lie about their condition.

But why do people lie, especially when they have been brought up to tell the truth, when they dislike being lied to themselves and when, on critical reflection, they must realise that social life could not work if everyone lied all the time? In everyday life, people move between telling the truth as an absolute moral value, to telling lies as a rational calculation of interests, a means towards an end. Telling lies can be selfish. It can be a means to attain money, honour or political power. Sometimes people tell lies against their own interests, to protect others or for the common good. People share the value and importance of communicating honestly and openly with each other. But they are also involved in power relations – in a competitive struggle to survive, to avoid being dominated, and to realise their interests against others. We move, often within moments, from wanting to tell the truth about the world, to wanting to realise our own interests and safeguard our social position and resources. People balance the interest in being ethical and social bonding with strategically pursuing material self-interest and power.[9]

The balance between being truthful and telling lies and perhaps saving one's life, face, career and fortune is at the centre of what happens in courts of law. Courts are supposedly based on people telling the whole truth and nothing but the truth, but they are in fact highly sophisticated mechanisms by which judges and juries decide who is telling the truth and who is being deceitful, distorting or being economical with the truth and, ultimately, who is telling lies. As Barnes writes:

> Trial procedures all over the world are designed to probe for indications that statements given in evidence are false, with the assumption, in general, that false statements are made with deceitful intent.[10]

The task, then, for judges and juries is to declare the truth and decide who has wilfully lied, deceived and distorted it. In any state, the ultimate power of the law and its representatives is to proclaim the truth or the facts about what happened.[11] This is central to the state maintaining a monopoly over the means of symbolic domination. To understand this process, we need to go beyond the nominal power of judges and the law and reveal how truth is negotiated and decided in court. What is the power of professional experts to name the truth? How are scientific facts presented as evidence? Do defendants and witnesses lie or are they simply dissembling, fabricating and being economical with the truth? Is lying in court an art or skill more likely to be found among those accustomed to giving evidence? Do the police lie? Are courts of law based as much on people telling lies, negotiating reality, and presenting the best case possible as on telling the truth? Finally, if judges have the power to produce and name the truth, who can judge judges and decide if they were lying or simply dissembling?[12]

The facts of the Kerry babies case

Under the Tribunals of Inquiry (Evidence) (Amendment) Act, 1979, Mr Justice Lynch had the task of sifting through all of the witnesses' testimonies and deciding the facts of the case: what had really happened; who was telling the truth and who was lying. At the beginning of his Tribunal Report, Mr Justice Lynch made an important announcement about how he would determine these facts:

> With one exception mentioned below the Tribunal finds facts only if the Tribunal is satisfied of such facts as a matter of substantial probability. This is a degree of proof in excess of the mere balance of probabilities and short of proof beyond a reasonable doubt. (TR, p. 9)

Mr Justice Lynch's distinction between 'beyond reasonable doubt' and 'on the balance of probabilities' corresponds to the distinction between the type of proof required in criminal and civil court cases. However, and this is crucial, the only part of the Report based on 'the balance of probabilities' is the chapter in which he claims that the members of the Hayes family discussed and planned in detail a trip to Dingle. For Mr Justice Lynch this explained the detailed accounts of the trip to Slea Head in the confessions.

A reading of the Tribunal Report suggests that the facts of the case were as follows. Joanne Hayes was a liar. She lied to her family, friends and fellow-workers. She lied about giving birth to the Tralee baby alone in the field. She lied about how the baby had died. She had, he decided, killed or 'done away with' her baby by choking and hitting it with a bath brush.

He concluded that the family decided to lie and cover up what had happened that night. Joanne Hayes lied to her friends, neighbours, colleagues, and her two other aunts. The rest of her family, he said, colluded in this lie. When the gardaí came and questioned them about what had happened, Joanne Hayes, her mother, two brothers and sister initially lied to them, some of them saying that they knew nothing about what had happened, and others that Joanne had given birth alone in the field. When the charges were dropped, members of the Hayes family lied to the media about having been assaulted. Mr Justice Lynch concluded that members of the family continued to lie during the Tribunal and that the gardaí were credible in comparison – they did not lie. They might have exaggerated, 'gilded the lily', and elevated 'honest beliefs and suspicions into positive facts' (TR, pp. 59, 61). But they did not lie.

So what is the truth about what happened? Who was lying? Did the gardaí lie? How was the truth produced within the juridical field? Before trying to answer these questions, it is necessary to address more fundamental issues about notions of truth.

Notions of truth

There are perhaps two key conceptions of truth. The first is that truth corresponds with reality and exists independently of people – facts speak for themselves. This fits in with a layman's notion of scientific truth, that truth is 'experiential and absolute, unconditional and unalterable'. This leads to a 'hard-hat' conviction that facts are facts, and sooner or later everyone comes up against reality. Objective reality can be empirically investigated. Statements about the world can be tested. When a crime is committed, people can be questioned in order to find out what really happened. This is not just the layman's notion of truth, it is an unquestioned orthodox belief about truth. Perhaps it is unquestioned because there is a feeling that unless there is an objective reality that can be ascertained, not only can there be no truth, but also no order, only chaos and anarchy.

The second notion of truth is that it is a matter of convention. This is syntactical truth. Truth comes from people sharing a similar way of reading, understanding and interpreting the world. What is true is what people agree to be true. Truth is agreed after rational debate among reasonable people. Truth is relative.[13]

Mr Justice Lynch was operating rigorously within the legal conventions by which truth is determined within the juridical field. When he stated that he had determined the facts of the case 'beyond reasonable doubt', this has to be understood within legal terminology. He is speaking as a sovereign. It does not mean that other reasonable people would not doubt the facts as he determined them, but that he has been ordained by state law to decide what is beyond reasonable doubt.

The problem with searching for truth within conventions is that it is dependent on people being like-minded and equally committed to discover the truth and the methods to achieve it. In other words, they leave aside whatever other interests they may have. They agree to search for truth by following certain procedures which strive to attain free, undistorted communication. However, the search for truth is compromised or undermined because people have other interests.[14] The problem is that, as noted above, as much as people struggle to attain the truth, they are also involved in a struggle for power.

Telling lies

We can move between two extremes in trying to decide what is a lie. We can focus not on individuals and what people say, but on language and discourse within which they speak. Some people see astrology, religion and political ideologies as lies.[15] This could be broadened to other discourses, for example psychiatry.[16] But what happens when we move between cultures and discourses? Does a truth in one conventional system become a lie in another? There would have been an outcry if during the Tribunal it had been suggested that to give birth to twins of different blood groups, Joanne Hayes had to have been a witch. Yet it was acceptable for a psychiatrist to say that she was a sociopath. Or do we simply say that people who operate within the discourse of witch-hunting are living in error, as might be decided about present-day psychiatry sometime in the future?

It is not only a question of distinguishing truth and lies from languages and discourses, it is also a question of the extent to which speech itself is a lie. The problem of truth and lies emerges when we make statements about the world. Any representation or statement about the world necessarily involves first a choice of some words over others and then a choice of the way they are put together. Since there could have been different choices, all representations of the world necessarily involve within themselves an element of misrepresentation. The question is how we distinguish true statements or representations of reality from statements which are only partial representations or misrepresentations.

This was a critical issue when, in order to sustain his ruling of the facts about what happened, Mr Justice Lynch played down the evidence of the State Pathologist that there was no evidence that the Tralee baby attained an independent existence, and chose instead words which represented Joanne Hayes as having killed her child. There is, of course, a difference between genuine attempts to represent the world, and deliberate attempts to misrepresent it. The latter is closer to dissembling, deceit and lying. But wherein lies the difference?

We could agree, perhaps, that lying is a deliberate attempt by someone to misrepresent the world and deceive people, and that this has to be distinguished from exaggeration, pretence and deception.[17] The emphasis on intention is important. To decide if someone has lied, we have to know that it was deliberate. However, intention is not just a personal moral issue. In social life it is not the person accused of lying but others who decide on the intention.[18] If we accept that lying involves a deliberate intention to deceive, we have also to accept that not all forms of deliberate deception can be treated as lies. We all engage in little acts of deception and fabrication in everyday life.[19] For example, a defendant who wears a suit, shirt and tie into court may deliberately try to deceive people into believing that he is no different from other men in the court. This, together with his posture and use of language, may be regarded as a deliberate attempt to create a false impression, to fabricate an image, to deceive people, but it could hardly be described as lying.

Consequences are just as important as intentions when it comes to determining lies.[20] Consequences are objective things. We can assess the consequences of a lie. To lie, causing disastrous unforeseen consequences indicates stupidity. The level of turpitude is low. However, when people lie knowing the consequences that will ensue, the turpitude is high. This is what happens when public figures divert attention from their own shortcomings and dishonesties by the use of scapegoats, for example, Jews, communists and illegal aliens.

Another problem is that lying is often seen as an issue of individual ethical behaviour and not as something done by groups and organisations. However, the state and military institutions often lie during a war.[21] An important question raised by the Kerry babies case is whether institutions of the state could be said to have lied; and, if they did so, was it to maintain power or for the common good?

Moral philosophers have identified instances when telling lies may seem excusable or justified. Examples include lying to the sick and dying, parents lying to their children, lying to protect peers and clients, lying to enemies, and lying to liars. One of the classic instances is the noble lie when public leaders lie not for selfish reasons, but for the common good. The argument revolves around the assumption that leaders know far more about the complexities of governing than ordinary people who need to be led and, sometimes, to be sheltered from the truth. For example, to prevent panic, the police might lie about the existence of an infectious disease or a serial killer. In both examples the state can claim that these lies were told for the greater common good. The right of the public to knowledge and information, and indeed the individual's right to life, is superseded by what public leaders decide is the common good. Another, more relevant example, is when the state and its institutions see themselves as under threat from subversive elements. If, as happened in the Republic of Ireland during the 1970s and 1980s, subversives begin to gain the upper hand, the gardaí may bend the law to achieve convictions, and the judiciary and politicians may turn a blind eye and accept the gardaí's account of events. It could be argued that in the interests of the greater common good and the state, it is necessary for the police to lie about the methods used to gain evidence against and extract confessions from terrorists and subversives. The problem is that there is no public control over what is deemed to be a threat to the public good. Consequently, Bok argues, the enemies of the state grow and their treatment becomes increasingly inhumane.[22]

Finally, while it may be desirable from a moral philosophical position to deal only with clear-cut lies, there is a grey area between truth and lies. Bailey makes a distinction between clear-cut and basic lies. A basic lie is when people 'knowing full well what that they are saying or doing is false, collude in ignoring the falsity'. This can be coercive or voluntary. The strong impose 'truth' on the weak but, he says, 'much of our untruthful "reality" is voluntary make-believe'. We live our lies, at a collective social as well as personal level. Basic lies are used to paper over the cracks when things go wrong and there is conflict: for example the cases of 'the emperor having no clothes' or of alcoholics always comparing themselves with those who drink more.[23]

There is, however, a difference between collusive or basic lies, and active connivance or collaboration in lying.[24] Connivance is the case where people appear to fall for or accept the lie that they are being told. For example, it could be argued that Joanne Hayes's family, friends, neighbours and workmates connived or collaborated in her lie that she was not pregnant again. At the same time, it could also be argued that there was a collective denial throughout the country, propagated by state prosecution lawyers and judges, that the gardaí abused or intimidated terrorist and criminal suspects while they were being interrogated. To the extent that Irish people accepted and joined in this pretence, they were collaborating in the lie. Within the state, it would appear (as we shall see in the next chapter) that most politicians knew that the gardaí were using abusive strategies to extract confessions, but collaborated in the gardaí's lie that they were not. We could say that in Ireland, in the years before the Kerry babies case, people colluded and lived the lie, partly voluntarily and partly because it was imposed by the state, that terrorists and criminals voluntarily confessed to the gardaí to crimes without being physically abused or intimidated. This is perhaps one of the basic lies that people in Ireland have lived with and colluded in during the last half of the twentieth century and it is at the heart of explaining the truth about what happened.

Truth, power and lies

Truth about the world is, then, structured within existing discourses and fields of power relationships. The production of truth and the telling of lies can be seen as a tactical struggle between the strong and the weak, the skilful and the not so skilful. Within each social field or area of social life, the strong use lies as if they have a right to control the weak. The strong lie, deceive and produce variations of the truth to suit themselves, not necessarily because they are cruel despots, but because they believe they are morally superior and that the weak are either ignorant and helpless or are a danger to themselves and others.[25] In the face of the resources and skill of the strong in producing and proclaiming their version of the truth, the weak often resort to telling lies and to spreading gossip and rumours about the strong.[26]

The strong are thus those who develop a monopoly over the means of producing and proclaiming the truth. In most areas of contemporary social life, the strong are representatives of the state. This ability to proclaim the truth about people and events that is central to the state's nominal power. Not only does the state dominate politically by developing a monopoly over the means of legitimate violence, it also dominates symbolically by developing a monopoly over the means of producing and proclaiming the truth. Representatives of the state are thus able to decide whether someone is guilty, criminal, mad or poor.

The most sophisticated and serious struggle for truth takes place in courtrooms. People like Joanne Hayes and members of her family might have been skilful at lying in their village, but when it came to 'presenting their case' to the Tribunal, they were completely out of their depth. The gardaí, on the other hand, were well skilled in the art of presenting their case.

Negotiating the truth in court

Despite the fact that we lie and that we know that others lie to us, we continue to believe in what Bok calls the principle of veracity. If we do not believe that people can and do tell the truth and that the truth can be discerned, social order would collapse.[27] This is one of the reasons why courts and tribunals have a crucial role to play in democratic societies. The rule of law presupposes shared common values and the existence of specific procedures, rules, sanctions and punishments within which juries and judges become the final arbiters of truth.[28] Within an adversarial system of justice, the truth is believed to emerge when the accused is both defended and prosecuted zealously within the bounds of the law. In other words, although courts are ostensibly based on people telling the truth, the examination and cross-examination of disputants and witnesses are based on the assumption that self-interest can lead to falsified evidence, exaggerated descriptions, and the truth hidden and dissembled. Courtroom trials procedures are designed 'to probe for indications that statements given in evidence are false, with the assumption, in general, that false statements are made with deceitful intent'.[29] The skill of the barrister in court is to help determine the truth. If a barrister can reveal that a piece or section of a witness's evidence is incompatible, inconsistent or contradictory, the prize is enormous since the whole of the witness's testimony comes under suspicion.[30]

The law operates within the 'juridical' field with its own language, discourse and practices.[31] The practice of those responsible for 'producing' or applying the law owes a great deal to the similarities which link the holders of this quintessential form of symbolic power. The juridical field has its own distinctive habitus – that is, its own preordained, unquestioned ways of thinking and acting which become second nature to regular participants. It is demonstrated in the protocols and assumptions, in the way people in the legal field think, act, talk and present themselves. The demand for strict adherence to this unwritten but highly specific habitus and code of practice becomes an unquestioned orthodoxy; it is a badge of honour among the legal profession. Success within the adversarial system requires a complete familiarity with this habitus and practice. In other words, in opposition to Mr Justice Lynch's claim (see p. 167) about the gardaí, familiarity can breed success just as much as contempt. Success comes from the respect of hierarchy, from reference to sacred texts and people, to being able to talk and give evidence using appropriate language and adopting proper postures and attitudes.

On the eightieth day of the Tribunal, Martin Kennedy was summing up for the Garda Superintendents whom he had been representing when he drew the following analogy between Slea Head and Portmarnock Golf Club:

> For the moment, if we take your Lordship as being an investigating Guard and your Lordship shall we say is a member of Portmarnock Golf Club, every inch of which is known to you, your Lordship is undoubtedly familiar with every blade of grass on the fairway and the rough – I am not too sure your Lordship would know about the rough as well. You are taking a statement from me and if I said I disposed of the body over the cliff beside the sixth green and you know there is no cliff beside the sixth green . . .

At this stage, Mr Justice Lynch intervened to say 'I think actually there might be a bit of one' (TT 80/29).

This habitus and code of practice, as well as the specific legal regulations, are central to the legal field creating and maintaining its independence and autonomy from the rest of society. Maintaining the symbolic domination of juridical professionals is, as Bourdieu points out, central to reproducing the supposed universality and neutrality of legal decisions. It is central to enabling judges to declare their opinions and theories as if they were facts. The practical content of the law that emerges in the judgement is the product of a symbolic struggle between professionals possessing unequal technical skills and social influence. They thus have unequalled ability to marshal the available juridical resources through the exploration and exploitation of 'possible rules,' and to use them effectively as symbolic weapons to win their case.[32] The institutionalised hierarchies and precedents along with the ongoing embodiment of unquestioned orthodoxies 'magically enables decisions of judges to appear as neutral and universally true'.[33]

The truth and lie of psychiatry

Knowledge exists in the form of discourses. A discourse such as psychiatry produces knowledge and truths about people. This knowledge and truth informs, enhances, limits and controls people's understanding of themselves and their behaviour. Foucault was anxious to overcome the negative conception of power as ideology.[34] He emphasised that discourses such as psychiatry are not something operated by the state or a ruling class to create and maintain power. Discourses not only produce positive effects, but are also positively and willingly embraced and embodied by subjects.[35] Psychiatry can help people to reveal and declare the truth about themselves, yet its power moves beyond understanding and can physically limit and control what people do and say. If the radical power of law is to decide the truth, the radical power of psychiatry is to decide what is madness. The negative power of psychiatry is its ability to limit and control what people do, not just by naming them as mad, but by being able to medicate and incarcerate them. When a psychiatrist declares that a person is a schizophrenic, psychotic or sociopath, he or she is producing truth. We cannot say they are lying. The only recourse to those who disagree with the truth of psychiatry is to resist and challenge its truth, by resisting and challenging its power. But it is difficult to produce an alternative truth that will have the same power as psychiatry in a court of law. Psychiatry has become the recognised expert discourse in the legal field on sanity, madness and personality defects.

When Dr John Fennelly, the pyschiatrist who attended Joanne Hayes, told the Tribunal that there was no doubt that Joanne Hayes was a sociopath, this was not a deliberate attempt to deceive (TT 54/64–87). However, saying that there is no doubt about Joanne Hayes being a sociopath is not in the same order as saying there is no doubt that the earth revolves around the sun. Brian McCaffery was another psychiatrist called as an expert witness during the Tribunal. He also testified about the personality of Joanne Hayes, but admitted he felt uncomfortable about testifying as he had not talked to or interviewed her. Nevertheless, he told the Tribunal that

> She [Joanne Hayes] has a personality disorder, she is inclined to tell lies to people in authority. She is expert at having attention drawn on herself, from what I have read and seen she catches a lot of public sympathy for a while.

He then named her personality disorder as 'pseudologica fantastica', a term given to individuals who repetitively tell major untruths (TT 68/82, 68/83).

The use of scientific evidence

In an adversarial system, it is up to each side to make the best case possible. The testimony of scientific experts is often crucial to developing a good case, but there are different types of scientific evidence. When a forensic scientist testifies that repeated tests show someone's blood to have been type O, this is a very different from a psychiatrist stating that someone suffers from 'pseudologica fantastica'. This statement is less valid and reliable. When scientists state that Joanne Hayes has blood group O, they do not say that this is a fact beyond reasonable doubt. Their statements tend to be more precise, such as if a blood sample were tested 1,000 times using this method, we would be 95 per cent certain that 999 times it would show it to be blood group O. Despite the rigorous methods employed by the state's own forensic scientists to test the blood groups, however, the gardaí rejected their validity. Instead they relied on the validity of their argument that the confessions of the Hayes family were given freely and spontaneously. To make a comparison with scientific statements, this is to suggest that if the Hayes family were questioned by other people, including other gardaí, they would be certain, perhaps even 99 per

cent certain, that they would have confessed in the same way as they did on
1 May 1984.

The production of what appears as good scientific evidence can flatter to
deceive. The case of the gardaí centred on proving that Joanne Hayes had twins
of different blood groups by becoming impregnated by two different men
within 48 hours. To justify this theory, legal counsel for the gardaí referred to
an article by Diane Settlage in the *International Journal of Fertility*. This was an
investigation into the conditions in which sperm survives in a vagina after intercourse. The article concluded that while it is possible for sperm to survive up to
96 hours, their concentration in vaginal mucus – which aids their survival – 'is
maximal from 15 minutes to 2 hours after vaginal deposition, and a steady
decline in total numbers is seen after 6 hours'.[36] This is not to say that superfecundation cannot take place. Cases recorded in medical history have been
reported in medical journals, from China[37] and the United States. In an article
reporting the American case, the authors refer to eight other cases between
1810 and 1940.[38]

Superfecundation is thus extremely rare: of the billions of births throughout
the last century, fewer than twenty cases appear to have been recorded, and
there seems to be no incident of superfecundation in Ireland or Britain. The
fact that superfecundation *can* take place in humans tells us nothing about how
likely it is to occur. Freak events in human health and biology are regularly
reported in medical journals, but this is simply to record that it is biologically
possible. However, apart from the long odds on this freak event having conveniently occurred in County Kerry in 1984, it was *also* implied that Joanne Hayes
had to be some kind of sexual freak for it to happen.

Unfortunately, it was not until the end of the Tribunal that the superfecundation theory was finally dismissed. If on the third day Mr Justice Lynch had
demanded evidence of the possibility of superfecundation before allowing questioning on this basis to proceed, he might have accepted that, as the Tribunal
was told by the State Pathologist, Dr John Harbison, it was such a rare
possibility that it could be safely discounted (TT 5/27). If Mr Justice Lynch had
followed Dr Harbison's advice, the theory that Joanne Hayes had sex with two
different men within hours – and for that reason could have given birth to the
Cahirciveen baby – would have been dismissed, and the Tribunal would
probably have lasted less than half the time it did.

The gardaí were not the only ones who might have misrepresented scientific
evidence. In his Report, Mr Justice Lynch seemed to overlook the scientific
opinion of Dr Harbison, who concluded from his examination of the Tralee

baby that he could not be certain that it had achieved an independent existence. Mr Justice Lynch, however, concluded beyond reasonable doubt that Joanne Hayes 'did away with' her baby. That she 'put her hands around its neck and stopped it crying by choking it' and that she then hit the baby with a bath brush 'to make sure it was dead' (TR, pp. 148, 19). This implies that the baby had achieved an independent existence.

Telling the truth about lies in the Kerry babies case

Mr Justice Lynch's explanation for everything that happened to Joanne Hayes and her family was that they engaged in subterfuge, lies and denials. His construction of *the* truth about what happened is careful and meticulous. It is important to emphasise that Mr Justice Lynch was not attempting to deceive, but rather chose a particular interpretation that he deemed to be generally beyond reasonable doubt or, in relation to what happened after the birth of the Tralee baby, to be on the balance of probabilities.

The notion that, on the balance of probabilities, members of the Hayes family had detailed discussions about a planned trip to Slea Head is central to the case, because it is central to the false confessions. To discover the truth about the case, it is necessary to discover why members of the Hayes family came up spontaneously, voluntarily and independently with a story about a trip to Dingle which, Mr Justice Lynch agreed, never took place. The answer, beyond reasonable doubt, was they were liars, fabricators and deceivers, and because they were guilty and ashamed of what happened to the Tralee baby. Given the independence of the judicial from the executive arm of the state, it was then just a coincidence that the truth about the Dingle connection served to maintain the honour and integrity of the gardaí.

The truth about the gardaí

There is, of course, another, equally plausible, explanation for what happened. Manning has argued that when it comes to pressing criminal charges and public-order maintenance, police officers 'are virtually required to lie'.[39] And Klockars found from his research that police lied regularly, particularly during the interrogation of suspects. The police officers he studied were morally comfortable with lying and saw it as an integral part of their role as law enforcers. He concluded that 'as the police officer becomes comfortable with lies and their moral justification, he or she is apt to become casual with both.' Barnes argues that success in lying leads not only to more lying but to its legitimation. We should no longer be surprised, he says, when police tell lies. However, deceit by police, 'can succeed only if their dupes believe that most of the time the police are honest'.[40]

Mr Justice Lynch claimed that the Hayes family, operating as a rational cohesive group, made a deliberate decision to lie about not knowing that Joanne Hayes was pregnant, and about her having given birth alone in the field at the back of the farmhouse. On the other hand, he argued that the gardaí did not lie but rather, operating as a rational cohesive group, developed an 'agreed line of defence' (TR, p. 60). This 'line of defence' was based on the insistence by all 28 members testifying that the confessions were given spontaneously and voluntarily and that, despite all the scientific evidence to the contrary, they all firmly believed that Joanne Hayes was the mother of the Cahirciveen baby. This 'agreed line of defence' was, Mr Justice Lynch argued, an unfortunate conse-quence that befalls gardaí who become over-familiar with court procedures. Now while 'an agreed line of defence' may not be a lie, it is a deliberate attempt to limit and control knowledge and the production of truth; and it could, therefore, pervert the course of justice.

As we saw in chapter 6, there were many other examples of contradictions in garda evidence which were more crucial. If Mr Justice Lynch had decided that there were conflicts of evidence in the testimonies of the gardaí, he might then have been left in the position of doubting the credibility of their evidence on other issues, particularly in relation to the completely voluntary and sponta-neous nature of members of the Hayes family's confessions.

Some years after the Tribunal, an appeal against a murder conviction was lodged under the Criminal Procedure Act 1993. The appeal was granted on a conflict of evidence in the testimonies of two of the investigating gardaí. One garda had testified that he took a piece of tissue which the suspect, Peter Pringle, had used to stop a nose bleed and that he had handed the tissue to a colleague; the intention was to obtain a blood sample for forensic evidence. However, the colleague testified that no such tissue was ever given to him. The court decided that the conflict in evidence concerning the tissue raised doubts about the credibility of the first garda's evidence. He had claimed that the suspect had made a self-incriminating statement about his involvement in the murder that had been crucial to his original conviction. The court decided that the conflict of evidence by the two gardaí rendered Pringle's conviction unsafe and unsatisfactory.[41] By avoiding any detailed analysis of conflicts in the evidence of the gardaí, and at the same time making out that the Hayes family were liars, Mr Justice Lynch was able to dismiss the credibility of the Hayes family and, in particular, their allegations of being intimidated and abused by the gardaí during their questioning.

What lies behind Mr Justice Lynch's truth?

Although Mr Justice Lynch did not consider the matter, it would appear that much of the nature and content of the questioning to which members of the Hayes family were subject contravened the 'Judges Rules' regarding the treatment of people in gardaí custody. These rules pertain to prisoners – that is, people who have been *formally charged and are in garda custody*. Mr Justice Lynch did not analyse the extent to which, even if members of the Hayes family had been in custody, their rights would have been violated. Rule 7 states: 'A prisoner making a voluntary statement must not be cross-examined, and no questions should be put to him about it except for the purpose of removing ambiguity in what he has actually said.' Rule 8 states:

> When two or more persons are charged with the same offence and their statements are taken separately, the police should not read these statements to the other persons charged, but each of such persons should be given by the police a copy of such statements and nothing should be said or done by the gardaí to invite a reply.[42]

Why this is significant is that Mr Justice Lynch did not analyse the extent to which members of the Hayes family, who were only helping the gardaí with their inquiries and therefore not effectively even in garda custody, were not only cross-examined, but rigorously interrogated. Neither did he analyse the extent to which the correspondence between the confessions of the members of the Hayes family came from suggestions made from statements given by other members.

When Mr Justice Lynch accepted the gardaí's version of events and dismissed the claims of physical abuse and intimidation, he did not pay sufficient attention to psychological and verbal intimidation. There is insufficient analysis in the Tribunal Report of the allegations members of the Hayes family made about threats, being roared and shouted at, of bad language and of tables being banged. When he ruled that what can be said and not said to an interviewee 'must vary with the circumstances of each case' he cited the Judgement of the Court of Criminal Appeal in *DPP* v *Pringle, McCann and O'Shea.* This was misleading, since that decision referred to people who had been charged and were in garda custody. Mr Justice Lynch indicated that the Tribunal was not established to find out or take an interest in investigating verbal intimidation or, as he put it, 'every allegation of a cross word that may or may not have been spoken' (TR, pp. 97, 83, 99). But the Tribunal was established to discover how innocent people confessed to a crime that they had not committed. It was strange, then, that the methods of interrogation used by the gardaí escaped even minimal scrutiny during the Tribunal. There was no examination of the techniques of persuasion and pyschological pressure. However, as O'Mahony has pointed out,

> While such a focus would have been informative and valuable, it is unlikely that many specific techniques would have been identified as always illegal or inappropriate. Police involved in criminal investigations must have some weapons at their disposal to counteract and expose the expected evasions and denials of guilty suspects. Police must be allowed to confront, contradict, trick, undermine and indeed sometimes to pressure suspects, although never to the degree that amounts to psychological duress.[43]

It may thus be that there is general collusion about the lie of enforcing the Judges Rules and the activities of the Murder Squad. The Squad had become experts at interrogating suspects in serious crimes. Over the previous 15 years they had been accustomed to obtaining confessions from a wide range of terrorists and criminals. They had been brutalised by a spiral of violence, often directed specifically at the gardaí, that had erupted in connection with the conflict in Northern Ireland. The sudden and dramatic experience of incarceration and rigorous interrogation must have made members of the Hayes family very vulnerable. Regardless of whether they were intimidated and abused, the collapse of their social world made them pliable in the hands of men skilled at obtaining confessions. At the end of the day's interrogation, the confessions were solid because, although there were inconsistencies, there was substantial similarity between those of Joanne Hayes, her sister Kathleen and her brothers Ned and Mike. They all made reference to the baby being stabbed to death and gave detailed descriptions of what happened on the car journey to and from Slea Head. Mr Justice Lynch could have argued that the enormous similarity in these descriptions meant that they could not have been given completely independently, spontaneously and voluntarily, as the gardaí argued. He could have argued that the gardaí were forced to create, collude in, and live by the lie that the confessions were spontaneous and voluntary, because the honour and credibility of the gardaí depended on it, as well as their own careers and prospects of promotion. Mr Justice Lynch could have ruled in this way, but instead he in effect exonerated the gardaí and blamed Joanne Hayes and members of her family.

CHAPTER TWELVE

Policing the state

If we look at the Kerry babies case in the context of long-term processes of social change and of changes taking place in Ireland in the 1970s and 1980s, it will help us to understand how the case happened. Throughout Europe the formation of states and subsequently nation states from the thirteenth century was one such long-term process of social change.[1] The nation state, as the term suggests, refers to the people, institutions, agencies and organisations which make decisions for the nation and the people as a whole. The state defines, defends and rules over a sovereign territory. It is the centre of power, the final power. It maintains, through the police and army, a monopoly over taxation, legitimate force and violence.[2] In its mature democratic form, the state is divided into three separate, independent powers: the legislature which devises policies and makes rules and laws; the executive and administrators who implement the rules and laws on a daily basis, including the police who see that laws and rules are enforced; and the judiciary which decides if the law has been applied correctly and fairly. The goal in maintaining the separation of the three powers of the state is to create a democratic nation state. The Kerry babies case provides insight into the way the state in Ireland operated during the 1980s when its monopoly over the means of violence was under threat from outlawed republican groups. Of course, what happened in Ireland has to be compared with what happened in Britain, especially with cases such as the Birmingham Six and Guildford Four.

The coercive power of the state is founded on physical force. Most democratic societies try to secure co-operation rather than having to rely on coercion and violence. However, having defined its goals and objectives, and having made its laws and policies, democratic states use whatever coercion and violence necessary to attain these goals and objectives. Once the state's successful claim to monopoly over legitimate physical force is established, the its territory becomes pacified internally.[3] This pacification increases trust and honesty in public and private life, mutual identification between its citizens, and the possibility of resolving conflict by reasoned argument rather than violence.

The everyday face of state power is the police, who have the power to break in to premises, and to capture, restrain, imprison and interrogate people.[4] Democratic states keep the possibility of physical coercion and violence in reserve – behind the scenes – and order and control are primarily maintained through law: the state has become a sophisticated legal machine of domination.[5] What is the relation between the police and this legal machine of domination when there is a threat to the state's monopoly on the use of force?

From a liberal-democratic perspective the state is legitimate when it expresses the authentic will of the people. In its ideal form, the state is seen as the collective representation of individual wills: in obeying the state, people are obeying the dictates of their collective will vicariously expressed.[6] The legitimacy of the state is negated when a space emerges between it and the general will of the people. It is when this space becomes large that elements of a police or authoritarian state can emerge. It could be argued that in the last thirty years the two principal threats to state legitimacy in the Republic of Ireland have been the excessive use of police force and the lack of trust in politicians and state officials.

The Kerry babies case raised questions about the gap between the state and the collective will of the people. Did the gardaí and, later, the Tribunal have the support of the collective will of the people? Moreover, it raises questions about what citizens of the state can do when they feel that the gardaí or the judiciary do not represent their will. How can people, individually or collectively, resist and challenge the gardaí and the judiciary?

At a fundamental level, the legitimacy of the state is undermined when it bends, disregards and breaks its own laws and rules. The Kerry babies case raises questions as to whether, up to 1984, the legislative and judiciary knowingly and willingly turned a blind eye to the way the state's elite corps of police operated. To what extent was this an inevitable, if unintended, consequence of the state securing convictions against 'hardened criminals', 'subversives', and 'terrorists'?

At another level, the case raises questions about the bias and unrepresentativeness of the state in the way that it favours particular interest groups and classes, and certain values, beliefs and attitudes.[7] To what extent can the police and the judiciary be deemed to be institutions representing and maintaining the interests, values and beliefs of a particular section of Irish society? 'The modern legal order', says Habermas, 'may be above all a rational system "characterized by positivity, generality and formality", but at the same time, modern law reflects the specific moral and cultural preferences of the bourgeoisie.'[8] Those who operate the law in Irish society may not be a breed apart, but they are different from non-legal people. They live and work in a different social field. Policemen, solicitors, barristers and judges know each other and how the field operates. They know intuitively what can and cannot be said and done. Ignorance of the law is no excuse for citizens of the state. But knowing how the law operates involves far more than knowing the specifics of legislative acts. Those who have no familiarity with the law – who have not been subject to its force – can be easily manipulated if not made fools of. In contrast, those who know the law, who know what happens when they become subject to it, who know what the police can and cannot do, who know their rights, what to say and not to say, how to remain silent, answer questions, make statements, give evidence in court and be subject to cross-examination, enter a highly specialised field where expert players dominate. Being able to survive and operate successfully in the legal field depends on a number of factors, not least of which are experience, social class background, and access to good advice and legal counsel.

The way the case was investigated, the way the Tribunal was conducted and the findings of the Report reveal the relationship between morality and law in Irish society. Any legal system in a mature democratic society has somehow to represent the moral beliefs and sentiments of the people. Once laws have been made, justice is served by their being implemented and adjudicated in a fair, open, transparent and equitable manner. This is deemed to be best achieved in some respects by moving more towards formal, rational, calculable law.[9] In other words, the first criterion for making good laws is to make them clear and unambiguous so that transgressions can be easily identified and prosecuted. That also enables judges and juries to assess if the law has been broken and, where necessary, to enforce appropriate penalties.

The law slowly but surely becomes an external force that stands above and beyond the ethics and morality of individuals.[10] Ethics and morality have more to do with the internal control of individual behaviour and less to do with the state regulating social order. Although laws are codified morals, modern law seemingly becomes detached from moral motives. When it comes to operating within the state or within the law, our personal moral convictions have little to no influence. We make choices not as moral actors, but as private legal persons.[11] It is only through the establishment of rational, formal, calculable law that the interference of religious preferences and personal moral convictions can be avoided. This is only possible when people recognise and accept that morality is separate from legality. This separation, in turn, leads to a rationalisation of morality. People recognise and accept different values and cultural traditions. They are critically self-reflexive rather than dogmatic about their values and morals.[12]

If law becomes removed or distant from the moral beliefs and values of the people, it will become an oppressive empty legalism. But if ethics and morality are put above the law, then this could lead to the danger that police, judges and juries make rules and enforce, interpret and assess laws on the basis of sentiments, feelings and maxims.[13] In reality, the separation of morality from law is an uneven process, in the Kerry babies case as in other instances of Western law. Throughout the case and within the enforcement and application of the law, another wider struggle was going on between Catholic fundamentalist ethics and liberal individualism.

The state under threat

Any understanding of what happened during the Kerry babies case has to take into account the troubled history of the Irish state, the conflict in the North, the strategies and tactics of Republican paramilitary groups, and the attempt by the gardaí to maintain law and order. The re-emergence of the Northern troubles in the late 1960s led to a resurgence of Republican military groups in the North and the South. The ambivalent relationship between the IRA and Fianna Fáil re-emerged in 1970 when two senior ministers were sacked and later tried and acquitted of illegally importing arms into the country to support the republican struggle in the North of Ireland.[14] The activities of proscribed republican groups, particularly the Provisional IRA, posed the greatest threat to public order in the South. This threat was dealt with firmly by the state. In 1972, the Fianna Fáil government set up the Special Criminal Court which held trials without juries. The Offences Against the State (Amendment) Act was also passed in December, following the explosion of two bombs in Dublin, which killed two and injured over a hundred people. There was growing agreement between opposition and government parties about the need to dispense with normal police and judicial standards if the state in the Republic was not to collapse in the same way as that in Northern Ireland.[15]

Conor Cruise O'Brien, Minister for Posts and Telegraphs, is adamant that the leaders of Cosgrave's coalition government between 1973 and 1977 believed that the greatest threat to the security of the state came from the IRA. He recalled a conversation he had with a Special Branch detective, shortly after the rescue of Tiede Herrema, the Dutch industrialist, who was kidnapped by a Republican group. O'Brien asked the detective how they had found Herrema:

One of the gang had been arrested, and we felt sure he knew where Herrema was. So this man was transferred under Branch escort from a prison in the country to a prison in Dublin, and on the way the car stopped. Then the escort started asking him questions and when at first he refused to answer, they beat the shit out of him. Then he told them where Herrema was.[16]

Garret FitzGerald, however, said that he was so distressed at the time of the heavy gang reports that he decided to raise the matter in the government and, if necessary, to force the issue to a conclusion by threatening resignation. He had received a visit from two 'responsible' members of the gardaí who were also worried about the activities of the heavy gang. They told FitzGerald that in some pending cases it was believed by some in the force that confessions had been extracted by improper methods, that Garda morale would be seriously damaged if the cases went ahead, and that some gardaí were persuaded to perjure themselves in the process.[17]

It is difficult to determine to what extent the conflict in Northern Ireland and the rise in terrorist activity in the Republic of Ireland contributed to a rise in criminal violence in Irish society. Crime increased generally in Ireland from the 1950s, a trend that has been linked to a number of social, cultural and economic factors, many of which were affecting Western society in general.[18] But from the time of the conflict in Northern Ireland there was a dramatic rise in the number of murders and armed robberies in the Republic. For most years from 1945 to the 1960s, the total number of murders in the Republic of Ireland was in single figures. Since the 1970s the figure has virtually always been greater than 20 and this rise can be attributed to terrorist incidents more than anything else.[19] An especially dramatic rise occurred in the 1970s and early 1980s in the number of gardaí murdered in the line of duty. There was an equally dramatic rise in the number of armed robberies; from 30 in 1971, to 228 in 1979, and 524 in 1989.[20] Although the rise in violent crime in the Republic is ostensibly linked with the development of the conflict in Northern Ireland, it must be borne in mind that a similar increase in crime and violent crime was happening elsewhere in Europe, for example in The Netherlands.[21]

It would be wrong to think that the state at any time, but particularly at the height of the conflict in the North, exercised a strict control over the gardaí by insisting that they operate within the letter of the law. It would always seem to be necessary to tap phones, intercept mail and watch and follow those who have been deemed to be a threat to the state. This became the specific skill of the Special Branch, which developed rapidly in the 1970s. So did the Murder

Squad, which specialised in interrogating suspect criminals. Like the Special Branch, they were to be given a relatively free rein when it came to interrogating suspect terrorists.[22]

The heavy gang

The history of the so-called 'heavy gang', the political environment in which it operated, and the attitudes and outlook of those who worked within it are relevant and important to a discussion of the Kerry babies case.[23] The Garda Technical Bureau is based in the Phoenix Park at Garda Headquarters. It has a number of technical and scientific experts, in fingerprinting, forensics and photography, who help in the investigation of cases. The Technical Bureau is called in by the local superintendent when detectives in that district need assistance in investigating a serious crime. One of the sections of the Bureau was the Investigative Section, a team of detectives specialising in identifying, locating and interrogating suspects. These detectives were skilled in taking statements and obtaining confessions deemed acceptable by the courts – that is, confessions that would be within the Judges Rules. Those nine rules specified what was permitted during the questioning of suspects.

Before the conflict in the North and the rise of subversive activity in the South, the Investigative Section was mainly brought in to help in serious crimes, particularly murders. This was how it received the name 'Murder Squad'. However, in the 1970s, the Murder Squad was brought in to help in the investigation of a broad range of crimes, especially when subversives were thought to be involved.

Questioning subversives, like questioning 'seasoned' criminals, was a skilled procedure, since those brought in for questioning on a regular basis would have learnt from others how to deal with the interrogation tactics of the gardaí. They knew their rights and what, at least legally, could be said and done to them when they were in police custody or, as members of the Hayes family were doing, 'helping the police with their inquiries'. The more that subversives became skilled at developing alibis and concealing any traces of their involvement in crime, the more the gardaí became dependent on obtaining statements and confessions. Yet the more the gardaí became dependent on confessions to obtain convictions, the more skilled subversives became at remaining silent, or repeating the same story.

The term 'heavy gang' emerged in the mid-1970s from within the gardaí, to describe detectives who became specialists in systematically extracting confessions from suspects. They were believed to use a variety of tactics including verbal intimidation, physical and mental abuse, and ultimately getting suspects to make confessions which were concocted or 'stitched up' by developing answers to questions which combined known facts with certain admissions. Ronan Bennett gives a vivid description of how he was interrogated about his possible involvement in a bank robbery in Belfast. He was eventually charged with the murder of a police inspector. Despite intimidation, he refused to confess, but suggests how his confession could have been concocted.

> I knew nothing of the bank robbery, nothing of the gunfight, nothing of the killing. What details would I have given, could I have given? I need have no worries, there would have been no problem about my lack of firsthand knowledge. The confession would have contained details known only to the guilty party. A detective would have asked: 'Did you meet so-and-so the morning before the robbery?' I nod. 'Did you tell him we had a job on?' Another nod or perhaps a weak yes. 'And did you go the next day in the blue four-door saloon to the bank? Was the car stolen earlier in the New Lodge area? Were you carrying the sub-machine-gun and so-and-so pistol? Did you shoot the officer when he ambushed you on emerging from the bank?' Yes to the first question, yes to the last. Yes to all of it. And in its statement form my confession would have read: 'I met so-and-so in the morning and told him we had a job on the next day. The car we got was a blue four-door saloon which had been stolen earlier in the New Lodge area. I carried the sub-machine-gun and so-and-so had the pistol . . .'. And the prosecution would have adduced this statement in court as formidable and conclusive evidence against me, convincing because why else would I have confessed (in the absence of any evidence of intimidation), and because it contained details which could only have been known to someone who had been involved. And, of course, by the detectives investigating the case.[24]

The O'Briain Commission

The number of allegations against the gardaí, particularly against members of the Murder Squad, grew throughout the 1970s.[25] The allegations usually emerged during court cases when defendants retracted their confessions, claiming that they had been beaten or intimidated into making them. The gardaí would claim in court that the statements had been made voluntarily, and in most cases their claim was accepted by the courts.

In 1977, following an upsurge in retracted confessions and allegations of abuse and intimidation of suspects while in custody, the government appointed a committee under Justice Bara O'Briain to recommend safeguards for persons in custody and for members of the gardaí. Justice O'Briain noted in the committee Report:

> Statistics can be misleading and we would not wish to attach undue significance to the figures quoted to us. However, the statement that 80% of serious crimes, in respect of which convictions are obtained, are solved by confessions i.e., as the end-product of questioning sessions – seems to indicate a high degree of reliance on self-incrimination, and an inability or reluctance to secure by scientific methods of criminal investigation and by persevering with police enquiries.[26]

The Committee received a dossier containing allegations by 26 people of ill-treatment at the hands of the gardaí.[27] The Committee realised that much of the problem centred on the 1939 Offences Against the State Act which empowered gardaí to arrest and detain people for up to 48 hours. It noted that the gardaí faced a particular problem in how they operated between inviting people to help them with their inquiries, and formally arresting them. The Committee recognised that if they formally arrested people, this could have serious consequences for the person arrested as well as for the garda himself.

> the practice has grown over the years to secure 'voluntary' attendance at Stations by refraining from advising the 'invitees' of the legal realities of the situation. We believe that most people who go to Garda stations to 'assist the police with their enquiries' do so under the misapprehension that they have no other choice than to do so. This practice has been condoned and as a result has become the established norm.[28]

The acid test of this was taken to be whether the invitee 'believes he is free to walk out the door at any time he wishes to do so'.[29] The Committee said it had been informed that it was normal for only one officer to interview an arrested person. However, two or more officers were likely to take part in questioning 'when the person is a habitual criminal, well-versed in the practices of police questioning and his own legal and constitutional rights'.[30] It may be remembered that when members of the Hayes family, who were not under arrest, were helping the gardaí with their inquiries, there were generally two officers present at all times. As Mr Justice Lynch said, 'none of them appreciated their rights or their status as persons in the Garda Station' (TR, p. 128). They did not know that they were free to get up and go at any time. More importantly, this funda-mental right was not made known to them, but in the rules of the legal game ignorance of the law is no excuse, and the gardaí knew the rules and how to play the game inside out. Mr Justice Lynch pointed out that when Joanne asked to bring the gardaí out to show where the body of her baby was hidden and was denied, she was effectively asking for permission to leave. He dismissed Superintendent Courtney's claim that there had been previous cases where such permission had not been granted, since they pertained to 'persons who had already been arrested and were therefore in Garda custody' (TR, p. 129).

The Committee made 22 recommendations. Its first recommendation was that 'the practice of taking people whom it is desired to question to a Garda Station "to help the police with their enquiries"' should be discontinued'. Its second recommendation was that a person arrested and brought in for ques-tioning should have a 'custodial guardian' – perhaps a member of the force not connected with the case – who would be responsible for 'the well-being of the person in custody and the safeguarding of his rights'.[31]

Six years later, in April 1984, none of the major recommendations of the Committee had been implemented. The state was turning a blind eye, in view of the problem it faced in dealing with serious criminals and subversives. It suited the state not to restrict the activities of the Special Branch and the Murder Squad, who might even have been informally encouraged in some of their less savoury practices. However, as in many other instances of states maintaining law and order, once members of the police were found to have 'overstepped the mark', or gone beyond the law, individual officers were held accountable.

There had been other important developments before the Kerry babies case. In September 1976, Vera Cooney was found murdered in a house in Sandymount, Dublin. She had been strangled and stabbed to death. A soldier, Christy Lynch, who had been doing some part-time work for her, was brought in for questioning. Twenty-two hours later he confessed to the murder. During the trial he retracted his confession saying that he been intimidated, kept awake, threatened and mildly assaulted. He said that the confession was made up through his being asked a series of questions to which he had given mono-syllabic answers. The questions were then 'stitched' together as statements to give an overall consistent confession. The judge and jury accepted his confession and Lynch was convicted and sent to prison. Three years later, after a number of appeals, Lynch was finally freed by the Supreme Court.

John Courtney was one of the detectives from the Investigation Section involved in the Lynch case. He was subsequently promoted to Superintendent and made head of the Investigative Section

On 30 March 1976, the postal train from Cork to Dublin was stopped and robbed. Six people were eventually accused of the robbery. On 7 April, four suspects – Nicky Kelly, Osgur Breathnach, Brian McNally and John Fitzpatrick – signed confessions about their involvement in the robbery. All four claimed that they had been beaten and intimidated into making their confessions. The only substantial evidence against them was their confessions. They were brought before the District Court and remanded in custody until the following day. They were split up, and contrary to existing regulations, two were put into a cell together. Dunne and Kerrigan, in their study of the case, suggested that there were two possibilities for what happened next, on which the whole case depended. The first possibility was they were in good health when they were put in the cells and the men beat each other up during the night, deliberately creating the bruising which they would later claim was inflicted by the gardaí. The second possibility was that the four accused had been beaten up by the gardaí and the gardaí deliberately kept them in cells two by two with the intention of setting up circumstances in which they could claim that the accused beat themselves up.[32]

The Court decided that the statements made by the accused were made voluntarily and not as a result of any assaults, ill-treatment or improper methods employed by members of the gardaí. The number of people arrested under Section 30 of the Offences Against the State Act 1939 grew dramatically in the late 1970s and early 1980s. It rose from 229 in 1972, to 912 in 1978, and to 2,308 in 1982. This means that in 1982 an average of 44 people were taken in every week under Section 30. Of the 2,308 people taken in, only 256 (11 per cent) were charged within 48 hours.[33]

By the time the case came to the Special Criminal Court, the charges against Fitzpatrick had been dropped. The Court held that the injuries Kelly, Breathnach and McNally suffered were self inflicted, or were inflicted by collaboration with persons other than the gardaí.[34] In concluding the case for the prosecution, the Senior Counsel Robert Barr said

There must have been a most incredible conspiracy among the Garda Síochana and civilian associates to lie and perjure themselves as well as to behave so disgracefully, as is alleged against them. That is so enormous as to be patently absurd.[35]

Some years earlier, in a judgement in the Birmingham Six case in Britain, Lord Denning, the Master of the Rolls, concluded that granting the six men an appeal would mean that the police were guilty of perjury, violence and threats, the confessions were involuntary and improperly admitted in evidence and the convictions erroneous. He concluded that this was 'such an appalling vista that every sensible person in the land would say: it cannot be right that these actions should go any further.'[36]

A number of events in the months leading up to April 1984 may have led the state to believe that the foundation of law and order were under threat, if not direct attack. In December 1983, a soldier and a garda were killed in the rescue of the kidnap victim, Don Tidey, a prominent businessman. This led to a major security review. In January the Minister for Justice, Michael Noonan, introduced a new Criminal Justice Bill. One of the main provisions of the bill was to limit a suspect's right to remain silent. This was heavily criticised by civil rights groups. In the debate that followed, the Association of Garda Sergeants and Inspectors announced that they were against any curtailment of the bill which was badly needed in the fight against crime. Figures released the following June showed that the number of serious crimes had reached an all-time high.[37]

Allegations made at about this time served to spread doubt about the methods being used to investigate crimes and gain convictions. In November, two detectives in the Garda Technical Bureau were deemed by the judge to have been fully vindicated in the High Court following a defamation case, even though they had lost their case. The case arose from the investigation of the murder of the British Ambassador, Christopher Ewart-Biggs. The detectives had been transferred after reporting that their superior had claimed that a fingerprint on a workman's helmet found at the scene belonged to a well-known IRA suspect, and that the superior was willing to testify to this in court. It transpired that the fingerprint belonged to one of the detectives who had carried out the testing.[38] In the Dáil debate on establishing a tribunal of inquiry into the Kerry babies case, Michael Woods (Fianna Fáil) referred to the case of Amanda McShane in Tallaght, whose statement it appeared had been written out by gardaí, and that she was simply told to sign it. He also alluded to the case mentioned earlier of Michael Ward, a 21 year-old traveller, who was supposed to have committed 26 burglaries; when the case was investigated it had been found that he was in Mountjoy Prison when some of the alleged offences were committed and, in regard to others, the householders had not reported any burglaries at all.[39]

Interrogating subversives

The political and policing climate at the time of the Kerry babies case therefore helps us to understand the investigation of the Kerry babies case. It was not just an unsettled time culturally and economically in Ireland, but also politically unsettled. There was political and public ambivalence about the rise in serious crime and subversive activities. The gardaí were expected to achieve results and yet operate within the letter of the law, which caused them difficulty when they had to deal with people who understood the law and knew how to play the legal game as well as they did. As Conor Brady suggested, the methods, achievements and results of the Murder Squad suited their superiors, including the Department of Justice.[40]

In the lead up to the Tribunal in November 1984, Brady interviewed a former member of the Murder Squad, who commented about the Murder Squad from Dublin becoming involved in a case:

> They're just bloody delighted to have somebody who knows the business, who's going to get stuck in and get to the bottom of what's going on. People don't know the sheer terror, the sheer paralysis, a bad murder creates in a rural area. They want whoever it is caught and they want it done fast and they're not too fussy about how it's done.

He said that the key to successful interrogation was relating to the people being questioned. It was important to enter into the minds and hearts of the suspects.

> You have almost to think yourself into their position, in under their skin. That's how you get to understand how they're thinking. And when you can think like they think, then you get the key to whatever it is you're after.

The problem, however, for the Murder Squad is that most of the time they are dealing with hardened criminals or trained subversives.

> You're interviewing a lot of decent people, of course, but nine times out of ten crime investigation leads you to scum. Bad, twisted, cunning perverts. They couldn't tell you the truth even if they wanted to, a lot of them.[41]

So what was the mentality of the Murder Squad when, like white knights riding out from the capital, they took the investigation of the Cahirciveen infanticide by storm? Did the local gardaí and the local people want the culprit caught? Were they not fussy about the means that had to be used? What was the attitude and mentality of the interrogators when they began their questioning of the Hayes family? In their evidence to the Tribunal, two of the main members of the Murder Squad, Detectives Browne and O'Carroll, were adamant that they sympathised with and understood Joanne Hayes's position. Det. Garda Browne told Mr Justice Lynch: 'My Lord, if ever I felt myself in a Police Station as a civilian, I would love to be treated the same way that Joanne Hayes was treated' (TT, 45/79). Det. Sgt O'Carroll said that he was fully aware of how susceptible to persuasion Joanne Hayes would have been.

> I have a little bit more experience than maybe some of my colleagues in that I lecture on cases of sexual rape, of infanticide and the mental state of a woman to kill an infant, a new-born infant, is surely a landmine or full of dangers for susceptibility and that is the one reason and the only reason I didn't suggest to Miss Hayes that she killed the Cahirciveen baby. (TT, 40/77)

If, however, Joanne Hayes and the rest of her family were treated with such care and caution throughout the time they were 'helping the gardaí with their enquiries', why then did they confess to a murder which they did not commit? To help answer this question we need – like the interrogators try to do with suspects – to enter into the minds and hearts of the interrogators, to understand that conscious and unconscious strategies and tactics that they use to get people to talk. The interrogation of suspect criminals has become a subtle and refined technique. Although there are regular allegations of intimidation and ill-treatment, it might well happen that skilled interrogators, such as those in the Murder Squad, have developed interrogating strategies which, although perfectly legal, if carefully and intensively applied produce confessions and statements which are made not because they are true, but because those who are being questioned cannot take – what they consider to be – mental torture any more.

Interrogation techniques

To understand this kind of oppressive questioning and its effects, and what took place in Tralee Garda Station on 1 May 1984, we have to consider what it is like to be suddenly lifted from the normal routine of everyday life and subjected to a barrage of questions from different people which, on and off, goes on for nearly twelve hours. Even when people are supposedly helping the police with their inquiries, it is, according to Mr Justice Lynch, no 'tea-party'. They can be expected to run the full gauntlet of an interrogation process. We need to be aware of the kind of strategies and tactics that members of the Murder Squad might have used on subversives and hardened criminals. Getting someone to talk and getting someone to confess to a crime are skilled procedures.

In their handbook on criminal interrogation, Inbau and his colleagues make three preliminary points: many criminal cases can only be solved through an admission of guilt; criminal offenders will ordinarily not admit their guilt unless interrogated in private sometimes for several hours; in dealing with criminal offenders, and necessarily with suspects who may actually be innocent, interrogators have to use less refined methods that are considered appropriate for the transaction of everyday affairs. They claim that when circumstantial evidence points towards a particular person, that person is usually the one who committed the offence. They stress the importance of having specialist interrogators, and insist that unethical means justify the ends of catching a criminal.[42] They identify seven broad tactics and techniques for the interrogation of suspects whose guilt seems definite or reasonably certain.[43] What is missing in the Kerry babies case is an exact knowledge of how each of the confessions came to be made, the nature of the dialogue between the interrogators and each of the members of the Hayes family, how things were elicited, and why they said what they did.

Since we do not know what exactly went on in Tralee Garda Station that day, it is hard to know the strategies and tactics of persuasion that were used to obtain the confessions. Once interrogation goes beyond persuasion, it can easily move into the realm of coercion. An experimental study of 75 college students showed how two thirds of them were coerced into making false written confessions about something that they had not done.[44] Some researchers have argued that the only reliable way of dispelling any hints of coercion is to tape-record the interrogation.[45]

Shuy has argued that building a confession is similar to the technique used in constructing a documentary film. 'The producer or director can, in such circumstances, select and edit at will toward the goal of yielding a product that suits his or her own intended outcome.'[46]

As we saw in chapter 6, Mr Justice Lynch firmly placed the blame for the Hayes's false confessions on the family. They were liars, they had guilty consciences, and they felt under pressure. He concluded that, besides feeling that they were not free to go, any feeling of pressure came from within themselves. The pressure was felt rather than real and had nothing to do with the interrogation strategies and tactics of the gardaí.

In his own careful analysis of the Kerry Babies Tribunal and, in particular, Mr Justice Lynch's Report, Paul O'Mahony emphasised how little attention was paid to why it was that the Hayes family made false confessions and lied against their own interests. He concluded that not enough attention was paid to the extensive findings from psychological research on techniques of psychological pressure, persuasion and compliance. He referred specifically to the well-known studies by Milgram and Lifton. Milgram showed that most people could be induced to comply with the instructions of an authority figure. Lifton described techniques which lead to personalisation, to a weakening of an individual's prior frame of reference, and eventually to a state of hypersuggestibility. These studies help us understand how people might comply under psychological duress, sign false confessions, and be partially convinced that they are true.[47]

When the Murder Squad orchestrated the interrogation of the Hayes family, whatever the political background, the moral beliefs and values of the interrogators, and the personal interest they may have taken in the case, they brought with them a range of sophisticated strategies and tactics for interviewing people and a reputation for obtaining spontaneous, voluntary confessions. When Mr Justice Lynch argued in his Report that the Hayes family were not put under any unusual pressure, he was, to use his own words in relation to the evidence of the gardaí, 'gilding the lily'. He was not declaring a fact, but telling a story, putting forward an 'unlikely, far-fetched and self-contradictory theory'.

It may well be that by blaming the Hayes family for having confessed to a crime they did not commit, Mr Justice Lynch was perhaps protecting the state and society from – to use Lord Denning's phrase – 'the appalling vista' that the confessions were the result of oppressive questioning, tried and tested methods of exerting psychological pressure, making people feel vulnerable and depersonalised and, ultimately, making them compliant enough to confess.

Finally, it is important to contrast the behaviour and methods of the Murder Squad – who had the task of policing the state – with those of Garda Liam Moloney who had the task of policing Abbeydorney. When Joanne Hayes was in the middle of her affair with Jeremiah Locke, it was Liam Moloney – following a request from Mrs Hayes – who drove out to the Hayes household to speak to Joanne. Similarly, when he received complaints about Aunt Bridie's drinking and driving, he spoke to Ned Hayes, who suggested that Liam Moloney should phone Bridie's sister, Sr Aquinas. This he did and, as a result, she wrote to Bridie who subsequently neither drank nor drove.[48]

Protesting against the state

One of the central arguments in this chapter is that not only does the state develop a monopoly over the means of violence, but that it also develops a monopoly over the truth and means of producing the truth. The Kerry babies case suggests that the maintenance of these two monopolies may be connected. When there is a threat to the state's monopoly over the means of violence, when it is challenged as being unjust or illegal, the state reserves the right to produce *the* truth about events surrounding this challenge. In mature democratic societies the judiciary is deemed to be independent of, and not directly account-able to, either the legislature or the will of the people. There may be debate and discussion in the media and the public sphere about judicial process and deci-sions, but the influence of this rarely goes beyond the weight of public opinion.

The Kerry Babies Tribunal generated widespread public interest. During the first three weeks it was regularly one of the lead stories in news reporting. As the Tribunal progressed public sympathy grew for Joanne Hayes, first in her local community and then nationally. The protest began as a form of support during the early days of the Tribunal when she was giving evidence. A woman from the Tralee Women's Group sent her a single yellow flower. Her example was followed by two other women. The support was broadcast on national radio. The next day Joanne Hayes received numerous individually wrapped yellow flowers. Many of these came from a group of women who had been contacted by the Tralee Women's Group. Sue Richardson of the Women's Community Press began to organise and co-ordinate the flower support. Other groups were contacted and asked to send a flower. Soon flowers began arriving for Joanne Hayes from all over the country. As well as flowers, Joanne Hayes received numerous letters and mass cards.[49]

In Abbeydorney, where the Hayes family lived, a local journalist, John Barrett, collaborated with the local butcher, Jerome Donovan, to contact every villager and local family in the parish who had a telephone. They organised the printing of streamers saying 'Abbeydorney supports Joanne'. The next day they picketed the Tribunal before its personnel arrived. The following day, a bus-load of women from Dublin, mainly members of women's groups, arrived to join the picket.

Mr Justice Lynch, with Garda escort to the Tribunal at Tralee.

Before the Tribunal proceedings began on 28 January 1985, Mr Justice Lynch made a statement about the protests that had taken place the previous week (TR, pp. 139–45). He said that the pickets, particularly that involving the women from Dublin, seriously threatened the continuance of the Tribunal hearings in Tralee and the freedom of the parties to make their respective cases to the Tribunal without hindrance from any outside party. He intended ensuring that the Tribunal would be carried out with total impartiality and total independence, and would give all parties the fullest possible opportunity of making their case fully and freely before it. He considered the pickets and assemblies outside the Courthouse grossly improper. He contrasted 'the silent and dignified assembly on behalf of the rural community of Abbeydorney with the raucous and ill-mannered assembly on Thursday gathered from the four corners of urban Ireland'. He criticised members of the Dáil who, he suggested, had made misleading and ill-informed statements about the Tribunal. He said that he was leaving it up to the Director of Public Prosecutions whether people who had taken part in the pickets should be prosecuted under the Tribunal Inquiry Act (1979) which, if they were convicted, could carry a fine of £10,000 and two years' imprisonment. He said that independent of this possibility he, as a High Court judge, could commit anybody to prison who threatened the integrity of the Tribunal. He therefore would not tolerate any more pickets in the vicinity of the Tribunal, or insults to the Tribunal, by any of the parties involved or their legal representatives.

There are two important points here. First, although Mr Justice Lynch was a High Court judge, he was not acting in this capacity as chairperson or head of the Tribunal, and under the Tribunal Inquiries Act (1979) he did not have the power to commit anybody to prison. The second and more important point has to do with the rights of citizens, including their elected representatives, to protest against the state, particularly the police and the judiciary who are not democratically accountable. Finally, while the judge criticised their behaviour, it was more than symbolic that members of the gardaí (including members of the Murder Squad) – whose conduct was being investigated by the Tribunal – escorted Mr Justice Lynch through the protestors (TR, pp. 144).

Shortly after the Tribunal Report was published, the Murder Squad was disbanded and for a time some of its leading figures were given desk jobs. Most, however, went on to have successful careers. Superintendent Courtney retired as Chief Superintendent in 1991. Det. Sgt Gerry O'Carroll became an Inspector and took early retirement. Det. Garda Browne became a Superintendent, as did Det. Sgt Shelly. Mr Justice Lynch went on to become a Supreme Court Judge before retiring.

Since the Kerry babies case, there has been an increase in critical reflection about the nature of the power of the gardaí and the state. A Garda Complaints Tribunal was established shortly after the case, although this operated more as an internal forum than as a fully independent watchdog. Throughout the late 1990s and early 2000s, there were major ongoing allegations of garda misconduct including lying under oath, obtaining a false confession to a murder, and the killing of a mentally ill man at the end of a siege. In November 2002, a Public Tribunal of Inquiry began into the conduct of gardaí in County Donegal where a family alleged that it had been systematically harassed by members of the gardaí over a number of years.

The integrity of politicians, state officials, policemen and members of the judiciary is now regularly questioned. Bishops and priests are no longer seen as paragons of trustworthiness and virtue. One of the consequences of increased liberal individualism is that people have become more self-assertive, confident and critical. There is no longer the same fear, awe and respect of those people in positions of power. Holders of power cannot now expect the type of obedience that obtained in the past. There is greater resistance and challenge to established forms of power. It is this resistance which is central to preventing the state from abusing its monopoly over the means of violence and producing 'the truth'.

CHAPTER THIRTEEN

The media

The media played a crucial role during the Kerry babies story. The case came to the attention of the public through investigative journalism. It was the media that kept the pressure on the state that eventually led to the establishment of the Tribunal. The hearings of the Tribunal were reported daily in newspapers, radio and television. Some of Ireland's leading journalists covered the Tribunal, four of them writing books about the case. The media reports during the early days of the Tribunal led to a public outcry from politicians, academics and priests. These reports helped galvanise support for Joanne Hayes and her family which, in turn, led to the pickets and protests against the Tribunal. When the Tribunal Report was published in October 1985 it was reported fully. There was an in-depth discussion of the Report on the *Late Late Show* on RTÉ television. The Report was criticised by Gene Kerrigan in *Magill*, and rejected in an editorial in the same edition. This led to a detailed rebuttal by Justice Kevin Lynch. He felt that criticisms were unfair and biased. He threatened legal action if they continued.

The part the media played in the case could be said to mirror the part they came to play in Irish society during the latter half of the twentieth century. During that time the media moved out from behind the coat-tails of the state and the Church and began to play the role of public watchdog, the fourth estate that represented public interest against the state, the Church and big business.[1] So the case might be seen as a triumph for mature, liberal, democratic society and the important role of the media in criticising and analysing state power and in generating public debate and discussion about issues that affect people's lives.[2] Yet Mr Justice Lynch was highly critical of the media in his Report. He suggested that without their interference there might not have been any case or Tribunal (TR, p. 135).

The reporting of the case

The murder of the Cahirciveen baby was slow to reach the national media. On 16 April 1984, it was reported in *The Irish Times* that Kerry gardaí were trying to identify a newly born baby boy found dead on a beach the previous Saturday night by a local man Jack Griffin. It said that a post-mortem examination was being conducted. The *Irish Independent* had an important addendum: 'The Gardaí say it could have been thrown into the sea at any point along the Kerry coastline'. This suggests that Slea Head might have been in the thinking of the gardaí from the outset.

Three days later, it was announced that gardaí were investigating the possibility that the baby was murdered. No post-mortem results were available, but it was reported that the baby had a broken neck and chest wounds. 'The baby boy appears to have fallen out of a plastic bag found beside the body. Gardaí believe the bag was washed on to the rocks.' Six days later it was reported that Murder Squad detectives had been sent to Cahirciveen. Post-mortem results showed that the baby had been beaten and stabbed before being thrown into the water.[3]

A crucial aspect of the case and of the Tribunal Report was the claim that the Hayes family, having read what happened to the Cahirciveen baby (including the stabbing), transferred this into what happened to the Tralee baby under pressure during garda questioning. But *The Kerryman* had no specific mention of stabbing. It reported (20 April 1984), under the headline 'Child May Have Been Murdered':

> The young baby found dead on a Cahirciveen beach at the weekend may have been murdered, according to Kerryman sources. The newly born male infant had a broken neck and chest wounds.
>
> There is no evidence that the child was put into the water in Cahirciveen, but it is thought it was probably put in somewhere in the South Kerry area.

The next week, *The Kerryman* (4 May 1984) gave front page coverage to a report that Joanne Hayes, a 25-year-old woman from Abbeydorney, had been charged with the murder of her newly born son and that her sister, two brothers and aunt had been charged with 'concealing the birth of the baby by secretly disposing of the body'. No specific mention or link was made in the Report to the Cahirciveen baby. Nor was there any mention that the Tralee baby had been found, although the paper would have gone to press a couple of days before its official publication date.

There were reports in the national media about the charging of Joanne Hayes and her family and, on 4 May 1984, of the finding of the Tralee baby. But although the Tralee baby was found in Abbeydorney, and although the woman and family were from Abbeydorney, there was no investigative reporting of the anomaly of someone being charged with murder before the body was found.

No coverage of the case appeared in the national media until the following October, when the charges against Joanne Hayes and her family were dropped. Interest was rekindled through a piece of investigative reporting by Don Buckley, a freelance journalist, who wrote mainly for the *Sunday Independent*. He had been given access to the Garda File and Report by a source within the gardaí. His report, written with Joe Joyce and published on 10 October 1984, was given front-page coverage and two full pages on the inside. The headline on their article 'Blood Test Key to Kerry Baby Deaths Riddle' was succinct and extremely accurate, given that it was written three months before the Tribunal began. The report detailed the history of the case, the discovery of the Cahirciveen baby, the murder hunt, the confessions, the murder charge against Joanne Hayes, the discovery of the Tralee baby, and the subsequent quandary for the gardaí when the 'twins' were found to have different blood groups. Buckley and Joyce said that the main problem was the similarity of the details of the confessions and the injuries suffered by the Cahirciveen baby. The report concluded that none of the theories put forward by the gardaí explained how members of the Hayes family confessed to a murder that fitted exactly, in execution and aftermath, with the death of the Cahirciveen baby.

The report in the *Sunday Independent* created enormous interest in the case. It must be remembered that the case occurred within the context of ongoing allegations – and categorical denials from the government and the gardaí – about the existence of a 'heavy gang' within the gardaí who extracted confessions through intimidation and abuse of those in custody. Perhaps the most significant coverage emerged in a report on *Today Tonight*, the flagship current affairs programme on RTÉ. The programme was produced by Barry O'Halloran.[4]

During the programme, Joanne Hayes talked about the birth and death of the Tralee baby and about giving birth alone out in the field at the back of the farmhouse. More significantly, members of the Hayes family made detailed allegations of abuse and intimidation during the time they were being questioned in Tralee Garda Station on 1 May 1984. Significantly, they said that it was because of this that they made and signed the statements about their involvement in the Cahirciveen baby's murder. Previously, reports and rumours about the mistreatment of people in garda custody would have been seen to involve political dissidents, subversives, or criminals. The Hayes family, however, seemed to be like any other family you would find in rural Ireland. Why, then, did they confess to a crime that they did not commit? As O'Halloran pointed out: 'The answer for most people in October 1984 was that they must have been pressurised or beaten. There was no other way that they could have come to make such incriminating confessions as far as the media and the public were concerned.'[5]

The coverage of the Tribunal in the media was extensive. For the first three weeks it was one of the front-page lead stories in the newspapers. The Tribunal was a major media event. The case had all the hallmarks to attract public attention – love, passion, sex, intrigue, crime, corruption and tragedy. It was unique and timely. Sex and extra-marital relations may have been the subject of dramas, novels and films, but they were only beginning to be discussed frankly and openly on the airwaves. The first few weeks of the case provided Irish people with the equivalent of a real, live soap opera. It was only when the Tribunal began to drag and get deeply involved in technical and scientific evidence and the detailed questioning of each garda that the coverage of the case began to decrease and move to the inside pages of newspapers.

Blame the media

Mr Justice Lynch was very critical of the role the media played in the case. He was adamant that they were biased, and that they misrepresented and sensationalised Tribunal evidence. He also blamed them for constructing the notion of a conspiracy on the part of the gardaí to frame the Hayes family for the death of the Cahirciveen baby.

> While references were made in the media to the persistence of the Gardaí with the charges against the Hayes family and Bridie Fuller despite compelling evidence to the contrary, the main disquiet expressed through the media was on the basis of a conspiracy on the part of the Gardaí to 'frame' or 'nail' the Hayes family and Bridie Fuller for responsibility for the death of the Cahirciveen baby at all costs. When one considers that the Gardaí involved in interviewing the Hayes family and Bridie Fuller on the 1st May, 1984, were drawn from all parts of Co. Kerry – Abbeydorney, Cahirciveen, Dingle, Killarney, Listowel and Tralee – as well as Detectives from Dublin, the idea of such a conspiracy becomes ridiculous – or, if it were true, monstrous. (TR, p. 135)

Instead of the media acting as the public watchdog, instead of engaging in fair and honest reporting, instead of stimulating critical debate and discussion about policing in Irish society, in Mr Justice Lynch's view they had engaged in inaccurate, biased and unfair reporting by promoting the notion of a conspiracy on the part of gardaí to frame the Hayes family for the Cahirciveen murder.

Mr Justice Lynch argued that while allegations of abuse made against members of the gardaí should be given publicity 'so that people may know what is going on', the media, he said, fell down 'in their failure to give equal prominence to the other side of the case'. He said there were many cases where allegations of abuse had turned out to be false. He noted that

> Sometimes indeed, allegations are made by a person and are then later abandoned by that person and yet the allegation will get the headlines whereas its abandonment, if published at all, invariably will be in small print. (TR, p. 75)

As an example of this Mr Justice Lynch referred to a report of the Tribunal in one of the Irish daily newspapers. The newspaper, he said, headlined its report in three eighths of an inch heavy typescript: 'Punched in the Stomach by Detective'. In the report it was stated that Mike Hayes told the Tribunal that he had been punched twice in the stomach as he was being walked around a room in Tralee Garda Station. But Mr Justice Lynch complained: 'How many of the people who read and were misled by the headlines read on into the small print to be put right again as to what Mike Hayes was really alleging had happened' (TR, p. 76).

What Mr Justice Lynch was referring to was in many respects the gap between the discourse and language of the legal field and of the media. He said in the Report that he was interested in establishing the facts of what had happened. The newspaper reported the fact that Mike Hayes said that he was punched in the stomach by a detective, but it was careful to put this in quotation marks, indicating that it was something said or claimed.[6]

Another issue is involved. The language and discourse of a Tribunal hearing are different from those of the media and, in particular, the popular press. Journalists, editors and sub-editors have to balance objectivity with the need to get their story accepted and printed, for readers to be attracted to the story and, in the final analysis, for the newspaper to sell. The people who work in newspapers have to balance accurate and fair reporting with the pressure of maintaining their competitive position in the market. One of the traditional ways which newspapers, particularly the tabloids, have used to advertise themselves and attract readers is through attractive banner headlines.

Mr Justice Lynch went further than just castigating the media for unfair and biased reporting. He suggested that, perhaps unwittingly, they were to blame for the Tribunal. In particular, he argued that the two programmes on *Today Tonight* had had the unintended consequence of leading members of the Hayes family to make false allegations of garda abuse and intimidation. Mr Justice Lynch maintained that the sudden and dramatic media coverage which emerged after the *Sunday Independent* story broke forced members of the Hayes family into giving plausible explanations, under the gaze of television cameras and reporters, why they had confessed to a crime they had not committed. The only way they could do this and, according to Mr Justice Lynch, 'the oldest way in the book' was to claim that their statements were obtained by grossly improper conduct by the gardaí against them (TR, p. 75).

It must be remembered that this theory is premised on Mr Justice Lynch's finding that there was no truth in any of the allegations of intimidation and abuse made about the gardaí by members of the Hayes family. The story the Hayes family told to the media was a complete concoction. This disregards the testimony of Pat Mann, the Hayes family solicitor, who told the Tribunal that the family had made allegations of abuse and intimidation as early as the day after being questioned.[7] It also important to realise that the pressure for the Tribunal did not come solely from the allegations of the Hayes family. An internal garda inquiry had been established the day after Buckley and Joyce published their story in the *Sunday Independent*. Moreover, they had been writing about allegations of garda abuse and intimidation for the previous seven years, and it could be said that the Tribunal arose more from investigative journalism than anything else.[8]

This is not to reject the plausibility of Mr Justice Lynch's explanation. Indeed it might well be that the vulnerability and suggestibility of people being questioned, their propensity to exaggerate or, in Mr Justice Lynch's terms 'gild the lily', may be just as strong in the presence of the media as the police.

The Kerryman

The media had another important role to play in the case. Mr Justice Lynch concluded in his Report that at 2.45 p.m. on 1 May 1984, Ned Hayes was the first to 'confess'. He gave a verbal statement in which he said that on the night in question he was told by his mother 'that Joanne Hayes had had a baby and that she had stabbed the baby to death with a carving knife'. Mr Justice Lynch argued that Ned Hayes made this up. He said Ned Hayes knew 'the two detectives wanted to solve the Cahirciveen baby murder case. He believed in any event that that was his sister's baby and he gave the Detectives a story to tie in with that belief' (TR, p. 100). While Ned Hayes might not have known where the Tralee baby was hidden on the farmlands, there must have been a reasonable doubt that he believed that his sister's baby was the one found in Cahirciveen. He might have wondered, suspected or feared. But this does not explain why Ned would say that his mother had told him that the baby had been stabbed. Accepting that Ned made up the part about his mother saying that the baby had been stabbed, where did the notion of the baby being stabbed come from? Mr Justice Lynch argued

> Ned Hayes gave them (the detectives) a story which was a combination first, of what had happened to the Tralee baby and what had gone on afterwards that night in the Hayes house and secondly, what would fit in with the stabbing or chest wounds of the Cahirciveen baby as reported in 'The Kerryman'. (TR, p. 100)

He repeated this later.

> The fact that Joanne Hays beat the baby with the bath brush made it easier for the other members of the family to believe, or suspect, or fear that she had stabbed it after death and broken its neck in a frenzy, when they read in 'The Kerryman' of the 20th April, 1984 of the finding of the Cahirciveen Baby and a short description of its injuries. (TR, p. 113)

As we saw above, the report in *The Kerryman* did not mention any stabbing. It simply said that the baby had a broken neck and chest wounds. However, there was coverage in the national media that might have reached the Hayes family and Ned in particular, which revealed that the baby had been beaten and stabbed before being thrown into the water. It might have been that although the Hayes family only bought *The Kerryman*, the news about the stabbing reached them through word of mouth. Nevertheless, in Mr Justice Lynch's argument, Ned Hayes conveniently transposed 'chest wounds' to mean stabbing with a carving knife, which coincidentally fitted in with the way that the Cahirciveen baby had been murdered.

The report in *The Kerryman* might also explain how the bath brush came to figure in Mrs Hayes's statement. Mr Justice Lynch pointed out that when

Detectives Smith and Coote were directed to talk to Mrs Hayes on 1 May, 'they knew little, if anything, more about the case than the ordinary citizen who reads "The Kerryman"' (TR, p. 109). He dismissed Mrs Hayes's claim that Detective Smith had suggested to her that the baby was beaten with the bath brush. He said 'there was absolutely no reason why the Detectives would invent or ever think of such a thing'. Mr Justice Lynch said that the notion of beating the baby with a bath brush was something Detective Smith 'would never have thought of in a month of Sundays' (TR, p. 112). But if Detective Smith believed that he was investigating the Cahirciveen murder, and if he had not been at the briefing the previous night and knew nothing about the stabbing, and if he was following the scant description in *The Kerryman* of the baby having died from a broken neck and chest wounds, he might not have been looking for a knife, but for some other implement that might have caused such injuries.

Criticisms of the Report

The task of the Tribunal was to establish the facts of the case. The state, and in particular the judiciary, reserves for itself a monopoly of declaring the truth. But if the media are to fulfil their role as public watchdog, or the social conscience of civil society, then it is crucial that they are able to analyse and criticise the state.[9] One of the distinguishing characteristics of the change in Irish society during the last half of the twentieth century was the growth in the been critical of governments, their departments and ministers, but during that time civil servants, the army and the police became the focus of media attention. However, while analysis and criticism of the legislative and executive arms of the state are not inherently problematic, criticism and analysis of judges and their decisions could jeopardise the independence of the judiciary.

Here we have a problem that lies at the heart of the case. If the media are prevented or inhibited from criticising judges and their determination of facts, how can they fulfil their task of public watchdog? Judges can be critical of the media, but to what extent is a mature democratic society founded upon the media being able to make fair comment and criticisms of judges and their decisions?

In the months after the Report was published there was praise as well as criticism of his conclusions. An editorial in the *Sunday Independent* (6 October 1985), which had originally broken the story, concurred with nearly all of Mr Justice Lynch's conclusions, particularly that Joanne Hayes was not the mother of the Cahirciveen baby, that she had killed her own baby, and that there was no physical abuse or intimidation. But it concluded that the Report failed to 'come up with a comprehensive explanation for the fact that the Hayes family confessed to a crime they had not committed'. *The Irish Times* (4 October 1985) made a similar criticism. It said that while his Report set out what happened in 1984, it did not explain why certain things happened. In particular, the editorial said, the Report did not explain how statements came to be taken from the Hayes family which tallied precisely in detail with what had since been shown to be false. It argued that to say that it was as a result of pressure and guilty consciences was not an answer. It also criticised the Report for not dealing with whether members of the Hayes family were under the impression that they could not leave the garda station and were therefore held in unlawful custody.

An editorial in *Magill* magazine said that the Report failed to answer the central question which it was established to answer, that is how people came to make detailed corroborative statements that were shown to be false. It called on the Minister for Justice to reject the Report. The conclusions of the editorial were based on a detailed analysis of the Report by Gene Kerrigan.[10] He criticised the Report for trying to elevate one possible version of events into the realms of factual reality. He called Mr Justice Lynch's story 'a fragile structure'.

> He has cited pieces of evidence and found them to be facts, then inferred other facts from these. If a serious doubt is raised about any substantial finding it removes a prop from several more. If we disbelieve any substantial part of Lynch's story we have to throw out the lot.[11]

In his analysis of the Report, Kerrigan began by examining the evidence for the birth being in the bedroom. He said that Mr Justice Lynch's assertion that Mrs Hayes, Kathleen and Bridie Fuller were present at the birth comes solely from Bridie Fuller's evidence. However, Kerrigan said that Bridie Fuller's evidence about what happened that night was full of contradictions about, for example, whether the baby was washed or not, and how long it had lived. If the baby was born in the bedroom, he asked, why did the forensic analysis by Louise McKenna find no trace of blood in the room?

Kerrigan challenged Mr Justice Lynch's categorical claim in his Report that 'Joanne Hayes got into a panic and as the baby cried again she put her hands around its neck and stopped it crying by choking it' (TT, 22/662–5) and 'the baby did not breathe again' (TT, 40/144–56). This, Kerrigan said, was crucial as it suggested that Joanne killed her baby. He argued that the evidence of Joanne putting her hands around the baby's neck was weak. Similarily, he argued that other than Mary Hayes's confession, there was little evidence for Mr Justice Lynch's claim that Joanne Hayes 'used the bath brush from the bathroom to hit the baby to make sure it was dead'. Kerrigan argued that the notion that Joanne Hayes hit her baby with the bath brush was problematic, given that the State Pathologist's evidence was that it was not certain if the Joanne's baby had achieved an independent existence, and that if the bath brush had hit the baby's head it would have fractured its skull. Finally, Kerrigan said that the Report's conclusions about how the false confessions came to be made were flawed. The issue, he claimed, came down to whether one accepted that the confessions were made freely, voluntarily and separately, and that they resulted from a mixture of guilty consciences and tough but fair questioning, or whether they resulted from unfair questioning and suggestions made by the gardaí.

On 18 October 1985, RTÉ's *Late Late Show* devoted the final section of the programme to a detailed discussion of the Tribunal Report. It began with the host Gay Byrne interviewing Joanne Hayes and John Barrett – a journalist from Abbeydorney who helped her write her book *My Story*. Joanne Hayes said that the reason she had come on the *Late Late Show* was to tell people that, contrary to what Mr Justice Lynch found, she did not kill her baby. She said that the reason she agreed to do the *Today Tonight* interview in October 1984 was to counteract claims being made that, despite the charges being dropped, the family were somehow implicated in the Cahirciveen baby's murder. Joanne Hayes was careful not to repeat any of the allegations of abuse and intimidation. Instead she suggested that it was unsatisfactory to think that she made the confessions voluntarily.[12]

After Joanne Hayes left, there was a discussion mainly between the host Gay Byrne and the various journalists who had written reports and books about the case. They were, generally, much more critical than supportive of the Report.

Mr Justice Lynch replies

In March 1986, Mr Justice Lynch wrote a detailed (approximately 6,000 word) response in *Magill* to Gene Kerrigan's article. While it has been common for judges to make orders in relation to the conduct of the media and reporters during a court hearing, it is still very unusual for judges to respond publicly to comments made in the media about verdicts or decisions that they have made. Not only does this bring them into public debate and discussion, but it can also be seen as an attempt to justify their findings. It brings them out of the legal field into the field of the media which, because of its different discourse and practice, operates under different rules and regulations. In leaving aside the established rubric within which legal people talk and write, judges face difficulties similar to those of other professionals, in this case how to remain true to legal discourse and reasoning – thus retaining the honour and respect of their colleagues – and, at the same time, write in a way that is accessible and meaningful to the general public. It should be remembered, however, that Lynch's Report was acclaimed for avoiding technical legal argument and language, and for balancing legal erudition and storytelling.

Mr Justice Lynch began the article with a further attack on the media.

> Since the Kerry Babies Report was published on 3 October 1985 it has naturally been widely discussed in the media. What is not natural or normal, however, is the fact that a section of the media have misrepresented the contents: the meaning and the bases of the Report, and appear to be maintaining a campaign to denigrate and discredit the Report and its author, myself, at the same time.[13]

He said that he had hoped when he produced his Report that it would be the end of the Kerry babies case for him. Instead, he said, 'I have had to endure totally unwarranted and snide attacks not only on the Report but on myself also'. He was particularly critical of the *Late Late Show*. He argued that the programme had great power and influence, but questioned whether it had dealt with the issues honestly and truthfully. He castigated Gay Byrne for allowing the media people present to claim that he had overlooked the evidence given by Professor Harbison, the State Pathologist, and the doubt that the Tralee baby had achieved an independent existence. He claimed that while he did not think Mr Byrne had deliberately intended to mislead the public about this, 'he did mislead them in assuring them that he had read the Report, when obviously he had no more than skimmed through it'.[14] If Gay Byrne had read the Report he would have been aware of the reference to Harbison's evidence on page 119 of the Report.

In Gay Byrne's defence, it is surely an overstatement to claim that he had only skimmed through the Report simply because he had missed one reference, especially as the particular reference was in the middle of a sentence in which he was primarily referring to Bridie Fuller's rebuttal of Harbison's evidence when she told the Tribunal that the Tralee baby had cried after birth. More importantly, however, when it was claimed on the programme that Mr Justice Lynch had overlooked the importance of Professor Harbison's evidence, this was more in the context of his not giving it due attention and significance. Since it was central to his argument that Joanne Hayes killed her baby, it was perhaps fair to say that he had overlooked the centrality of Professor Harbison's evidence.

In his defence, Mr Justice Lynch pointed out that at the beginning of his Report he had made it very clear that any painstaking perusal of the transcripts 'could find passages which contradict some of the passages' to which he referred. It was 'the province of the Tribunal to decide what evidence is or is not reliable and acceptable'. He went on to say that at the end of the Tribunal he had 'a complete grasp and recall of the evidence'. In preparing his Report, he 'overlooked none of the evidence'. To support this conclusion, he quoted Deirdre Purcell, the *Sunday Tribune* reporter, who had written about 'his frightening powers of concentration and memory'. He had deliberately not included all the relevant references to the evidence for everything he wrote about the Report, because he said it 'would have become unreadable as each sentence would have had to be followed by lines and lines of references'. It was, he said, 'absurd' to assume that his findings were based solely on the passages in the transcripts of the evidence referred to in the Report.[15]

As an example, he pointed out that in relation to the evidence for writing that Joanne Hayes put her hands around the baby's neck and stopped it crying by choking it, he said he could also have referred to Joanne Hayes telling the doctors in St Joseph's Hospital in Limerick 'that she had killed her own baby, but had nothing to do with the Cahirciveen baby'.[16]

There is some justification for Lynch's remarks. During his evidence Dr John Fennelly was asked:

Q. In her account to you she feels she actually killed her child?
A. Yes.
Q. . . . that this was a deliberate killing rather than an accidental one?
A. Certainly, she said . . . that when the baby cried she put her hand on his mouth. (TT, 18/19)

What Mr Justice Lynch did not say was that Dr Fennelly immediately put this in context:

I suppose you could say it is deliberate, whether the girl at that stage intended to kill the child or just to stop it from crying would be very difficult to say, particularly in the distraught state she was in at the time. What I am saying is that there was no premeditated thought of killing the baby, I would say, but that this was a possibly spontaneous deed in response to the child crying and tremendous tension and the problem of not knowing, she is on her own in the dark and she has a baby and he cries, this could be the last straw. It wasn't premeditated, certainly this was just a spontaneous act I would say. (TT, 18/10)

Given that his conclusion that Joanne Hayes killed her baby was a vital element in his construction of the truth about what had happened, and that Dr Fennelly's evidence was crucial to this, it is puzzling that Mr Justice Lynch did not give it greater prominence or refer more specifically to it in his Report.

Mr Justice Lynch went on to attack Kerrigan's conclusion that he had relied solely on Bridie Fuller's evidence in placing the birth of the Tralee baby in the bedroom. He pointed out that he referred twice in his Report (TR, pp. 73, 107–8) to Mike Hayes's evidence that the baby was born in the bedroom. Moreover he said, 'What right has Mr Kerrigan to say what I did or did not take into account in reaching my conclusions?'[17]

Mr Justice Lynch went on to emphasise the importance of finding that the Tralee baby was born in the bedroom was to explaining what had happened.

If Joanne Hayes's own baby had been born in the field then the family's statement to the Gardaí could not have come into existence without there having been gross misconduct, almost certainly including physical abuse, on the part of the Gardaí. If on the other hand Joanne Hayes's own baby was born in her own bedroom, to the knowledge of the whole family, then the family's statement to the Gardaí could well come into existence without any such gross misconduct on the part of the Gardaí.[18]

Once the birth and death of the Tralee baby had been located in the bedroom a number of things would thus fall into place. If members of the Hayes family could be deemed to be lying about this crucial issue, this meant that one element of their so deemed 'false' confessions were true. If the birth in the bedroom was not, as suggested, part of the frame-up, then maybe the details about a planned trip to Dingle was not a frame up. In other words, if the trip to Dingle were taken in the mind, it could with a guilty conscience enter a realm where, under rigorous questioning, the members of the Hayes family might have actually believed that such a journey had been undertaken. But if the baby was born in the bedroom, the question remained why a detailed forensic examination of the bedroom could not find any trace of blood? Mr Justice Lynch's response to this was that the family had had two weeks in which to wash and clean everything in the bedroom. Again, however, given the centrality of this to his determining the truth about what had happened, one would have imagined he would have dealt with this in his Report.

Mr Justice Lynch concluded his defence with a stirring admonition and warning:

> Much of what has been written in the media and spoken on radio and television has gone far beyond *bona fide* discussion of the Kerry Babies Report and its findings and has deteriorated into personal attacks upon me, its author. In so doing there has been much written, and said, and implied about me, that is grossly untrue and clearly defamatory.
>
> I have so far refrained from availing of my legal rights in this regard, but these rights remain alive and available to me at any time that I may wish to avail of them.[19]

Suing for libel

As it turned out, it was not Mr Justice Lynch who sued for libel, but members of the Murder Squad. Detectives Gerry O'Carroll, P. J. Browne and John Harrington brought a High Court action against those involved in writing, publishing and distributing Joanne Hayes's *My Story*. The book had contained various references to the 'heavy gang'. In particular, there was a reference about how Joanne Hayes had felt a fellowship with Nicky Kelly. Lines were quoted from 'The Wicklow Boy', a song by Christy Moore which suggested that Nicky Kelly had been forced to sign a false confession. But Mr Justice Lynch had found that there was no intimidation or abuse by any of the gardaí of members of the Hayes family. The implication that there was any association between what happened to Nicky Kelly and what happened to Joanne Hayes was therefore libellous. The three members of the Murder Squad were successful in achieving an out-of-court settlement which, including costs, was estimated to be close to £100,000. The defendants issued an unreserved apology.[20]

The objectivity of the media

The coverage of the case raises important questions about the media and their role, in Ireland and in modern democratic societies. When it comes to news and current affairs, the media have an important role to play in creating and maintaining a civil society through telling the truth, through presenting objective, unbiased news reports, and through critical commentaries and analyses.[21] Factual accounts of events – and critical analysis of other accounts – which are not constrained by other interests and agendas, are central to people knowing, understanding and forming opinions about what is happening in the world in which they live.[22] Such reporting and analysis are central to understanding the power of the state and to limiting and controlling its power. The media have come to play an important role in creating and maintaining public debate and discussion about the nature of society. But it has also come to play an important role in guarding the public interest, in trying to ensure that the state, or the system of money and power, does not colonise or destroy civil society and the lifeworld or culture through which people communicate with each other and maintain and develop a shared understanding of the world.

It could be argued, then, that by revealing what happened in the Kerry babies case, the media played a crucial role as public watchdog over the state and the gardaí. The media kept the public informed, pressed for a Tribunal, and prevented the symbolic domination of the state – that is to say its version of the truth – becoming a monopoly.[23] Mr Justice Lynch may have been right to say that the criticisms of the Report were unbalanced and unfair. However, it could be argued that any curtailment of knowledge and information, and of fair criticism, is detrimental to the creation of a mature, democratic, civil society.[24] At an extreme level, the curtailment of knowledge and criticism is enacted through state censorship. This is what makes the state's monopoly of the means of producing the truth, and the media's important role as a critique of the state and its truth, so vital to maintaining a democratic society.[25]

The guiding principle – or indeed law – of news reporting is the public right and need to know. In representing this right, journalists often come in conflict with institutions and organisations. The role of the state can, for example, be to uphold and protect other rights which can clash with the public's need to know and right to discuss and engage in fair comment. In banning members of Sinn Féin from radio and television under the Broadcasting Act 1973, the state decided that the right to know was not as great as the need for law and order and maintaining the security of the state.[26] Within the judicial field, courts have issued bans on reporting and have halted trials in the interests of justice and fairness. The other way the state controls the media is through libel law. Here the state decides on the balance between the public right to know and an individual's right to protect his or her good name, honour and status in society.[27] This raises the question of what constitutes fair comment and how is this to be judged in relation to the public's right to know and the individual's right to a good name.

It would be wrong to think that the debate about the role of news and current affairs in civil society is confined to a simple struggle between the interest in reporting facts and the interest in maintaining social order and people's honour. In the first instance, the producers of news and current affairs often have hidden interests and agendas which distort their neutrality and objectivity. Objectivity can be distorted by attempts to attract viewers, listeners and readers; it is no coincidence that some stories get reported more than others. When it comes to news factors, or the criteria which make some news stories more interesting and attractive than others, the Kerry babies case ranked very high.[28]

Objectivity can be distorted by the type of news product being produced, the editorial line taken, and the economic and political interests of the owners.[29] This is often reflected in the different headlines and approaches to a story taken by tabloid and broadsheet newspapers.[30] Nevertheless, those who work in gathering and disseminating news are generally committed to reporting the facts and making fair comment. Objectivity is a primary value in news organisations and is ritually enforced.[31] But even though journalists may have the intention of reporting facts, they can be influenced by their background, interests, values and beliefs.[32] It could be argued that the Kerry babies case was created and developed by the type of journalist who represents urban, liberal, left-wing values, who is sceptical of the state and its institutions, and is far from representative of mainstream Ireland.[33] Finally, journalists' objectivity and their will to tell the truth about what happened in a case such as this can be undermined by the format or the way the story has to be told.[34] It is no coincidence that the coverage of the Kerry babies case died down in the media when the Tribunal became heavily involved in technical and scientific issues. Once Joanne Hayes, her colleagues, lover and family had given their evidence, the human interest was lost. Indeed, it is the requirement to develop human interest that can lead journalists to select some events more than others and to highlight or sensationalise them.

While journalists may write their own reports, they are not the sole producers. They are dependent on sources. When the news of the Cahirciveen baby's murder broke, journalists were dependent on official garda sources for their reports. What the police tell journalists can vary between nothing (a news blackout) and a full and frank disclosure of everything that happened. In between, we enter the world in which some events or aspects of a story are selected and where these are given a certain spin. The problem for journalists is to know in what way their sources are being economical with the truth and what kind of spin is being put on the story.[35] For example, the report in the *Irish Independent* (4 May 1984) two days after Joanne Hayes and her family had been charged and the Tralee baby found might have been objective, but appears to have been heavily reliant on garda sources who were economical with the truth.

> Gardaí were last night investigating the grim discovery of a second dead baby in Co. Kerry within three weeks.
>
> The body of the first infant – a boy – was found on the beach at White Strand near Cahirciveen. Then on Wednesday evening, the remains of another baby were discovered in a water hole on marshy ground near Abbeydorney village, about six miles from Tralee.
>
> The dead baby was wrapped in a plastic bag and Gardaí said it was a fully formed infant. They were unable to establish the child's sex.

It is significant that there was no mention that the water hole where the body of the second baby was found was on the farm of Joanne Hayes who, earlier that morning, had effectively been charged with the murder of the Cahirciveen baby, and members of her family with concealment and disposal of that body. The reference to being unable to establish the child's sex is peculiar as this was readily known. It is as if garda sources were anxious to reduce any possible links being made between the Tralee and Cahirciveen babies.

Reliance on sources is a particular problem for crime reporters. Crime is generally a big news story. Reporters are dependent on official police sources for informal, backstage information as well as 'scoops'. The police realise that it is not an equal relationship; reporters are more dependent on them. This enables police to drip feed stories at a pace that best suits their interests and to patrol the facts, which often forces crime reporters into giving the official line, not questioning the information they are given, not being critical of police actions, and not engaging in rigorous investigative reporting.[36]

As we saw above, the story of the case broke not so much because Don Buckley had been conducting an investigative report on the Murder Squad. It came through a source within the gardaí who, apparently, not only drew his attention to the Garda File and Report, but also allowed him access to make a copy. So what was the interest and motivation of the source within the gardaí? It may have resulted from an internal struggle or conflict between the rank and file and an elite squad. It may have been the return of a favour to Don Buckley. Perhaps it was a mixture of both, but the reality is that the case probably came to light from a mixture of these alliances and power struggles.

CHAPTER FOURTEEN

Unruly bodies

Dramatic changes occurred in Irish society during the second half of the twentieth century – modernisation of social and economic life, entry into Europe, conflict in Northern Ireland – but perhaps the most subtle and yet significant change was in Irish culture. The monopoly that the Catholic Church had developed over Irish morality began to fragment. Young men and women began to distance themselves from the rhetoric of piety, humility, purity and chastity developed by the Church and inculcated in the homes, schools, community and everyday life in which they were brought up, and in which they became constituted as sexual subjects.[1] It would be wrong to think that the change from the conservative Catholic to a liberal, pluralist approach to sexuality and sexual morality was a smooth and easy transition. There were many conflicts and struggles throughout Ireland, in sitting rooms at home, in school classrooms, in radio and television programmes, in pubs.[2]

From the late 1960s, the battle was being fought for the hearts and minds of young Irish people and also for their bodies – particularly the sexuality, fertility and bodies of women. Young people increasingly came under the influence of media messages. The content of these messages in advertisements, soaps and serials – sometimes overt, sometimes hidden – was a mixture of individualism, liberalism, consumerism and hedonism. At the same time, the symbolic domination of the Catholic Church through its teachings, exemplars, and sacred images – particularly of Our Lady and panoply of virgin martyrs – was fading rapidly.

It was not a straight vote for liberalism and hedonism. The switch away from a rigorous Catholic morality was often fraught with inner turmoil and conflict. What happened to Joanne Hayes was, in some respects, not dissimilar from what happened to Anne Lovett and many other young women. The demand to remain pure and virginal was met with an equal and opposite demand to give free rein to sensual desires, to let go of the moral harness, and to taste and indulge in bodily pleasures. At a macro level, this battle was being fought out over issues such as contraception, abortion, illegitimacy and unmarried mothers.[3] In these ideological struggles, younger women generally had to compete against the older men who dominated the state, the judiciary, the police and the Catholic Church. It was these older men who generally made, interpreted and enforced the laws concerning sexual freedom and fertility control.

One of the strategies used by those who adhered to a traditional conception of women was to root out and expose those who transgressed sexual norms. Sexual transgressors were a different order from sexual deviants who could, as long as they were remorseful, be quietly dealt with behind closed doors. They were 'good' sinners who sought forgiveness. They may have sinned, they may have broken the rules, but they did not openly challenge the rules which constituted them as sinful. In the past in Ireland, many sexually deviant women were quietly forced to migrate or to go into a Magdalen home.[4] Sexually transgressive women who did not go quietly and seemed to make a virtue out of their transgression were in danger of being pilloried, vilified and demonised.

In this chapter, I want to suggest that what happened to Joanne Hayes and in the case as a whole might not have been a coincidence. Was it a coincidence that an ordinary Irish woman was plucked from obscurity and made infamous? Was it a coincidence that, as a sexual transgressor, she was made into a kind of exotic, sexual predator, who was not just very different from other Irish women, but represented a threat to them and to every decent Irish man? In the second half of this chapter, I investigate the claim, made in its early days, that the Tribunal represented a latter-day witch-hunt.

The question we have to ask is whether it was a coincidence that Joanne Hayes was brought into the public gaze and pilloried. Within a week of the Cahirciveen baby being found, there was a police investigation, or what McCafferty called a 'woman-hunt', in which every potentially sexually transgressive woman was tracked down and questioned.[5] Women were interviewed who had broken romances, were known or suspected of being involved in affairs, or were forced into marriage because of pregnancy. To what extent did Joanne Hayes become – as expressed in the title of Nell McCafferty's book on the case – 'a woman to blame'.

Creating infamous women

Was it, then, simply a stroke of misfortune that someone as unknown as Joanne Hayes was picked out from obscurity to become an infamous Irish woman? History is scattered, particularly in times of social upheaval, with the relics of scapegoats on whom social disorder can be blamed. Throughout the last three hundred years in Europe, in a lightning flash of power, authorities descended on resisting, recalcitrant, individuals who were elevated to notoriety as disturbers of the peace. There is a process at work that suddenly makes ordinary individuals out to be extraordinary criminals.[6]

Michel Foucault claimed that in the nineteenth century there was a shift in emphasis from crimes to criminals, which occurred within the emergence of the psychiatry of crime. What makes some crimes more significant than others is that they have been committed by demented and pathological people, by dangerous individuals. Foucault argued that the task of the criminal psychiatrist is to locate the nature of the pathology that makes people dangerous and a threat to the existing social order. What is the dementia that leads a woman to kill her husband or child? Finally, he pointed out that murders which have most social significance, that attract attention and demand explanation, take place in a domestic setting.[7]

The process of rooting out dangerous individuals helps reveal the nature and structure of power, the way domination is enacted, the strategies by which the powerful dominate. Normally, power operates subtly and discreetly as well as obscurely. It is denied and hidden. Power, Foucault argued, is revealed when its forces are provoked through unexpected resistance. He was particularly interested in those dark legends in which ordinary individuals, wretched scoundrels and unsuspecting transgressors, suddenly provoked power into revealing itself.[8]

So it was no coincidence that an insignificant woman like Joanne Hayes was plucked from obscurity to become an infamous national figure. She had, according to Mr Justice Lynch, done away with her baby in her own bedroom. What made Joanne Hayes infamous in the first place was her sexual transgression. It was the act of putting her eye on a married man and having an affair with him that led, almost inevitably, to her downfall. That is why sexually transgressive women have to be rooted out, pilloried, and exorcised as some form of contemporary demons that destroy the moral order.

What happened to Joanne Hayes has to be put within the context of the mythical stories of transgressive Irish women.[9] In Ireland, the idealisation of the traditional mother and the stigmatisation of those who transgressed from the ideal were perpetuated by Church and state, by priests, politicians and judges. In the 1930s there was a growing fear that many working-class women 'whose sexual behaviour was not influenced by the dominant middle-class, Catholic sexual values' were contaminating Catholic moral order.[10] But Joanne Hayes was more than just a sexually transgressive woman. She became, in Said's terms, the archetypal 'other', the opposite of the good, pure, chaste Irish mother whose status and honour had to be defended.[11] Revealing and rooting out sexually transgressive women in Irish society became a means through which the identity of Irish women was created and maintained.[12]

In the discourse and practice of contemporary Irish sexuality, Joanne Hayes was a perverse, sexually deviant woman. She abandoned the essential biological identity of woman as naturally caring and submissive. She was direct in her opposition to and transgression of the essential identity of married Irish women.[13] But what made Joanne Hayes sexually transgressive was not that she used her sexuality to control and manipulate men – the use of sexual capital to attain other forms of capital have probably always been a feature of women's struggle for power – but that she was open and public in her transgression.

In order to understand what happened to Joanne Hayes, it is necessary to understand that she was vilified because she became the opposite of what she should have been. By openly having an affair with a married man, by becoming pregnant by him, and by giving birth to two children, she challenged the sexual morality of the Church in which she had been constituted as an ethical subject. Her resistance and public challenge to traditional Catholic morality meant that she gradually became subjective to the disciplinary gaze of those in authority. She slowly moved from the initial support of family, friends and colleagues, to strategies of engendering guilt, shame and embarrassment, to interrogation by the gardaí, to incarceration in gaol and then in a psychiatric hospital, to, finally, the clinical, legal dissection of her character in the witness box. This was the process that made her into an infamous woman.

Mythical tales and heroes can play a part in the production of what Foucault calls resistant discourses or counter-memory.[14] Myths can be liberating and help to create and sustain collective identity. The birth of the Irish nation state is associated with mythical tales of the men who fought in the 1916 rebellion. They were the heroes deemed to have liberated Catholic Ireland from Protestant England. But over time these myths can themselves become an oppressive regime of truth defining the essence of a people.[15] Joanne Hayes is not, by any means, a mythical hero, but her story is part of a resistance against the received truths about women, sex, justice and equality in modern Ireland – truths produced by the state, the Catholic Church, law, medicine and science. The origins of the story of the Kerry babies began with the local resistance of Joanne Hayes, but its mythical status is reproduced through the way she, like many other women, were blamed for what the state did to them and for the decline of moral order. In this respect, it is not a question of whether the story remains in the realm of historical truth or fiction, but rather its political effect.[16]

Sexually transgressive women as exotic scapegoats

During the Tribunal, the legal team for the gardaí attempted to fictionalise or manufacture Joanne Hayes as a sexually transgressive woman. The purpose of asking witnesses if they knew a Tom Flynn was to establish the sexual history of Joanne Hayes. This was the beginning of the superfecundation theory. Joanne Hayes was not simply sexually transgressive, she was unique among women in being a superwoman, someone able to have sex with two different men within 48 hours and become pregnant both of them. The gardaí argued that Joanne Hayes was unique among her kind – but her uniqueness was the complete opposite of Our Lady who had become pregnant while remaining a virgin.

Said points out that 'the construction of identity . . . involves establishing opposites and "others" whose actuality is always subject to the continuous inter-pretation and re-interpretation of their differences from "us"'.[17] Consequently, the rooting out and castigation of dangerous individuals are part of the process of creating and maintaining our identity. Who 'we' are is dependent on defining ourselves in opposition to who 'they' are. Each age and generation require the construction of 'others' against which self-identity can be established. Establishing differences, the construction of 'others' – and it is always a construction – is part of the process of identity formation. In this respect, the demonisation of Joanne Hayes can be seen as part of securing the identity of Irish women.

There is a process in which sexually transgressive women become not just dark and unacceptable but, as Said points out, exotic.[18] And it is as this dark, unacceptable and exotic other that they become the scapegoat for gender and sexual equality. Consequently, to understand contemporary sexuality and gender relations in Ireland, it is necessary to understand the process by which certain women become mythologised as sexually infamous. In discussing the construc-tion of Arabs as 'others', Said describes how their difference was seen as essential and biological as well as sexual. The difference of Arab men was defined in terms of their sexual prowess and powerful sexual appetite. He demonstrates how Arabs are counted as 'mere biological beings; institutionally, politically, culturally they are nil'.[19] And we can see how Joanne Hayes was constructed similarly. She was depicted by the counsel for the gardaí as a nymphomaniac – so sexually voracious as to put her eye on a married man and have regular sex with him – and, at the same time, to be having sex with at least one other man, and to have written his name at the end of her bed as if he were a trophy, some kind of notch on her sexual gun.

Joanne Hayes as a scapegoat

Said's theory of the construction of the exotic 'other' can be linked to René Girard's theory of the 'scapegoat'. The 'scapegoat' is often constructed by persecutors who convince themselves that an individual, despite his relative weakness, is extremely harmful to society.[20] The 'scapegoat' is deemed to have committed a crime that is so diabolical that it reaches in and threatens the heart of the social body. The persecutors become an undifferentiated crowd, and eventually a mob, who speak with one voice. Another characteristic of the scapegoat is that they often 'belong to a class that is particularly susceptible to persecution'.[21] Joanne Hayes was thus vilified not because she was a woman, but because she belonged to a class of sexually transgressive women – women who behaved like men. This fits in with Girard's argument that scapegoats arise in a time of social crisis. 'Men', he declared, 'feel powerless when confronted with the eclipse of culture'.[22]

This helps to explain why Joanne Hayes became infamous. It was less to do with any crime she might have committed, and more to do with challenging the traditional Catholic habitus within which Irish male power had been created and maintained for generations.[23] What was central to this crisis was not so much that Joanne Hayes might, as Mr Justice Lynch claimed, have done away with her baby, but that she was seen as a sexual predator luring men to their downfall. This could unleash a fear of the social world being turned upside down, of women behaving like men. This could in turn be linked to an undeclared, repressed fear of women's sexuality which, if not controlled, could undermine if not destroy culture and society. Women like Joanne Hayes consequently became infamous, exotic, scapegoats, because they were a threat not only to the traditional Catholic conception of sexuality, women and mothers, but to a patriarchal order centred on the sexual oppression of women.

What happened to Joanne Hayes is a particular example of the complex relation between male dominance, the idealisation of motherhood, and the control of female sexuality.[24] In Ireland, this has to be understood in terms of the Catholic Church's monopoly over morality, its obsession with sexual morality, the veneration of Our Lady as the ideal chaste mother, and the dominance of males in the Catholic church and state.[25] Only one among the 28 gardaí who investigated the case was a woman. None of the 15 lawyers was female. The judge who wrote the Tribunal Report and decided the facts of the case was male.

A modern-day witch-hunt?

Joanne Hayes was not unique. What happened to her was not very different from what happened to other sexually transgressive women. Sometimes the process of shaming, demeaning and demoralising women can become indistinguishable from demonising them. To demonise a woman is to make out that she is so harmful, so disruptive, so deviant and so depraved, that she is not just extraordinary, but unnatural: so much so that she infects and destroys the existing social order. Joanne Hayes was antithetical to the good Irish mother. In Purkiss's terms, Joanne Hayes

> appears as a kind of 'antihousewife', the antithesis of the true housewife's carefully constructed, socially approved and fragile identity, the dark side which the good wife 'must suppress, define herself against, in order to fashion her own identity as a housewife.[26]

Various claims made during and after the Tribunal suggested that much of what happened was the equivalent of a modern-day witch-hunt. In an interview in *Hot Press*, Professor Brendan Kennelly, a Kerryman, said: 'It's like a medieval witch hunt with the victims burning at the stake and the crowd dancing around the fire'. Six days later, Members of the Oireachtas Committee on Women's Rights described the questioning of witnesses, particularly of Joanne Hayes, as 'harrowing and quite horrific', 'frightening' and 'mental torture'. In the Senate, Brendan Ryan said that 'legalised torture' was being conducted in Tralee.[27]

In her book on the case, Nell McCafferty argued that the Tribunal was just another incidence of hypocritical, prejudicial, moralising men standing in judgement over women, particularly in relation to their purity, fertility and sexuality. She argued that the two detectives from the Murder Squad who interviewed Joanne Hayes were prejudiced, narrow-minded and naïve when it came to understanding women. For her, the implication of Det. Sgt Gerry O'Carroll's evidence was that

> An Irishman could scare afford to blink his eyes then, lest his women have sexual intercourse with the fellow next door, and it would take a sharp-eyed fellow indeed to notice that she was pregnant, never mind know if she was pregnant by him.[28]

She claimed that the attitudes of the detectives were no different from a long line of 'moral policemen' including bishops, priests, politicians, doctors and pharmacists who, long before Joanne Hayes came to public attention, had controlled the lives of Irishwomen.

When it came to analysing the Tribunal, McCafferty was equally scathing. None of the 15 legal men in the Tribunal had witnessed childbirth and yet they pondered and deliberated whether it was possible for woman to give birth standing up.[29] She pointed out that it took a scientific test for a male medical expert to discover that a woman can break an umbilical cord on her own.[30] They wondered what a woman the size of Joanne Hayes would look like if she were carrying twins. Then they had to consider if it was possible for a woman to give birth alone in a field to one baby and then go back into the house and give birth to another and manage all the time to remain calmly secretive about the first. But McCafferty also suggested that there was some connection between the Tribunal and a witch trial. The notion that Joanne Hayes had twins by two different fathers was, McCafferty suggested, diabolically clever.[31]

Numerous different references were, then, made to diabolical events and a witch-hunt. But to what extent are analogies possible to the witch-hunts of three to four hundred years ago?[32] It is important to emphasise that I remain sceptical about any analogy. I have pursued the analysis on the basis of a hypothesis. If it is assumed from the outset that there is no connection whatsoever, then having looked at some of the literature on the witch-craze of medieval times, we can see to what extent the hypothesis of there being no connection can be rejected.

Mr Justice Lynch and legal representatives of the Tribunal look into the spot where Joanne hid the body of her baby. Joanne and Kathleen Hayes are standing on the left.

Medieval witch-hunts

History is about retelling the past, but some stories are so degrading and inhuman that they are extremely painful to tell. They become suppressed. Eventually they are buried so deep in the collective psyche, that bringing them back up is seen as revolting. Trevor-Roper was aware that many critics would see his study of the witch-craze of medieval Europe as 'a disgusting subject, below the dignity of history'.[33] The purpose of witch-hunts was to expose and eradicate deviant, heretical behaviour. Although essentially a social movement, Trevor-Roper pointed out that the witch-craze was deliberately extended to destroy dangerous persons. 'When a "great fear" takes hold of society, that society looks naturally to the stereotype of the enemy in its midst. Once the witch had become the stereotype, witchcraft was the universal accusation.'[34] He went on to argue that if the folklore of witches had not become such a centralised force within the intellectually approved cosmology of the time, 'then psychopathic persons would have attached their sexual hallucinations to others, perhaps more individual figures'.[35]

Witch-hunts were, he argued, an attack by church and state on social non-conformity. People who did not integrate into mainstream religion and society were used as scapegoats for personal and social ills. Priests and lawyers wove together a number of deviant and dissident behaviours into a social stereotype called a witch.

Although Trevor-Roper is recognised as having opened up the historical investigation into the witch-craze, he overlooked one major issue. Barstow concluded that of the 200,000 people accused of being witches – half of whom were convicted and killed – more than eight in ten were women.[36] Besides being predominantly female, they tended to come from isolated rural areas and were seen as overly assertive sexually.

The classic statement from the *Malleus Malificarum*, the witch-hunter's manual, is that 'all witchcraft comes from carnal lust, which is in women insatiable'.[37] This summed up the widespread belief that women were by nature oversexed, wicked, and therefore dangerous to men. Indeed, it has been argued that the witch-hunts can be linked to a fear in men of being desired by sexually assertive women not of their choosing.[38] Bastow argues that this fear could have real foundations. Western European women were asserting themselves more in the sixteenth century, and taking greater responsibility for their sex lives than they did in any other period until the 1960s. Because premarital sex was the norm and premarital pregnancy was not condemned, 'young women and men were freer to learn about themselves sexually, to experiment sexually, and to try out partners'.[39] From her examination of the records of witch-trials in Essex – where the most virulent accusations were made and where the best records in England were kept – Hester suggests that as many as one third to one half of the women were accused of sexual deviance such as lewdness, fornication and incest.[40] Karlsen argues that having an illegitimate child as well as abortion and infanticide were specifically linked to witchcraft accusations in New England.[41] In Irish folk tradition, notes O'Connor, 'the popular perception of the woman who takes the life of either her own or another woman's newborn child is that of a demonic and unrepentant murderer'.[42] She argues that the diabolical nature of infanticide relates to the belief that the dead child would suffer unending misery by its separation from God and that this belief was current among Irish people up to the 1950s.[43]

Accused women were seen as independent-minded and traitors to their families. They also tended to be older, widowed and from the poorest section of society.[44] They were generally poor, often single or widowed and with children, and seen as strong, independent-minded women who were traitors to the system. Their heretical practices and inherent sinfulness posed real threats to existing social order.[45]

While very little of what happened during the Tribunal corresponds substantially with the witch-trials of the sixteenth and seventeenth centuries – they were very different times and circumstances with very different personnel involved – the questions that were put, the suggestions that were made, the way women were conceptualised and written about, had some structural similarities. Sometimes the process of shaming, demeaning and demoralising women can become indistinguishable from demonising them; to make out that they are so harmful, so disruptive, so deviant, so depraved that they are not just extra-ordinary but unnatural.

Of course, one of the main characteristics of witch-trials was torturing the victims who would then make incredible confessions, even to crimes of which they had not been accused. These included having sex with, marrying and offering babies to the devil. What was remarkable about these confessions was the amount of fantastic detail they contained about events that did not happen.[46] One of the main questions which historians of witchcraft have had to answer is how the confessions of witches were obtained. As Trevor-Roper noted:

> If the confessions were freely given, we have to admit at least the 'subjective reality' of the experiences confessed, and then the remarkable identity of those confessions, which converted many a sixteenth-century sceptic, becomes a real problem. On the other hand, if the confessions were obtained by torture, that problem hardly exists. The similarity of answers can be explained by a combi-nation of identical questions and intolerable pain.[47]

Trevor-Roper conceded that 'witches' confessions became more detailed with the intensification of the inquisitorial procedure' and that 'torture lay, directly or indirectly, behind most of the witch-trials of Europe, creating witches where none were and multiplying both victims and evidence'.[48] However, the problem is to explain why witches confessed to absurd crimes in England where there was no judicial torture.[49] The answer, for Trevor-Roper, lay in the power of the current discourse, and how this belief became deeply internalised in the habitus or mindset of peasants, clerics, judges and intellectuals alike.[50] That is, victims came to see themselves as and believe themselves to be witches.

Although they spoke the same language as their victims, the investigating gardaí operated in a completely different manner from for example the local guard, Liam Moloney, whom the Hayes family had known. Barstow argued that victims of witch-hunts, 'Faced with legal procedures they did not under-stand and threatened with torture, they struggled to say what they thought the judges wanted to hear.'[51] Like many other victims of modern methods of police interrogation, Joanne Hayes said she felt brainwashed. 'They kept roaring and shouting at me to tell them that I had stabbed the baby and in the end I was convinced I had done it'; 'I didn't think my mind was my own'; 'at that stage I would have believed anything'.[52] The accusers of witchcraft were experts in extracting confessions to things which had not happened and which the accused could not have done; they were also experts in persuading the accused to describe these fictitious events in their language. Witches willingly testified to having had sex with the devil, breastfeeding demons, flying on broomsticks, making men impotent and their genitals disappear. This is how Det. Sgt Gerry O'Carroll described Joanne Hayes's confession.

> She shouted again that, or more or less half shrieked, that she was insane, that she was a murderess, that she killed her baby and she said that the knife, that the Dectectives had brought in, was the knife she had stabbed her baby with. (TT, 40/34)

This is how Garda Michael Smith described how Kathleen Hayes during her confession physically re-enacted the murder scene for him:

> I said to her: 'Wouldn't a woman be very weak after giving birth to a baby to be able to stab it?' She actually pulled out the chair that she was sitting on from behind the desk; she was sitting on the opposite side from me; and she knelt up on the chair crossways and she indicated with her hand how Joanne stabbed the baby. (TT, 61/68)

Another possible analogy to the witch-craze needs to be examined. A key features of witches was that they were over-sexed and sexually deviant, which meant that 'if a man could not resist a woman, it was, by nature, her fault'.[53] This could be linked to another magical power attributed to witches – the possession of an evil eye which, through a look, could render a victim helpless and affect their physical and spiritual well-being. The possessor of such an eye was said to be a malicious or covetous person, a witch.[54]

In Mr Justice Lynch's estimation Joanne Hayes was 'the main or dominant force in the liaison between herself and Jeremiah Locke'. Jeremiah Locke had married his wife Mary, 'before Joanne Hayes put her eye on him'. After this he 'gladly accepted the sexual favours which he knew were so readily available to him' (TR, pp. 15, 146, 16).

In his Report, Mr Justice Lynch could not understand the sympathy and support that had been shown for Joanne Hayes, a woman whom he saw as infatuated, selfish and uncaring and who led Jeremiah Locke astray, in comparison to Mrs Mary Locke. He argued that Joanne Hayes continued the affair with Jeremiah Locke 'with total disregard for the feelings, much less the rights, of Mrs Locke'. He went on to say that she 'tried to get Jeremiah to desert his wife and the one lawful child which he then had and to set up house with herself'. The image here is of helpless man, being led astray by sexual favours, who had no control or responsibility for what happened (TR, p. 146).[55]

At the heart of most witchcraft accusations would be some extraordinary, inexplicable coincidence. Someone fell ill and perhaps died. It would be recalled that the accused witch, who was already suspect for other reasons, had visited the house. It was not known how she did the deed, but she was obviously to blame. Throughout the Tribunal, the gardaí continued to reject all the scientific evidence which said that Joanne Hayes was not the mother of the Cahirciveen baby. Maybe she was superfecund, maybe she killed another baby in exactly the same manner, but it had never been found. For the gardaí Joanne Hayes was obviously guilty – hadn't she confessed to her guilt? – and all the scientific evidence could not dislodge that belief. For some people, scientific evidence is secondary to belief. There were many coincidences throughout the Kerry babies case, but for Joanne Hayes and her family it was fortunate that the blood group of the Cahirciveen baby did not coincide with that of the Tralee baby.

In making an analogy between what happened to Joanne Hayes and medieval witch-hunts, the evidence is not just tenuous, but highly controversial and contested. The controversy is as much over of how we see the past, and how and why we study history. For some feminist historians there are structural features of the way women have been seen and treated throughout the history of the West which are repeated at different times in different formats. Hester, for example, concludes:

> Overall, the witch-hunts were an instance of male sexual violence against women, relying on a particular sexual construct of female behaviour. The hunts were a part of the apparently on-going attempt by men to control women socially, and to reimpose the male-dominated status quo in a period of many changes including economic restructuring and pressure on economic resources. In other words, the witch-hunts of the sixteenth and seventeenth centuries were a part of the 'dynamics of domination' whereby men at the time maintained dominance over women.[56]

Sharpe, however, argues strongly against this feminist interpretation of witch-hunts. He disagrees with the notion that witches were some kind of 'proto-feminists, strong women who dared speak out for themselves and cause trouble'. Rather than witches being seen as victims of a patriarchal plot against them, it is better to see them as social actors – admittedly within a patriarchal society – who had goals and concerns of their own. They were involved in a struggle for power in a complex system of social hierarchy which in many cases led them to be their own worst enemy or accusers.[57]

CHAPTER FIFTEEN

Conclusion

The Kerry babies case is unresolved. Many questions remain unanswered. Most of the gardaí still appear to believe that Joanne Hayes had twins. She has not given an interview or talked publicly about the case since 1986. She was adamant throughout the Tribunal that she gave birth alone in the field at the back of the farmhouse. Mr Justice Lynch, who decided the facts of the case, ruled that Joanne Hayes gave birth to only one baby – the Tralee baby – but did so in her bedroom with members of her family present. The Hayes family claimed that the reason they confessed to their involvement in the murder of the Cahirciveen baby was because of the abuse and intimidation of their interrogators. The gardaí insisted that all the confessions were voluntary, spontaneous and independent. Mr Justice Lynch ruled that there was no abuse or intimidation, and that members of the Hayes family made up stories the gardaí wanted to hear out of a sense of guilt from witnessing Joanne Hayes 'do away with' the Tralee baby.

It is important at a practical level to retell the story of the Kerry babies case because while the Tribunal Report was critical of the way the case was investigated, it essentially exonerated the gardaí and by and large accepted their account of what happened during the interrogation of the Hayes family. Although the Murder Squad was disbanded and a Garda Complaints Board established in the aftermath of the Tribunal, many of the gardaí involved in the case went on to have long and successful careers in the force. On the other hand, the Tribunal effectively deemed Joanne Hayes to be a killer and members of her family as uncaring, devious liars some of whom were more obsessed with protecting the family name rather than the life of the Tralee baby.

Retelling the story is also important because justice may have been improperly or incompletely done.[1] Whatever happened to the Tralee baby remains in doubt, particularly as the State Pathologist could not be certain whether it had achieved an independent existence. More significantly, whatever else the Tribunal Report achieved, it did not explain satisfactorily how members of the Hayes family made detailed confessions about a crime they did not commit. It should be remembered that if the Cahirciveen baby had been blood group O, Joanne Hayes and her family could well have been convicted on the basis of their confessions. Many Irish people were quick to blame the British state for the injustices done on Bloody Sunday in Derry, and in the aftermath of the bombings in Guildford and Birmingham when innocent people were convicted of crimes they did not commit. Perhaps the Kerry babies case is an ongoing and unwelcome skeleton in the Irish cupboard.

But the Kerry babies case is an important part of understanding how we have come to be the way we are. The latter half of the twentieth century in Ireland was a transition from a predominantly traditional, rural, conservative and Catholic society to a more modern, urban, liberal and secular society. Lifestyles, attitudes and values changed rapidly. An old-established order, often accepted without question, was yielding place to new. But the birth of any new order is rarely simply and straightforward. It is about people, transgressive individuals, doing things differently, challenging and resisting the way things are.

The case represents a watershed for women in Irish society. During the last decades of the twentieth century there was a struggle for greater equality between the sexes.[2] Women strove to achieve equality in the workplace, home, education, health, social welfare, before the law, and in the way they were portrayed, related to and treated in everyday life. Men continued to dominate symbolically, socially, economically, politically and legally. What we see in this case is how Irish men, particularly the lawyers, Mr Justice Lynch and the gardaí, perceived and understood Joanne Hayes and Irish women in general. Is it a coincidence that with one exception all the gardaí involved in the case and all the legal personnel involved in the Tribunal were men? Given this imbalance, we have to ask if was it a coincidence that sexuality, fertility and the character of a transgressive Irish woman like Joanne Hayes was publicly put on display and clinically and legally dissected.

The case is a reminder of how attitudes to sex, love and marriage have changed in the last twenty years. During this period there was a shift from a traditional culture based on self-denial and self-sacrifice, to a culture that revolved around self-expression and self-indulgence. Social relations were becoming less formal and rigid. There were important changes in the relations between the sexes. Women began to go into pubs, sometimes unaccompanied.

But again, the transition was not a smooth one. We saw during the Tribunal the negative reaction to the notion of a married woman going to the pub with a man other than her husband. A married man was seen as being unsafe in the company of such a woman who, in Mr Justice Lynch's phrase, might 'put her eye on him'. As long as there were temptresses like Joanne Hayes, happily married men like Jeremiah Locke would be easily led into accepting what was, again in Mr Justice Lynch's phrase, 'so readily available to him' (TR, p. 146).

Other dramatic changes were taking place in sexual attitudes and practices. Sex was breaking out of the traditional confines of marriage. Young people began to imitate what they saw in films and in television programmes such as *Dallas*. It was not so much that Ireland was a sexually promiscuous society, rather that love and romance were becoming sexualised. The sexual revolution was late in reaching into Ireland, and perhaps later still in arriving in rural Kerry; and while it had to do with increased sex outside marriage, it also had to do with a decreased sense of guilt and shame about sex.

About one birth in twenty used to be outside marriage with 'fallen' women spirited away by family and church to a Magdalen asylum, sometimes never to be seen again. For a single woman to become pregnant was a major sin and source of shame. It was a time when people like Mr Justice Lynch could refer to a 'lawful child'.[3] But stories such as those of Anne Lovett and Joanne Hayes have to be put in the context of the struggle by the Catholic Church to maintain control of sexuality and women's fertility. The events in Kerry took place a year after abortion had been made unconstitutional and during a time when Dr Kevin McNamara, Bishop of Kerry, led a campaign against the liberalisation of the contraceptive laws. What happened to Joanne Hayes is the story of what happened to a young woman who, having grown up in a culture of self-denial in which religion, family and community were everything, was swept up by an incoming tide of sexual liberation and self-indulgence. For many Irish people at that time, she became a type of transgressive, exotic sexual 'other' – completely different from 'us'. In this sense, Joanne Hayes became a scapegoat for the decline of the type of pure, chaste Irish virgin epitomised by Our Lady, which for generations had been central to creating and sustaining Catholic Ireland.

Joanne Hayes was a young woman who played the game of sex, love, and romance – and lost. She played the game differently from the way it might be played today. She refused to use contraceptives. She was adamant that it was ludicrous to think that the Church's opposition to contraception had anything to do with her wanting to become pregnant. But in arguing that the use of contraceptives would have been a barrier in the expression of her love for Jeremiah, she revealed how much she was a product of her Catholic upbringing. She expressed her love by not using contraceptives and becoming pregnant.[4] She wanted to become pregnant and have Jeremiah Locke's children. It was both a selfless act – a surrender to love and life – and, at the same time, a deliberate tactic to win his love and loyalty. It was a peculiarly Irish way of playing the game of love and sex. But it had disastrous consequences. Whatever support she had when caught out the first time she became pregnant, it was not there the next time. She did not live up to the standard of the moral adage 'once bitten, twice shy'. She paid a high price for that and her newborn son 'Shane', the Tralee baby, paid the price of his life.

Mr Justice Lynch was right to argue that honour was at the heart of understanding what happened. The honour and respect of others is fundamental to our social being and to our sense of self. Honour legitimates our social position, possessions and place in the community. Our sense of self, our sense of well-being is closely linked to honour. In Ireland today, but especially in Kerry in 1984, honour and sense of self are closely tied to family. The Hayes family were not strange. They were a close-knit unit, well established and well integrated into the local community. For them, family was everything. Maintaining the honour of the family, the family name, was crucial. It was more important than the state against which it had to defend itself when attacked. This seems to have been a sentiment shared by the people of Abbeydorney, who came out publicly to support the Hayes family.

It would be wrong, however, to think that it is was just the Hayes family who were obsessed with honour. I have argued that it was a sense of honour, of maintaining their good name and reputation, which led the gardaí, and particularly the Murder Squad, to proceed with the criminal charges against Joanne Hayes and her family even though the forensic evidence was stacked against them. Honour plays a crucial role in legitimating power. Unless the gardaí attain honour among the people they serve, they are closer to being a power that has to be obeyed than to an authority to be respected. The Kerry babies case emerged as part of a long line of rumours and complaints about the existence of a heavy gang within the gardaí who, it was alleged, bent the rule of law particularly in relation to the interrogation of suspects. The honour of the gardaí was at stake because it appeared that they lied. If this was the case, a cornerstone of the establishment could not be trusted. Since then, we have discovered that not only gardaí but also other important cornerstones of the Irish establishment tell barefaced lies, sometimes under oath, including a former Taoiseach, government ministers, civil servants, bank managers, priests and bishops. Indeed what we have learnt most from all the tribunals that followed the Kerry babies case is the skill of members of the establishment in being unable to remember, dissembling reality, being economical with the truth, and telling lies. It is not that members of the establishment never told lies before, it is that so many people thought they never did.

As well as everything else, then, the Kerry babies case is about lying, and of course one of the main reasons people lie is to protect themselves, particularly their honour and good name. It was easy for Mr Justice Lynch to castigate members of the Hayes family as liars. It was less easy for him to say the same about the gardaí. Instead he castigated them for exaggeration, 'gilding the lily' and following fanciful theories. There is, however, sufficient evidence to believe that the gardaí did more than this.

Lying is a complex matter. It ranges between dissimulation and deliberate deception. Many people in Ireland lived a collective lie that the gardaí never intimidated or abused people in custody. But the lie was perpetuated because, when there was a rapid rise in violent crime and the state's monopoly of the legitimate means of violence was being challenged during the 1970s, it suited the legislature and judiciary to turn a blind eye to the behaviour of some of its gardaí. In times of need the state, in particular the police, will always tend to bend the laws to attain the greater good of protecting the social order. Almost twenty years after the Kerry babies case, major investigations of the gardaí's role are still in train. These include allegations of a man confessing to a murder he did not commit, of gardaí lying under oath, of a mentally ill man being unnecessarily shot in the back, and of a deliberate and concerted effort to frame members of a family for crimes they did not commit. When the gardaí are discovered to have bent the law they have sometimes been disowned and abandoned. This is what happened to the Murder Squad, who became scapegoats.[5] Yet despite everything that happened in the Kerry babies case, the gardaí still appear to use methods of questioning and interrogation which result in people making confessions to crimes that they have not committed.[6]

The Kerry babies case reminds us that the creation of a mature, democratic, civil society is a precious and fragile exercise and that, as in every other society, members of Irish society need to reflect critically and continually on the way power operates. They need to keep a watch on the state, to question the actions of politicians, police and judges, and to make them accountable for their actions. During the second half of the twentieth century the media increasingly took on this role, and played a crucial part in bringing the case to the attention of the public. Perhaps, however, the media 'ran with the story' not out of any duty as the 'fourth estate' or public watchdog of Irish society, but because it was good entertainment – a sensational story that sold copies.

The truth about ourselves

We may all tell lies and live with lies. It seems to be a necessary consequence of the will to power and order. But there is also a will to truth, and to tell the truth about the past as it really was. This is what I have tried to do here. But there is another dimension to telling the truth which centres on the need to tell the truth about ourselves.[7] It is a compulsion that goes back to the origins of Christianity and the development of confession.[8] However, with the move away from a god-centred world from the Enlightenment onwards, the practice of speaking the truth about ourselves gradually moved away from priests and confessors. Humans became the measure of all things.[9] Now it is psychologists, psychiatrists, sociologists and a range of other human scientists who speak the truth about individuals and society and help people to speak the truth about themselves. Discovering and revealing the truth about oneself has moved beyond Christian confession to become the code of belief and practice of liberal individualism. Increasingly cut off from the ties of church, family and community, and left isolated as a rational actor in the marketplace, the modern individual fulfils the interest in being ethical by searching for the essence of self – the true, authentic self which becomes the rock on which a moral life can be built. Within this search for self, the discovery and declaration of one's sexuality – the truth about one's sexual self – becomes crucial. To discover oneself, it is imperative to discover the nature of one's desires and pleasures. To explain the Kerry babies case, we have to realise that this new search for self and new ways of speaking the truth about oneself – something at the heart of the sexual revolution – only began to emerge in Ireland during the latter half of the twentieth century. But – and this has been central to my argument – we can never understand the truth about ourselves unless we see how we are caught in times, places and circumstances not of our choosing.

The Kerry babies case is important in holding up a mirror to Irish society. It moves the truth about people away from an overly individualised conception of self. To understand the truth about ourselves, we need to understand the way we are shaped, moulded and constituted by discourses, social structures and long-term processes of social change. Here the focus is quite different. We see and understand ourselves as products of a certain society, at a particular time in history, operating within different discourses (liberalism, Catholicism), living within social structures and institutions (capitalism, the state and the Catholic Church). Also central to my argument is an understanding of how these macro processes work by connecting them to the micro processes of every-day life and the lives of ordinary individuals. The case of the Kerry babies shows what it is to be a woman or man, to be a member of a family, to feel free, to fall in love, to feel ashamed, to become subject to the law, and to be examined and interrogated by police and lawyers. The search for truth – the search to understand the truth about oneself – becomes a search to understand the terms and conditions of one's life.[10]

Revealing the truth about oneself is thus closely tied in with revealing the truth about social life, the way it is structured and changes over time. Sociological explanation tries to take into account the macro world of large formal institutions and mechanisms of social control with the micro world of communication, exchange, co-operation, and conflict. The task is to develop a way of using sociology to remain at once true to the subjective world of communication, meaning, feelings and emotions and, at the same time, to the objective world of discourses, structures and processes of change. This necessitates making links between structures and discourses that have a real and independent existence outside particular individuals. We thus have to show how these structures and discourses shape habitus, the way people see, read and understand the world. But habitus enables as much as it limits. It structures but never determines what individuals do and say. Indeed, as we have seen throughout this case, it is the way people transgress, the way they bend the rules, which continually reshapes not only the habitus, but also discourses and structures.[11]

We therefore have to make a connection between the abstract theoretical understanding of the structures and processes that exist outside us, and how people react, transgress and live out their daily lives, the practical logic of living in families, communities, groups, organisations and wider society. The success of producing a balanced macro-micro understanding of social life depends on providing a rich or 'thick' description of the practice of everyday life which captures the intuitive feel for the social games in which people are involved.[12] The danger always exists of sociologists assuming or believing that they understand the logic of everyday life, that they have 'a feel for the game', but what they in effect do is to misconstrue the logic of their theories for the logic of practice.[13] To counteract this threat sociologists must reflect continually and critically on how they look at the world through a sociological framework and how, in speaking from a designated, symbolically legitimated position in society, as an academic, intellectual, lecturer or researcher, they become an active participant in symbolic domination.[14]

One way of trying to overcome the gap between the abstract theoretical language of sociology and the logic of everyday practice is to tell stories which combine the two. By telling or retelling, in a sociologically informed way, stories that are relevant, meaningful and accessible to participants in everyday life, the likelihood of symbolic domination can be reduced. Sociologists are not different from everyone else, except that the stories they tell tend to be highly formulated and regulated within the parameters of social scientific field and discourse. Indeed, it is through telling stories about ourselves that we create a shared symbolic world and constitute ourselves as individuals. Every day we listen to stories which tell us about people, who they are, and the events in their lives. And we tell our own stories.[15]

Since there is a choice about what to include and omit, and how to tell them, stories about oneself and the time and place in which we live reveal truths about ourselves. By telling stories about the past, we can understand not only how things were different then, but also what legacies remain from that time in the way we see the world and ourselves. We can understand how we came to be the way we are. Stories become the images and reflections left behind as we move on through time. Some stories, over time, become mythical. They last because they tell the truth better. They become part of the collective subconscious imagination of who we are. Kearney argues that Irish myths have been obsessed with martyrdom and motherland and that we need to repossess the myths we create about ourselves.[16] The Kerry babies story can be regarded as one of mythical proportions, capturing the truth about the struggle in Ireland during the latter half of the twentieth century and how, despite attempts to turn the country into a mature, modern, liberal democracy, we were caught up in telling stories about death, sacrifice and mothers, and cleansing society of unruly bodies and transgressive women.

Mr Justice Lynch claimed that he had for the most part identified the facts of the case beyond reasonable doubt. His tribunal was part of the process in which the state reserves a monopoly over the production of truth and which, following Bourdieu, can be seen as part of its monopoly over the means of symbolic violence. The production of Mr Justice Lynch's truth was dependent on a careful piecing together of different pieces of information, a downplaying or disregard for other pieces and, consequently, the stitching together of a very clear, coherent and seamless account of the facts. When he published his Report, it could be said that the state proclaimed the truth about itself.

Critically reflecting on and telling the truth about power, the state, and the way it operates in people's lives are important components of a mature, democratic and civil society. Fair comment and critical reflection should be permitted and encouraged. What has been handed down or given as established, absolute and unquestionable should be resisted and challenged. Our interest in speaking the truth is also the interest we have in trying to live an ethical and free life. I have argued that the truth about the Kerry babies case is as much about discovering the truth about Irish people as it is about establishing the facts. The case of the Kerry babies is part of the past in Ireland, part of the past that should not be forgotten. If it is, we are in danger of repeating its mistakes.

Notes

References to the following publications are given in the text in brackets:

TR *Report of the Tribunal of Inquiry into The Kerry Babies Case* (Dublin: Government Publications, 1985).

TT Transcripts of the Public Tribunal of Inquiry into the Case of the Kerry Babies. References take the following format: Day 7, page 64 is given as TT, 7/64.

Chapter 1 Telling stories

1   The story was covered in the provincial and national media, particularly during the Tribunal of Inquiry in 1985 (see chapter 13). There have been numerous books and articles, including Nell McCafferty, *A Woman to Blame* (Dublin: Attic Press, 1985); Barry O'Halloran, *Lost Innocence: The Case of the Kerry Babies* (Dublin: Raytown Press, 1985); Gerard Colleran and Michel O'Regan, *Dark Secrets: The Inside Story of Joanne Hayes and the Kerry Babies* (Tralee: The Kerryman, 1985); Joanne Hayes, *My Story* (Dingle: Brandon Press, 1985). See also Gene Kerrigan, 'The Kerry Babies Case', *Magill*, 30 May 1985: 16–51; 'The Kerry Babies Case: An Analysis of Mr Justice Lynch's Report', *Magill*, Nov. 1985: 4–34. There have also been academic articles, see Paul O'Mahony, 'The Kerry Babies Case: Towards a Social Psychological Analysis', *Irish Journal of Psychology* 13 (2) 1992: 223–8. The story has been written into songs and poems. Finally, although the setting was changed to New Hampshire, the story formed the content of a novel, see Jean Hanff Korelitz, *The Sabbathday River* (London: Macmillan, 1999).

2   Richard Kearney, *On Stories* (Harmondsworth: Penguin, 2001), p. 3.

3   As Fulford argues: 'Stories are how we explain, how we teach, how we entertain ourselves, and often how we do all three at once. They are the juncture where facts and feelings meet. And for those reasons, they are central to civilization.' See Robert Fulford, *The Triumph of Narrative: Storytelling in the Age of Mass Culture* (Toronto: Anansi Press, 1999), p. 9.

4   Richard Kearney, *Postnationalist Ireland: Politics, Culture, Philosophy* (London: Routledge, 1997), p. 121.

5   R. F. Foster, *The Irish Story* (Harmondsworth: Penguin, 2001), p. 187.

6   Bourdieu sees this struggle between objectivism and subjectivism as central to sociological analysis. See Pierre Bourdieu, *The Logic of Practice* (Cambridge: Polity, 1992), pp. 30–51.

7   Fulford reminds us that

> [S]tories inevitably demand ethical understanding. There is no such thing as *just a story*. A story is always charged with meaning, otherwise it is not a story, merely a sequence of events. It may be

possible, as social scientists imagine, to create value-free sociology, but there is no such thing as a value-free story. (*Triumph of Narrative*, p. 6).

8   Kearney, *On Stories*, p. 31 (emphasis in the original). Kearney rejects the constructivist argument that it does not matter what story is told or how it is told, as long as it works (p. 43).

9   This raises a range of questions about relativism. How can we say that one description is truer than another? Following Foucault, we can say that truth always exists and is always determined within discursive rules, whether they be juridical, scientific or sociological. There is truth, but truth is always produced within rules. He argued that success does not depend on trying to disclose a truth beyond rules, but rather on seizing the rules, inverting their meaning and redirecting them against those who had initially imposed them. In this sense the production of truth is a like a combat, with offensive moves and resistances. 'Humanity does not gradually progress from combat to combat until it arrives at universal reciprocity, where the rule of law finally replaces warfare; humanity installs each of its violences in a system of rules and thus proceeds from domination to domination.' (Michel Foucault, 'Nietschze, Genealogy, History' in *Language, Counter-Memory, Practice: Selected Essays and Interviews*, ed. D. Bouchard [Ithaca, N.Y.: Cornell University Press, 1977], p. 151). In Foucault's terms, my strategy in this book is not to replace the truth of events produced within the rules of the dominant discourse of the Tribunal and others, but to extend, subvert, undermine, resist and challenge these truths.

10   Max Weber famously defined a state as 'an organisation which successfully upholds a claim to binding rule making over a territory, by virtue of commanding a monopoly of the legitimate use of violence' (*Economy and Society*, Berkeley, CA: University of California Press, 1978, 1, p. 54. [Originally published 1922.]). Bourdieu notes: 'One may say of the state, in the terms Leibniz used about God, that it is the "geometral locus of all perspectives". This is why one may generalise Weber's formula and see in the state the holder of the monopoly of legitimate symbolic violence. Or, more precisely, the state is a referee, albeit a powerful one, in struggles over this monopoly.' See Pierre Bourdieu, 'Social Space and Symbolic Power' in *In Other Words: Essays Towards a Reflexive Sociology* (Cambridge: Polity, 1990), pp. 136–7.

11   In this respect, Foucault reminds us, it is not a question of whether the story remains in the realm of historical truth or fiction, but whether it has a political effect.

> As to the problem of fiction it seems to me to be a very important one; I am well aware that I have never written anything but fictions. I do not mean to say, however, that truth is therefore absent. It seems to me that the possibility exists for fiction to function in truth, for a fictional discourse to induce effects of truth, and for bringing it about that a true discourse engenders or 'manufactures' something that does not as yet exist, that is, 'fictions' it. One 'fictions' history on the basis of a political reality that makes it true, one 'fictions' a politics not yet in existence on the basis of a historical truth.

(Michel Foucault, *Power-Knowledge: Selected Interviews and Other Writings 1972–77*, ed. C. Gordon [New York: Pantheon, 1980], p. 193.)

12   Kearney, *On Stories*, pp. 68–9.

13   For an analysis of this distinction, see Jeffrey Alexander, *Theoretical Logic in Sociology*, vol. 1, *Positivism, Presuppositions and Current Controversies* (Berkeley: University of California Press, 1982), pp. 2–5.

14 The gathering of 'indisputable' facts led to the dominance of what Lawrence Stone calls 'scientific history' between the 1930s and 1960s. But then historians began to believe that 'the culture of the group, and even the will of the individual, are potentially at least as important causal agents of change as the impersonal forces of material output and demographic growth'. It is a return to narrative which has helped 'new historians' discover 'what was going on inside people's heads in the past, and what it was like to live in the past' (Lawrence Stone, 'The Revival of Narrative: Reflections on a New Old History', *Past and Present* 85, 1979: 7, 10, 13).

15 Durkheim became renowned for his positive empirical study of the social facts of suicide and was able to show, using demographic data, that something as individual as suicide was related to social facts such as whether people were Protestant or Catholic, married or single, members of the military, or living in a time of economic crisis (Emile Durkheim, *Suicide: A Study in Sociology* [New York: The Free Press, 1951]). However, he insisted that social facts included moral maxims and conventions which limited and constrained individuals. 'If I do not submit to the conventions of society, if in my dress I do not conform to the customs observed in my country and class, the ridicule I provoke, the social isolation in which I am kept, produce, although in an attenuated form, the same effects as a punishment in the strict sense of the word.' (Émile Durkheim, *The Rules of the Sociological Method* [New York: The Free Press 1964], pp. 2–3).

16 This task of linking analytically real, objective, material structures which exist independently of individuals and which limit and constrain what they do and say, with the way people read, understand and live their lives and how they adapt to, bend, resist and reshape these limits and constraints, is at the heart of sociology. See Pierre Bourdieu, *Outline of a Theory of Practice* (Cambridge: Cambridge University Press, 1977), pp. 1–71.

17 See Pierre Bourdieu, 'Some Properties of Fields' in *Sociology in Question* (London: Sage, 1993), pp. 72–7.

18 On *habitus*, see Pierre Bourdieu, *Pascalian Meditations* (Cambridge: Polity, 2000), pp. 128–63.

19 It would be wrong to think that there are an agreed set of rules and strategies as to how sociology should be written and produced. Like all other fields, there are differences (competing knowledges) about the best way to produce sociological truth. Moreover, as Bourdieu pointed out, one of the fallacies of the sociologist is to believe that it is possible to be neutral, placeless and unclassifiable. In this respect, the field of sociology is like other social fields in that it induces and presupposes dispositions which tend to disguise all its arbitrary content as 'timeless, universal self-evidence'. Sociologists continually need to reflect critically on the social position they occupy and the limits and constraints of the scholastic field in which they operate (Bourdieu, *Pascallian Meditations*, p. 29).

20 For an overview of historical research on Irish women, see M. Cullinan, 'Bibliography: Irish Women', *Journal of Women's History* 16 (4) 1995: 250–77.

21 In comparison with the number of stories about men, stories about Irish women have been few and far between. Even when women were deemed to have made a contribution to the modernisation of Irish society – particularly at the time of the foundation of the Irish state in 1922 – it has tended to be seen as a kind of adjunct to what was seen as essentially a male act. See E. Mahon, 'From Democracy to Femocracy: The Women's Movement in the Republic of

Ireland' in P. Clancy, S. Drudy, K. Lynch and L. O'Dowd (eds), *Irish Society: Sociological Perspectives* (Dublin: Institute of Public Administration, 1995), pp. 674–708.

22 Although the revision of Irish women's history is growing rapidly, there is still a dearth of women's biographies and autobiographies. The major exception is Angela Bourke's biography of Bridget Cleary which, not unlike this study, tells the story of what happened to a woman who, in 1895, was caught between an old world of folk beliefs and fairies and a new world of science and rationality, and ended up being tortured and burnt to death by her husband (Angela Bourke, *The Burning of Bridget Cleary* [London: Pinlico, 1999]).

The absence of female biographies and autobiographies is remarkable given that feminist research methodologies have emphasised the importance of producing a phenomenological, interpretative understanding of the lived experiences of women. See A. Byrne and R. Lentin, 'Introduction' in A. Byrne and R. Lentin (eds), *(Re)searching Women: Feminist Research Methodologies in the Social Sciences in Ireland* (Dublin, Institute of Public Administration, 2000), pp. 38–41. A post-positivist, feminist perspective of social understanding demands not only that women tell their own stories, but that they also do so in a way which, as much as possible, breaks analytical or epistemological distinctions between describing subjective experiences and analysing women objectively. This is at the heart of the feminist philosophy that 'the personal is political'. See C. Stivers, 'Reflections on the Role of Personal Narrative in Social Science', *Signs* 18 (2) 1993: 411.

There are, however, inherent problems in telling tales about women. If phenomenological understanding is to be at the forefront, does this mean that if stories about women are not autobiographical, they are best written by other women? This, in turn, raises questions of symbolic domination and violence. Is it possible for intellectuals who are not, in Gramsci's terms, organic – that is who do not come from or belong to the same class, group or community, and who do not have direct personal experience of the people about whom they write – to be able to write anything which contributes to their emancipation rather than their symbolic domination? (Antonio Gramsci, *Selections from the Prison Notebooks* (New York: International Publishers, 1975). If the knowledge that I produce about Irish women does not accurately reflect their lived experiences it may not just be invalid, it may contribute further to their domination and oppression. It is for this reason that feminist research emphasises the importance of the active collaboration of the subject in the research process and that the research outcome must contribute to rather than subtract from their freedom and emancipation. See J. Acker, K. Barry and J. Esseveld, 'Objectivity and Truth: Problems in Doing Feminist Research' in M. M. Fonow and J. A. Cook (eds), *Beyond Methodology* (Bloomington: Indiana University Press, 1991), pp. 133–53.

This leads to an ethical and methodological issue. What if the subjects, in this case members of the Hayes family, do not want to participate, and consider that any writing or research is detrimental to their interests? Is it good enough to argue that because the story, for whatever reasons, has entered the public domain, that it has been central to an understanding of who we are, it can no longer be considered as belonging to them alone?

23 See Tom Inglis, *Moral Monopoly: The Rise and Fall of the Catholic Church in Modern Ireland*, 2nd edn (Dublin: UCD Press, 1998), pp. 178–200.

24   Frances Finnegan, *Do Penance or Perish: A Study of Magdalen Asylums in Ireland* (Pilltown [Kilkenny]: Congrave Press 2001). See also M. Luddy and C. Murphy, '*Cherchez la Femme*: The Elusive Woman in Irish History', in M. Luddy and C. Murphy (eds), *Women Surviving: Studies in Irish Women History in the Nineteenth and Twentieth Centuries* (Dublin: Poolbeg Press, 1990).

25   This is a reference to Bourdieu's sociology and, in particular, his monumental study of working-class life in France. See Pierre Bourdieu *et al.*, *The Weight of the World: Social Suffering in Contemporary Society* (Cambridge: Polity, 1999). The emphasis on everyday life and the tactics which people employ in their daily struggles – and how these differ from the strategies of institutions and organisations – is at the heart of the work of Michel de Certeau and Henri Lefebvre. See Michel de Certeau, *The Practice of Everyday Life* (Berkeley: University of California Press, 1984); Henri Lefebvre, *Everyday Life in the Modern World* (New Brunswick: Transaction Press, 1984).

26   Maria Luddy, *Women in Ireland 1800–1918: A Documentary History* (Cork: Cork University Press, 1995).

27   Margaret Ward, *Maude Gonne: Ireland's Joan of Arc* (London: Pandora, 1990), p. 21.

28   Kearney, *Postnationalist Ireland*, p. 189.

29   C. W. Mills, *The Sociological Imagination* (Harmondsworth: Penguin, 1970), pp. 10–12.

30   Kearney, *On Stories*, p. 69.

31   Pierre Bourdieu, *Masculine Domination* (Stanford: Stanford University Press, 2001), pp. 22–33.

32   Pierre Bourdieu, 'Forms of Capital' in J. Richardson (ed.), *Handbook of Theory and Research for the Sociology of Education* (Westport [Conn.]: Greenwood Press, 1986), p. 245.

33   Pierre Bourdieu, *Language and Symbolic Power*, ed. J. Thompson (Cambridge: Polity, 1991), p. 50.

34   See Pat O'Connor, *Emerging Voices: Women in Contemporary Irish Society* (Dublin: Institute of Public Administration, 1998), pp. 109–24; Tony Fahey, *Family Formation in Ireland* (Dublin: Economic and Social Research Institute, 2002).

35   Reviewing examples of the new genre of storytelling by historians such as E. Le Roy Ladurie, Eric Hobsbawm, E. P. Thompson, Natalie Zemon Davis and Keith Thomas, Stone notes five differences from previous approaches.

> First, they are almost all without exception concerned with the lives and feelings and behaviour of the poor and obscure rather than the great and powerful. Secondly, analysis remains as essential to their methodology as description . . . Thirdly, they are opening up new sources, often records of criminal courts . . . Fourthly, they often tell their stories in a different way . . . they gingerly explore the subconscious rather than sticking to the plain facts. . . . they try to use behaviour to reveal symbolic meaning. Fifthly, they tell the story of a person, a trial or a dramatic episode, not for its own sake, but in order to throw light upon the internal workings of a past culture and society. (Stone, 'Revival of Narrative', p. 19).

36   This raises questions about the relation between individual action and social structures and long-term historical processes. See Anthony Giddens, *The Constitution of Society* (Cambridge: Polity, 1984); J. Alexander, 'The New Theoretical Movement' in Neil Smelser

(ed.), *Handbook of Sociology* (London: Sage, 1988), pp. 77–101; P. Bourdieu, 'Men and Machines' in K. Knorr–Cetina and A. V. Cicourel (eds), *Advances in Social Theory and Methodology* (London: Routledge & Kegan Paul, 1981), pp. 304–17.

37 Of course, the problem in telling the story of the Kerry Babies is that Joanne Hayes is not a famous woman, but an infamous one. As Foucault reminds us, it may not have been a coincidence that someone like Joanne Hayes was plucked from obscurity to become a national figure. Chance and power go together. Throughout the last 300 years in Europe, individuals have been elevated to notoriety as disturbers of the peace. (Michel Foucault, *Power, Truth and Strategy*, ed. M. Morris and P. Patton [Sydney: Feral, 1979], p. 81).

38 See, for example, Jonathan Culler, *Structuralist Poetics* (London: Routledge, 1975).

39 O'Mahony, 'The Kerry Babies Case'.

40 See Carlos Ginsberg, *Clues, Myths, and the Historical Method* (Baltimore: Johns Hopkins University Press, 1989).

41 This concept of 'other' occurs in many other writings. As Said notes, the concept of identity is always subject to continuous interpretation and reinterpretation of how others are different from us. (Edward Said, *Orientalism: Western Conceptions of the Orient* [Harmondsworth: Penguin, 1995], p. 332).

42 See Bourdieu, *Language and Symbolic Power*; Foucault, *Power, Truth and Strategy*; Foucault, *Power-Knowledge*, 1980.

43 P. Bourdieu, 'The Force of Law: Toward a Sociology of the Juridical Field', *The Hastings Law Journal* 38 (1987): 805–53.

Chapter 2 The investigation

1 Barry O'Halloran, *Lost Innocence: The Case of the Kerry Babies*, Dublin: Raytown Press 1985: 18. The fertiliser bag, along with the two other bags, was taken back to the Garda Station and the three bags to play a crucial role in the case. After an inexplicable delay, the bags were eventually sent for forensic examination. They were never tested for fingerprints. As Mr Justice Lynch pointed out in the Tribunal Report, while the sea might have eroded any prints on the fertiliser bag and the brown plastic bag in which the dead baby had been wrapped, this might not have been the case with the clear plastic bag (TR, p. 132).

2 Gerard Colleran and Michel O'Regan, *Dark Secrets: The Inside Story of Joanne Hayes and the Kerry Babies* (Tralee: The Kerryman, 1985), p. 69.

3 Nell McCafferty, *A Woman to Blame* (Dublin: Attic Press, 1985), p. 9. This was significant as it would be part of the garda case against the Hayes family that it only took about 24 hours for the body of the baby to make a journey, a hundred times longer and more precarious, from Slea Head across Dingle Bay, around Doulus Head, and into White Strand.

4 O'Halloran, *Lost Innocence*, pp. 21–2. The absence of a blood sample turned out to be crucial since it was claimed later that the lung tissue became contaminated and did not provide an accurate sample.

5 Colleran and O'Regan, *Dark Secrets*, pp. 73; O'Halloran, *Lost Innocence*, p. 23.

6 In the Tribunal Report, Mr Justice Lynch points out that the interpretation and practice of the 1949 Act was that 'the mother [*sic*] should be charged with murder in the first instance'

(TR, p. 37). It would then be at the discretion of the District Justice to reduce the charge to infanticide if there were the extenuating circumstances described in the Act.

7   John Creedon, Consultant Obstetrician and Gynaecologist in St Catherine's Hospital in Tralee, told the Tribunal that he himself had encountered at least five cases of self-delivery in which the babies were found dead.

> We had cases of a similar nature in the past which had been resolved within the law, without any apparent criminal formality. In other words we could persuade patients to give us their consent and we could proceed to notify the Coroner and appropriate authorities with the baby brought into hospital and the post mortem examination carried out and the cause of death established, natural cases and we could proceed to sign a death certificate. (TT 7/64)

8   See TT, 36/62.

9   The breakthrough was a result of dogged police work. Tralee General Hospital had been checked out several times before. Det. Sgt Dillon had not been involved in the case previously, but he had contacts in the hospital that proved invaluable. See O'Halloran, *Lost Innocence*, p. 28.

10   Given that there were three plastic bags found at White Strand, it was a coincidence that Joanne Hayes made reference to two plastic bags. The reference to a pool of water does not seem to have struck a chord with the gardaí. Abandoned dead babies are often found near or in water.

Chapter 3   Preparing the case against the Hayes family

1   Bourdieu defines those things which are neither discussed nor disputed as the universe of doxa. They are almost self-evident and taken for granted. It is where social convention eliminates alternatives, a complete merging of the subjective individual with objective institutional structures. Orthodoxy, on the other hand, allows for debate, discussion and argument. The tight seal of doxa can be broken at a time of crisis, but it has to be in the interests of the dominated to expose the taken-for-granted world being promoted by the dominant order. It might have been possible for some gardaí to have suggested that not all confessions were given voluntarily and spontaneously, but it would have had to have been in their political interests to have done so. (Pierre Bourdieu, *Outline of a Theory of Practice*. Cambridge: Cambridge University Press, 1977), pp. 168–9.

2   The Tralee baby's umbilical cord turned out to be crucial evidence since it contradicted Joanne Hayes's claim that she gave birth alone in the field and tore and broke the cord with a blade or scissors. If the cord had been cut, who cut it, where, and with what?

3   See G. Kerrigan, 'The Kerry Babies Case', *Magill*, 30 May 1985: 46.

4   Colleran and O'Regan claim that in the draft report they used the full term 'grotesque, unbelievable, bizarre, and unprecedented' to describe the events in the Hayes home that night. These were the words used by the Taoiseach Charles Haughey in 1982 when Malcolm MacArthur, a murderer, was arrested in the flat of the Attorney General Patrick Connolly. (Gerard Colleran and Michael O'Regan, *Dark Secrets* [Tralee: The Kerryman, 1985], pp. 133–4).

Although Det. Sgt Mossie O'Donnell was the more senior, it is generally accepted that the report was mostly written by P. J. Browne. The Report is signed solely by Superintendent John Courtney. See Barry O'Halloran, *Lost Innocence* (Dublin: Raytown Press, 1985), p. 154.

5   John Courtney gives a description of this case in his memoirs. Interestingly, he notes: 'We were accused of extracting that statement [from Liam Townson] by brutal means, but we never used violence of any nature in our interviews with suspects.' John Courtney, *It was Murder* (Dublin: Blackwater Press, 1996), p. 25.

6   O'Halloran suggests that the 'floury language used in the more colourful passages' of the report can be linked to the fact that P. J. Browne was born and reared in Listowel which 'has long abounded in poets, novelists and dramatists' (O'Halloran, *Lost Innocence*, p. 154). Coleran and O'Regan claim that much of the flowery language of the first draft, including the phrase 'slaughter of infants' was taken out on the insistence of Superintendent Dónal O'Sullivan (Coleran and O'Regan, *Lost Innocence*, p. 134.

7   O'Halloran concludes that the report 'is a highly subjective account which makes few if any concessions to the conflicts and contradictions contained in the available evidence' (*Lost Innocence*, p. 162).

8   *Today, Tonight,* 16 October 1984.

9   Quoted in O'Halloran, *Lost Innocence,* p. 174.

10   *The Irish Times,* 17 Oct. 1984.

11   *The Irish Times,* 24 Oct. 1984.

12   Colleran and O'Regan, *Dark Secrets,* p. 138.

13   Mr Justice Kevin Lynch had been appointed to the High Court the previous year. He was 57 and lived in Dublin. He was the son of a Kerryman, Fionán Lynch, who was from Cahirciveen.

Chapter 4 The Hayes family story

1   Tribunals of inquiry have become a central element in the creation and maintenance of a mature democratic civil society. For a detailed discussion and critique of recent tribunals, see M. Corcoran and A. White, 'Irish Democracy and the Tribunals of Inquiry' in E. Slater and M. Peillon (eds), *Memories of the Present* (Dublin: Institute of Public Administration, 2000), p. 196. The Tribunal was the third since the 1979 Act. The first two, the Whiddy Island (when an oil tanker caught fire and sank in Bantry Bay) and Stardust (when a fire at a disco in Dublin killed over 40 young people) were marked by stark conflicts of evidence. In the case of the Whiddy Island Tribunal, it was directed that certain witnesses be charged with perjury (*The Irish Times* 24 Jan. 1985). For an account of the Stardust Inquiry, see Neil Fetherstonhaugh and Tony McCullagh, *They Never Came Home: The Stardust Story* (Dublin: Merlin, 2001).

2   During the Tribunal, Mr Justice Lynch elaborated on this rationale:

> I am going to have to report to the Minister in due course, report to the Minister on what I think is the truth of this whole matter and it is not just the evidence that is given but the various witnesses that can be helpful in arriving at where the truth lies. But some times if there is cross examination which is shown to have good foundation then that can be helpful at ascertaining the truth in accordance with cross examination, but if it turns out that there was cross examination which had little or no foundation, then this can be equally helpful to me in judging the case which puts forward that cross examination. So I am not going to restrict cross examination. It is up to the representatives of all parties what they want to ask. (TT, 13/2)

3   See Barry O'Halloran, *Lost Innocence* (Dublin: Raytown Press, 1985), pp. 52–3.

Chapter 5 The gardaí's story

1   It should be noted that Martin Kennedy uses the name 'Joanna' to refer to Joanne Hayes. This may seem a slip of the tongue. On the other hand, Joanne Hayes said that Superintendent Courtney repeatedly referred to her as 'Joanna' when interviewing her on 1 May 1984. In her confession she also referred to herself as Joanna, a name she said she detested and which nobody called her.

Chapter 6 Blaming the Hayes family

1   Kerrigan pointed out that, contrary to Mr Justice Lynch's claim, in his statement of complaint Ned said that he was 'turned' not 'lifted' upside down. Kerrigan argued that this would be no great feat for a tall and heavy man: 'School kids do it to one another all the time' (*Magill*, 14 Nov. 1985, p. 28).

2   *Ibid.*

Chapter 8 The context

1   *The Irish Times*, 20 Jan. 1984.

2   *The Irish Times*, 20 June 1984.

3   *The Irish Times*, 11 Aug. 1984.

4   *The Irish Times*, 7 Dec. 1984.

5   *The Irish Times*, 29 June 1984.

6   *The Irish Times*, 19 Oct. 1984.

7   *The Irish Times*, 1 Dec. 1984.

8   *The Irish Times*, 30 Nov. 1984.

9   *The Irish Times*, 12 Dec. 1984.

10   *The Irish Times*, 1 Mar. 1984.

11   See A. Mulcahy, 'The Impact of the Northern "Troubles" on Criminal Justice in the Irish Republic' in P. O'Mahony (ed.), *Criminal Justice in Ireland* (Dublin: Institute of Public Administration, 2002), pp. 275–96

12   *The Irish Times*, 10 Jan. 1984.

13   *The Irish Times*, 27 Nov. 1984.

14   *The Irish Times*, 23 Mar. 1984.

15   *The Irish Times*, 23 Aug. 1984.

16   *The Irish Times*, 24 May 1984.

17   *The Irish Times*, 29 May 1984.

18   *The Irish Times*, 29 Aug. 1984.

19   *The Irish Times*, 19 Sept. 1984.

20   *The Irish Times*, 23 Mar. 1984.

21   *The Irish Times*, 7 Apr. 1984.

22   *The Irish Times*, 3 Aug. 1984.

23   *The Irish Times*, 3 Oct. 1984.

24   See C. Wouters, 'Formalization and Informalization: Changing Tension Balances in Civilizing Processes', *Theory Culture and Society* 4 (2/3) 1986: 1–18.

25   For a description of the public debate in County Kerry before the Referendum, see Nell McCafferty, *A Woman to Blame* (Dublin: Attic Press, 1985) pp. 35–9.

26   *The Irish Times*, 10 Jan. 1984.

27   *The Irish Times*, 18 July 1984

28   *The Irish Times*, 7 Jan. 1984.

29   *The Irish Times*, 10 Jan. 1984.

30   *The Irish Times*, 13 Jan. 1984.

31   *The Irish Times*, 21 Jan. 1984.

32   *The Irish Times*, 29 Aug. 1984.

33   *The Irish Times*, 10 May 1984.

34   *The Irish Times*, 11 Oct. 1984.

35   *The Irish Times*, 21 Feb. 1984.

36   For a more detailed discussion of these changes, see Tom Inglis, *Lessons in Irish Sexuality* (Dublin: University College Dublin Press, 1998); T. Inglis, 'From Sexual Repression to Liberation?' in M. Peillon and E. Slater (eds), *Encounters with Modern Ireland* (Dublin: Institute of Public Administration, 1998), pp. 99–104; T. Inglis, 'Foucault, Bourdieu and the Field of Irish Sexuality', *Irish Journal of Sociology* 7, 1997: 5–28.

37   *The Irish Times*, 7 Feb. 1984.

38   *Ibid.*

39   Quoted in Fintan O'Toole, *The Lie of the Land: Irish Identities* (Dublin: New Island, 1998), p. 146.

40   *The Irish Times*, 25 Feb. 1984.

41   *The Irish Times*, 23 Oct. 1984.

42   *The Irish Times*, 22 Jan. 1985.

43   TR, p. 148. It should be noted that, partly as a result of this social change, it became politically incorrect to use the term 'illegitimate' or 'unmarried mother' to describe 'births outside marriage' or 'single mothers'.

44   *The Irish Times*, 12 June 1984.

45   *The Irish Times*, 6 Nov. 1984.

46   *The Irish Times*, 5 Jan. 1985.

47   *The Irish Times*, 8 Feb. 1984.

48   *The Irish Times*, 5 July 1984.

49   *The Irish Times*, 18 Feb. 1985. In an essay in May 1985, Fintan O'Toole gave a more detailed description of this event. See Fintan O'Toole, 'Seeing is Believing' in *A Mass for Jesse James: A Journey through 1980s Ireland* (Dublin: Raven Arts Press, 1990), pp. 16–22

50   Fintan O'Toole interviewed one of the children's parents who linked the statues' beginning to move in Asdee not just to the Kerry babies case and the national publicity it received, but to two murders in the Listowel area and a man in Tarbert who was having sex with his two nieces, one of whom became pregnant (*Ibid.*, p. 16).

51   For a more detailed description and analysis of this habitus, see Tom Inglis, *Moral Monopoly: The Rise and Fall of the Catholic Church in Modern Ireland*, 2nd edn (Dublin: University College Dublin Press, 1998), pp. 24–30.

52   Ann Swidler uses the term 'settled' to a describe a homogeneous culture similar to Catholic Ireland before the 1960s and 'unsettled' to describe a culture in which there are contradictory visions of society associated with ideologically opposed interest groups (A. Swidler, 'Culture in Action: Symbols and Strategies', *American Sociological Review* 51 (2) 1986: 273–86). Pierre Bourdieu uses the term 'hysteresis' to refer to what happens when a field such as Irish sexual morality undergoes a major transformation and the traditional habitus becomes destabilised. This can result in people occupying contradictory positions, such as bishop and lover, not only causing suffering for the individual but also making the traditional habitus – the way Irish people read, understand and interpret sexuality – visible (Pierre Bourdieu, *Pascalian Meditations* [Cambridge: Polity, 2000], p. 160.)

53   O'Toole, *Lie of the Land*, p. 76.

Chapter 9   Long-term processes of change

1   This raises the relation between social structure and individual agency, and between macro- and micro-level analysis. See R. Münch and N. Smelser 'Relating the Micro and the Macro' in J. Alexander, B. Giesen, R. Münch and N. Smelser (eds), *The Micro–Macro Link* (Berkeley: University of California Press, 1987), p. 357. Randall Collins argues that since culture, the economy, states, organisations and classes do not act, any causal explanation in sociology has to start with the empirical world and the real live actions of individuals (R. Collins, 'Interaction Ritual Chains, Power and Property' in Alexander *et al.* (eds), *The Micro–Macro Link*, p. 195, emphasis in original.

2   See Tom Inglis, *Moral Monopoly: The Rise and Fall of the Catholic Church in Modern Ireland*, 2nd edn (Dublin: University College Dublin Press, 1998), pp. 17–38; 205–10.

3   See Steve Bruce, *Religion in the Modern World: From Cathedrals to Cults* (Oxford: Oxford University Press, 1996).

4   See Inglis, *Moral Monopoly*, pp. 209–13.

5   See Tom Inglis, *Lessons in Irish Sexuality* (Dublin: University College Dublin Press, 1998): 50–69.

6   Joanne Hayes, *My Story* (Dingle: Brandon Press, 1985), p. 25.

7   *Ibid.*, p. 60.

8   *Ibid.* Deidre Purcell, who covered the Tribunal for the *Sunday Tribune*, phoned Fr Hickey to speak to him but he told her that 'he did not want to get involved at all in the situation' (*Sunday Tribune*, 27 Jan. 1985).

9   Hayes, *My Story*, p. 34. As O'Halloran points out, Mrs Hayes and a neighbour, Mary Shanahan, went to the local garda, Liam Moloney – and not to the local priests – to ask him to talk to Joanne (*Lost Innocence*, p. 49).

10   For a detailed analysis of the role of small-scale land holders in Irish agricultural production and the strategies they employed, see D. Hannan and P. Commins, 'The Significance of Small-scale Landholders in Ireland's Socio-economic Transformation' in J. Goldthorpe and C. Whelan (eds), *The Development of Industrial Society in Ireland* (Oxford: Oxford University Press, 1992), pp. 79–104.

11　See Hilary Tovey and Perry Share, *A Sociology of Ireland* (Dublin: Gill & Macmillan, 2000), pp. 51–2.

12　Peter McKevitt, *The Plan for Society* (Dublin: Catholic Truth Society of Ireland, 1944), p. 9.

13　*Ibid.*, p. 41.

14　Daly argues that the Catholic vision of Irish society was founded on spiritual ideals of frugal comfort lived out in the fellowship of family, friends and neighbours (M. E. Daly, 'The Economic Ideals of Irish Nationalism: Frugal Comfort or Lavish Austerity?', *Eiré/Ireland* XXIX (4) 1994: 77–100).

15　For a history of the farm, see Gerard Colleran and Michael O'Regan, *Dark Secrets* (Tralee: The Kerryman, 1985), pp. 28–9.

16　See Barry O'Halloran, *Lost Innocence* (Dublin: Raytown Press, 1985), p. 29.

17　*Ibid.*, p. 31. For how the Hayes farm compared with other farms in Kerry in the 1980s, see M. Shutes, 'Kerry Farmers and the European Community: Capital Transitions in a Rural Irish Parish', *Irish Journal of Sociology* 1, 1991: 3.

18　For an analysis of the marriage options and strategies of inheriting sons, see D. Hannan, 'Peasant Models and the Understanding of Social and Cultural Change in Rural Ireland' in P. Drudy (ed.), *Ireland: Land, Politics and People* (Cambridge: Cambridge University Press, 1982), pp. 141–65. As Salazar has argued, these strategies were part of kinship system and cultural domain of meaning in which an understanding of self was constituted within a number of spheres of meaning including blood, sex, name, land and home (C. Salazar, 'On Blood and Its Alternatives: An Irish history', *Social Anthropology* 7 (2) 1999: 166).

19　Hannan and Commins, 'Significance of Small-scale Landholders', p. 82.

20　See O'Halloran, *Lost Innocence*, p. 32.

21　See Inglis, *Lessons in Irish Sexuality*, pp. 34–6.

22　O'Halloran, *Lost Innocence*, p. 30.

23　See Judith Perkins, *The Suffering Self* (London: Routledge, 1995), pp. 2–3.

24　See Michel Foucault, *The Use of Pleasure*, vol. 2, *The History of Sexuality* (London: Penguin, 1987), p. 138.

25　Hugh Connolly, *The Irish Penitentials* (Dublin: Four Courts, 1995). Over the next 1,400 years, asceticism and self-denial became central to Irish morals and the daily struggle to live an ethical life. Ó Ríordáin argues that they became so ingrained in the Irish mind and body that they became an essential part of the Irish social character (John Ó Ríordáin, *Irish Catholic Spirituality* [Dublin: Columba, 1998], p. 19.

26　For a detailed description and analysis of the origins and development of these practices see Michael Carroll, *Pilgrimage: Holy Wells and Popular Catholic Devotion* (Baltimore: Johns Hopkins University Press, 1999).

27　See Joseph Glynn, *Matt Talbot* (Dublin: Veritas, 1977); Simon O'Byrne, *Matt Talbot: Secular Franciscan* (Dublin: Veritas, 1979). There is street in Tralee named after Matt Talbot.

28　See Michael Mason, *The Making of Victorian Sexual Attitudes* (Oxford: Oxford University Press, 1994); Steven Seidman, *Romantic Longings: Love in America 1830–1980* (London: Routledge, 1991).

29　See Carroll, *Pilgrimage*, pp. 135–66.

30　Inglis, *Moral Monopoly*, pp. 26–49.

31   For an autobiographical description of relationships and sexuality education in the 1940s see Gráinne Flynn, 'Our Age of Innocence' in M. Cullen (ed.), *Girls Don't Do Honours: Irish Women in Education in the 19th and 20th Centuries* (Dublin: WEB, 1987), pp. 79–99 For an indication of the sexual ignorance of women in the 1950s see Alexander Humphreys, *New Dubliners* (New York: Fordham University Press, 1966), and Inglis, *Lessons in Irish Sexuality*, pp. 29–39.

32   See T. Inglis, 'Foucault, Bourdieu and the Field of Irish Sexuality' *Irish Journal of Sociology* 7, 1997: 5–28.

33   For further discussion of this transformation See T. Inglis, 'Pleasure Pursuits' in M. Corcoran and M. Peillon (eds) *Ireland Unbound: A Turn of the Century Chronicle* (Dublin: Institute of Public Administration, 2002), pp. 25–35; T. Inglis, 'From Sexual Repression to Liberation' in M. Peillon and E. Slater (eds), *Encounters with Modern Ireland* (Dublin: Institute of Public Administration, 19980, pp. 99–104.

34   Hayes, *My Story*, p. 27.

35   For a discussion of the impact of Dallas on Irish society, see M. Kelly, 'Television Content: Dallasifiction of Culture' in K. Suine and W. Trietzschler (eds), *Dynamics in Media Politics* (London: Sage 1992), pp. 75–101; Barbara O'Connor, *Soaps and Sensibility: Audience Response to Dallas and Glenroe* (Dublin: RTÉ, 1990), pp. 27–8; Ien Ang, *Watching Dallas: Soap Opera and the Melodramatic Imagination* (London: Methuen, 1985), p. 136.

36   See C. Wouters, 'Etiquette Books and Emotion Management in the Twentieth Century: Part 2 – The Integration of the Sexes' *Journal of Social History*, 29, 1995: 325–40.

37   See E. Mahon, 'From Democracy to Femocracy: the Women's Movement in the Republic of Ireland' in P. Clancy, S. Drudy, K. Lynch and L. O'Dowd (eds), *Irish Society: Sociological Perspectives* (Dublin: Institute of Public Administration, 1995), pp. 675–708.

38   For a history of the Irish women's movement, see Linda Connolly, *The Irish Women's Movement: From Revolution to Devolution* (Basingstoke: Palgrave, 2002).

39   Norbert Elias, *The Civilising Process*, ed. and trans. Eric Dunning, Johan Goudsblom and Stephen Mennell (Oxford: Blackwell, 2000); C. Wouters, 'Formalization and Informalization: Changing Tension Balances in the Civilizing Processes' *Theory, Culture and Society* 3 (2) 1986: 1–18. For a fuller summary of the debate about the 'permissive society' and informalisation in the light of Elias's theory, see Stephen Mennell, *Norbert Elias: An Introduction* (Dublin: UCD Press, 1998), pp. 241–6.

40   See C. Wouters, 'Manners' in *Encyclopedia of European Social History from 1350 to 2000*, vol. 4 (New York: Scribner's Sons, 2001), pp. 371–82.

41   Colleran and O'Regan, *Dark Secrets*, p. 31.

42   O'Halloran, *Lost Innocence*, p. 35.

43   Nell McCafferty, *A Women to Blame* (Dublin: Attic Press, 1985), p. 43.

44   *Ibid.*, p. 42.

45   Quoted in S. McAvoy, 'The Regulation of Sexuality in the Irish Free State, 1929–1935' in G. Jones and E. Malcolm (eds), *Medicine, Disease and the State in Ireland 1650–1940* (Cork: Cork University Press, 1999), pp. 253–66.

46   See K. H. Connell, 'Peasant Marriage in Ireland after the Great Famine', *Past and Present* XII, 1957: 76–91; K. H. Connell, 'Peasant Marriage in Ireland: Its Structure and Development

since the Famine', *Economic History Review*, 2nd ser. XIV, 1961–2: 501–23; D. McLoughlin, 'Women and Sexuality in Nineteenth Century Ireland' *Irish Journal of Psychology* 15 (2–3) 1994: 266–75.

47 See K. H. Connell, *Irish Peasant Society* (Oxford: Clarendon, 1968), pp. 126, 121.

48 See P. McNabb, 'Social Structure' in Jeremiah Newman (ed.), *Limerick Rural Survey* (Tipperary: Muintir na Tire, 1964), pp. 222–3.

49 Clarkson has pointed out that, while Connell argued strongly that there was a swing from young and unrestricted marriage to old and regulated marriage, we know little about the intimacies and relationships between lovers and husbands and wives in the nineteenth century. In effect, the same is true for much of the twentieth century (L. A. Clarkson, 'Marriage and Fertility in Nineteenth-Century Ireland' in R.B. Outhwaite (ed.), *Marriage and Society* [London: Europa, 1982], pp. 237–55).

50 See Declan Kiberd, *Inventing Ireland: The Literature of the Modern Nation* (London: Vintage, 1996); Terence Brown, *Ireland: A Social and Cultural History 1922–79* (London: Fontana, 1981).

51 See Seidman, *Romantic Longings*, pp. 60, 17.

52 Quoted in Dorine Rohan, *Marriage Irish Style* (Cork: Mercier, 1969), p. 32.

53 Quoted *Ibid.*, p. 39.

54 *Ibid.*, pp. 71, 75.

55 See Conrad Arensberg and Solon Kimball, *Family and Community in Ireland* (Cambridge [Mass]: Harvard University Press, 1940); John Messenger, *Innis Beag* (New York: Holt Rinehart Winston, 1969).

56 See Hugh Brody, *Inniskillane* (London: Jill Norman & Hobhouse, 1982).

57 O'Donoghue speculates that sexual dysfunction – difficulties in engaging in sexual intercourse – would affect 20 per cent of the Irish adult population but does not speculate how this compares with other societies (F. O'Donoghue, 'Sexuality and the Irish' in C. Keane (ed.), *Mental Health in Ireland* [Dublin: Gill & Macmillan, 1991]), p. 54.

58 T. Fahey, 'Marital Fertility Control in Ireland: Some Evidence Examined' (Dublin: Economic and Social Research Institute Seminar Paper, 1983), p. 12

59 Hayes, *My Story*, p. 27.

60 See Seidman, *Romantic Longings*, p. 4.

61 McAvoy notes that the draft legislation to ban birth control in the 1930s had all-party agreement, because there was general agreement that matters of sexuality were not suitable for public debate. See McAvoy, 'Regulation of Sexuality', p. 257.

62 This was at the heart of 'The Bishop and the Nightie' episode when in 1965 a woman was asked on the popular television programme *The Late Late Show* what colour nightie she had worn on her honeymoon and replied that could not recall and that perhaps she had not worn any. Bishop Tom Ryan sent a telegram to RTÉ saying he was disgusted and the following day gave a sermon on the episode and the programme. See M. Earls, 'The Late, Late Show: Controversy and Context' in M. McLoone and J. MacMahon (eds), *Television in Irish Society* (Dublin: RTÉ–IFI, 1984), pp. 107–22.

63 See Colleran and O'Regan, *Dark Secrets*, pp. 15–16.

64 Hayes, *My Story*, p. 28.

65   Colleran and O'Regan, *Dark Secrets*, p. 39.

66   The car has a special place in the history of twentieth-century courting practices. While not necessarily the most suitable or comfortable place to make love, it provided a generally warm but, more importantly, private space for intimacy which could be created in obscure parts of cities, towns and rural areas. Bailey sees the car as playing a crucial role in transforming American courtship practices. See Beth Bailey, *From Front Porch to Back Seat: Courtship in Twentieth Century America* (Baltimore: Johns Hopkins University Press, 1988), p. 86. In relation to Britain, see S. Humphries, *A Secret World of Sex* (London: Sidgwick & Jackson, 1988), p. 104. It would seem that courting couples in Ireland also quickly latched on to the possibilities of the car. The Carrigan Report (1931), which examined juvenile prostitution, referred to the notorious indecency in Irish society, both in urban and rural areas, 'a feature of which is the misuse of motor cars'. Quoted in McAvoy, 'Regulation of Sexuality', p. 262.

67   Hayes, *My Story*, p. 34.

68   McAvoy concludes that the effect of the investigations, reports and subsequent social legislation to deal with what was perceived to be rampant sexual indecency in the 1930s was subtly to place 'responsibility and "blame" for sexual nonconformity on women' (McAvoy, 'Regulation of Sexuality', p. 264).

Chapter 10 Honour and shame

1   The notion of 'others' has been developed by Said in relation to how Arabs came to be seen by Westerners. See Edward Said, *Orientalism* (Harmondsworth: Penguin, 1995). The notion of scapegoats has been developed by René Girard in *The Scapegoat* (London: Athlone Press, 1986). I return to these issues in the last two chapters.

2   Bourdieu has developed the concept of habitus to explain the shared mental framework into which people are socialised and through which they read, understand and interpret the world similarly. One of his earliest and most enduring definitions described habitus as 'a system of lasting, transposable dispositions which, integrating past experiences, functions at every moment as a *matrix of perceptions, appreciations and actions* and makes possible the achievement of infinitely diversified tasks'. Pierre Bourdieu, *Outline of a Theory of Practice* (Cambridge: Cambridge University Press, 1977), pp. 82–3.

3   For a good introduction to these and other issues central to Bourdieu's sociology see L. Wacquant 'Toward a Social Praxeology: The Structure and Logic of Bourdieu's Sociology' in Pierre Bourdieu and Löic Wacquant (eds), *An Invitation to Reflexive Sociology* (Cambridge: Polity, 1992), pp. 1–59.

4   The study of honour and shame has been a feature of anthropological studies, particularly in Mediterranean societies. See J. Pitt-Rivers, 'Honour and Social Status' in J. G. Peristiany (ed.), *Honour and Shame: The Values of Mediterranean Society* (London: Weidenfeld & Nicolson, 1965), p. 21.

5   See Frank Stewart, *Honor* (Chicago: Chicago University Press, 1994), p. 129.

6   *Ibid.*, p. 59.

7   The relationship between honour and symbolic capital is at the centre of Bourdieu's work. Symbolic capital comes from 'the esteem, recognition, belief, credit, confidence of

others'. See Bourdieu, *Pascalian Meditations* (Cambridge: Polity Press, 1999), p. 166. In everyday life, people are constantly trying to present themselves in a good light. Symbolic capital makes people look good. In this way it can legitimate the other capitals that they have accumulated. The struggle for symbolic power, as in the gift relationship, subverts commercial relations. It is the refusal to reduce social relations to economic relations. It is the game of power played by different means. See Pierre Bourdieu, *The Logic of Practice* (Cambridge: Polity, 1992), 112–21.

8   While Bourdieu developed a theory of different forms of capital, most notably economic, cultural and social, his whole work may be seen as a hunt for symbolic capital in its varied forms. See Bourdieu and Wacquant, *An Invitation to Reflexive Sociology*, p. 119.

9   For an analysis of the link between symbolic capital and cultural capital, see P. Bourdieu, 'Forms of Capital' in J. Richardson (ed.), *Handbook of Theory and Research for the Sociology of Education* (Westport [CT]: Greenwood Press, 1986), pp. 252–3.

10   For a thorough analysis of social position and how this is derived from different forms of capital, see Pierre Bourdieu, *Distinction* (London: Routledge & Kegan Paul, 1984).

11   See J. K. Campbell, 'Honour and the Devil' in J. G. Peristiany (ed.), *Honour and Shame: The Values of Mediterranean Society* (London: Weidenfeld & Nicolson, 1965), p. 146; J. Schneider 'On Vigilance and Virgins' *Ethnology* 9, 1971: 1–24; D. Gilmore, 'Introduction' in D. Gilmore (ed.), *Honor and Shame and the Unity of the Mediterranean* (Washington: American Anthropological Association, 1987), p. 4; J. Davis 'Family and State in the Mediterranean' in Gilmore (ed.), *Honor and Shame*, p. 26; C. Delaney, 'Seeds of Honour, Fields of Shame', in Peristiany (ed.), *Honour and Shame*, p. 36.

12   Pitt-Rivers, 'Honour and Social Status', pp. 42, 46.

13   For the link between family and honour, see P. Bourdieu, 'On the Family as a Realized Category', *Theory, Culture and Society* 13 (3) 1996: 21.

14   'It [the family] is one of the key sites of the accumulation of capital in its different forms and its transmission between the generations. . . . This is seen clearly in the transmission of the *family name*, the basic element in the hereditary symbolic capital.' Bourdieu, 'On the Family', p. 23.

15   Bourdieu sees social life as based on people operating strategically within different social fields to attain and retain different forms of capital. One of the crucial strategies in passing on capital from one generation to the next, particularly in traditional rural areas, is making a good marriage. See P. Bourdieu 'Marriage Strategies as Strategies of Social Reproduction' in E. Foster and P. Ranum (eds), *Family and Society* (Baltimore: Johns Hopkins University Press, 1976), pp. 117–44.

16   Nell McCafferty, *A Woman to Blame* (Dublin: Attic Press, 1985), p. 134. Bridie Fuller died in the week before the Tribunal Report was published.

17   Scheff argues that shame exists in modern societies just as much as it does in traditional ones. The difference is that in traditional societies they have a language to express shame. In modern societies, the language to express shame has disappeared and, consequently, it remains hidden, bypassed and unacknowledged. See Thomas Scheff, *Microsociology* (Chicago: University of Chicago Press, 1990), p. 79; Thomas Scheff, *Bloody Revenge: Emotions, Nationalism and War* (Boulder: Westview Press, 1994), pp. 49–50.

18   Joanne Hayes, *My Story* (Dingle: Brandon Press, 1985), p. 32.

19   Scheff, *Microsociology*, p. 179.

20   See John Whyte, *Church & State in Modern Ireland 1923–1979*, 2nd edn (Dublin: Gill & Macmillan, 1980), pp. 196–272.

21   Hayes, *My Story*, p. 27.

22   Infanticide would be a classical example of Scheff's theory of shame–rage spiral when the sense of shame is built up to such an extent over nine months that in the trauma of giving birth the shame turns to anger which is directed at the source of the shame, the newborn baby. It is perhaps ironic that as a contrast to the shame–rage response sequence, Scheff refers to the pride–love process by which mother and child develop an emotional bond. See Scheff, *Bloody Revenge*, p. 178.

23   As Bourdieu notes: '[I]n the game of honour, although unmeasurable stakes are involved, each party must consider the other capable of choosing the best strategy, namely that which consists of playing according to the rules of the code of honour.' See Pierre Bourdieu, 'The Sentiment of Honour in Kabyle Society' in *Honour and Shame: The Values of Mediterranean Society*, ed. J. G. Peristiany (London: Weidenfeld & Nicolson, 1965), p. 204.

24   See Bourdieu, *Outline of a Theory*, p. 17.

25   See *ibid.*, p. 15.

26   On social honour as a game, see Bourdieu, *The Logic of Practice*, p. 100.

27   See Bourdieu, 'The Sentiment of Honour', pp. 197–205.

28   *Ibid.*, p. 205.

29   '[T]he indefinable thing which makes a man of honour, is as fragile and vulnerable as it is imponderable.' *Ibid.*, p. 218.

30   See J. H. Berke, 'Shame and Envy' *British Journal of Psychotherapy* 2 (4) 1986: 262–70.

31   Berke suggests, wrongly I believe, that shaming strategies do not devolve so much from a struggle for power as from a personality defect on the part of the shamer. *Ibid.*, p. 265.

32   In September 1999, Sonia O'Sullivan, a world champion and probably Ireland's most famous female athlete, was denounced from the pulpit of a Catholic Church as being a 'common slut' for the unashamed public manner in which she undermined Catholic values by having a child outside marriage and allowing herself to become the focus of media attention (*The Irish Times*, 4 Sept. 1999).

33   See Scheff, *Bloody Revenge*, p. 49.

Chapter 11   Telling lies

1   Friedrich Nietzsche, *Philosophy and Truth: Selections from Nietzsche's Notebooks of the early 1870s*, ed. and trans. D. Breazdale (Atlantic Highlands, N.J.: Humanities Press, 1979), p. 80.

2   With some exceptions mentioned below, lying has not received the attention it deserves in sociology. Perhaps this is because it falls between two theoretical stools. On the one hand, it is ignored by Habermasians since it comes within the realm of strategic action that is oriented to success rather than understanding. See Jurgen Habermas, *The Theory of Communicative Action*, vol. 2 (Boston: Beacon Press, 1987). On the other hand, for Foucauldians, the emphasis is not so much on the way power lies, but the way it produces truth. See Michel Foucault,

Power/Knowledge: Selected Interviews and Other Writings 1972–1977, ed. Colin Gordon (Brighton: Harvester Press, 1979). There have been some important analyses of lying, particularly Bok's moral philosophical study. See Sisela Bok, *Lying: Moral Choice in Public and Private Life* (Hassocks [Sussex]: Harvester Press, 1978). There have also been studies of lying in politics; see Hannah Arendt, *Between Past and Present: Eight Exercises in Political Thought* (New York: Viking, 1968); R. Rasberry, *The 'Technique' of Political Lying* (Washington [D.C.]: University Press of America, 1981); and in the media, see Glasgow University Media Group, *Bad News* (London: Routledge & Kegan Paul, 1976). However, much of the empirical research on lying comes from psychology. See M. Eck, *Lies and Truth* (New York: Macmillan, 1970); P. Ekman, *Telling Lies: Clues to Deceit in the Marketplace, Politics and Marriage*, 2nd edn (New York: Norton, 1992); B. DePaulo and R. Rosenthal 'Telling Lies', *Journal of Personality and Social Psychology* 37, 1979: 1713–72; D. Paulhus, 'Self–deception: Where Do We Stand?' in J. Lockard and D. Paulhus (eds), *Self–deception: An Adaptive Mechanism?* (Englewood Cliffs: Prentice-Hall, 1988, 251–7).

3   This concept of established and outsiders comes from Elias and Scotson's study of an English urban community in the 1950s. See Norbert Elias and John Scotson, *The Established and the Outsiders: Sociological Enquiry into Community Problems*, 2nd edn (London: Sage, 1994). However, Mennell has argued, relations between established and outsiders can be broadened to other power relations (Stephen Mennell, *Norbert Elias: An Introduction* (Dublin: UCD Press, 1998, p. 124). On informalisation and changes in power relations between social classes see C. Wouters, 'Etiquette Books and Emotion Management in the 20th Century, Part One – The Integration of Social Classes', *Journal of Social History* 29, 1995: 107–24 and 'Changing Patterns of Social Controls and Self–Controls', *British Journal of Criminology* 39 (3) 1996: 416–32.

4   See John Barnes, *A Pack of Lies: Towards a Sociology of Lying* (Cambridge: Cambridge University Press, 1994): 103–8.

5   Anthropologists have shown how lying is ingrained in the social life of diverse cultures. See Fred Bailey, *The Prevalence of Deceit* (Ithaca [N.Y.]: Cornell University Press, 1991), p. x; M. Gilsenan, 'Lying, Honor and Contradiction' in Bruce Kapferer (ed.), *Transaction and Meaning: Directions in the Anthropology of Exchange and Symbolic Behaviour* (Philadelphia: Institute for the Study of Human Issues, 1976): 191–219; M. Anderson, 'Cultural Concatenation of Deceit and Secrecy' in R. Mitchell and N. Thompson (eds), *Deception: Perspectives on Human and Non–Human Deceit* (Albany [N.Y.]: State University of New York Press, 1986), pp. 32–48; J. du Boulay, 'Lies, Mockery and Family Integrity', in J. Peristiany (ed.) *Mediterranean Family Structures* (Cambridge: Cambridge University Press, 1976), pp. 389–406.

6   See Barnes, *A Pack of Lies*, pp. 75–8.

7   See T. Scheff, 'Negotiating Reality: Notes on Power in the Assessment of Responsibility', *Social Problems* 16 (1) 1986: 3–17.

8   See Friedrich Nietzsche, *The Will to Power*, ed. Walter Kaufmann (New York: Random House, 1967), p. 84. Nietzsche not only considered lying conventional, he also believed it to be an a necessity for social survival. 'There is only *one* world, and that world is false, cruel, contradictory, misleading, senseless. . . . We need lies to vanquish this reality, the "truth," we need lies in order to live.' (p. 451).

9   It may be that as that everyone has to lie, that social life without lying is impossible. See H. Sachs, 'Everyone Has To Lie' in M. Sanches and B. Blount (eds), *Sociocultural Dimensions of Language Use* (New York: Academic Press, 1975), pp. 57–79. Deutscher, for example, pointed out that there is often an inevitable gap between what we say and what we do. See Irwin Deutscher, *What We Say/What We Do: Sentiments and Acts* (Glenview, IL: Scott, Foresman, 1973). Goffman demonstrated how fabrications – inducing false beliefs about what is going on in social situations – is endemic in social interaction. See Erving Goffman, *Frame Analysis* (Boston: Northwestern University Press, 1986).

10   Barnes, *A Pack of Lies*, p. 37.

11   Foucault insisted that lawyers and judges have become the experts not just in naming the truth, but producing, discovering and guaranteeing it. See Foucault, *Power/Knowledge*, p. 141.

12   Leaving aside the presupposition that there is an objective state of affairs independent of the technique of assessing the truth through interrogation, much depends on the techniques of interrogation and the relative power of the participants who participate in negotiating the facts of the case and assessing blame and responsibility. See Scheff, 'Negotiating Reality', p. 14. See also P. Bourdieu, 'The Force of Law: Toward a Sociology of the Juridical Field', *Hastings Law Journal* 38, 1987: 814–53.

13   Bailey, *The Prevalence of Deceit*, pp. 16, 123.

14   This is one of Bourdieu's main criticisms of Habermas. See Pierre Bourdieu, *Pascalian Meditations* (Cambridge: Polity, 2000), p. 65.

15   Nietzsche, for example, referred to religion as 'the holy lie'. It was, he argued, invented by priests and philosophers to gain and maintain power, authority and credibility over ordinary people (*Philosophy and Truth*, pp. 89–90)

16   See T. Szasz, 'The lying truths of psychiatry' in R. Duncan and M. Weston-Smith (eds), *Lying Truths: A Critical Scrutiny of Current Beliefs and Conventions* (Oxford: Pergamon Press, 1979), pp. 121–42

17   Bok focuses on 'clear-cut' lies which she defines as intentionally deceptive messages in the form of a *statement*. See Bok, *Lying*, p. 15.

18   See Gilsenan, 'Lying, Honor and Contradiction', p. 192.

19   See Goffman, *Frame Analysis*, pp. 83–123.

20   See Bailey, *The Prevalence of Deceit*, p. 13.

21   Arendt pointed out the American military and state institutions deliberately engaged in strategies of disinformation and deception to mislead people as to what was happening during the Vietnam War (Hannah Arendt, *Crises of the Republic* [New York: Harcourt Brace Jovanovich, 1972]).

22   See Bok, *Lying*, p. 144.

23   See Bailey, *The Prevalence of Deceit*, pp. 35, 34.

24   Barnes, *A Pack of Lies*, p. 91.

25   Bailey, *The Prevalence of Deceit*, p. 83.

26   *Ibid.*, p. 91.

27   Bok, *Lying*, p. 31.

28   This raises fundamental questions about the nature of truth and the way truth is discerned. As Habermas points out:

The world as the sum total of possible facts is constituted only for an interpretation community whose members engage, before the background of an intersubjectively shared lifeworld, in processes of reaching understanding with one another about things in the world. (Jürgen Habermas, *Between Facts and Norms* (Cambridge: Polity, 1996, p. 14)

The validity of positive law, its binding force and capacity for social integration are based on the idea of self-legislation (the supposition of the political autonomy of the united citizens) and the constitutional state which legitimises the rule of law in the first instance (*Between Facts*, pp. 38–9). Habermas is fully aware that the legitimacy and validity of law can be contaminated by money and power with the result that 'often enough, law provided illegitimate power with the mere semblance of legitimacy' (*Between Facts*, p. 40). The problem, of course, is the extent to which legal language and norms and courtroom procedures, in themselves jeopardise the possibility of justice and, consequently, the validity of the law. At the heart of this problem is whether the law operates as an independent social field, the extent to which it separate from other arms of the state, and to what extent it is founded on an 'intersubjectively shared lifeworld'. To what extent could the Hayes family, the police, Mr Justice Lynch and members of the legal profession be said to share such a lifeworld? This is what distinguishes Bourdieu and Habermas in their interpretation of how the law operates.

29   Barnes, *Pack of Lies*, p. 31.

30   Of course, this relates not just to court cases, but also to social life in general. See J. Dean, J. and W. F. Whyte, 'How Do You Know If the Informant is Telling the Truth', *Human Organization* 17 (2) 1958: 34–8.

31   Bourdieu, 'The Force of Law', p. 814.

32   *Ibid.*, pp. 828–9.

33   *Ibid.*, p. 840.

34   See Michel Foucault, *Power*, vol. 3, *The Essential Works* (Harmondsworth: Penguin 2001), p. 119.

35   Foucault, *Power*, pp. 326–48.

36   D. Fordney-Settlage, 'A Review of Cervical Mucus and Sperm Interactions in Humans', *International Journal of Fertility* 26 (3) 1981: 166–7.

37   See Lu, Hui-Ling, Chuan-Xi Wang, Feng-Qiang Wu, Jian-Jin Li 'Paternity Identification in Twins with Different Fathers', *Journal of Forensic Sciences* 39 (4)1994: 1100–2.

38   See P. Terasaki, D. Gjertson, D. Bernoco, S. Perdue, M. Mickey and J. Bond, 'Twins with Different Fathers identified by HLA', *New England Journal of Medicine*, 14 Sept. 1978: 590–2.

39   Peter Manning, *Police Work: The Organization of Policing* (Cambridge [Mass.]: MIT Press, 1977), p. 181.

40   Carl Klockars 'Blue Lies and Police Placebos', *American Behavioural Scientist* 27, 1984: 543; Barnes, *A Pack of Lies*, p. 44.

41   *DPP* v *Peter Pringle Court of Criminal Appeal* (*Irish Law Reports*, 1995): 575.

42   See Report of the Committee to Recommend Certain Safeguards for Persons in Custody and for Members of an Garda Síochána, Dublin: Government Publications, 1978.

43   P. O'Mahony, 'The Kerry Babies Case: Towards a Social Psychological Analysis', *Irish Journal of Psychology*, 13 (2) 1992: 237.

Chapter 12 Policing the state

1   On the development of the modern nation state from within towns, feudal rule and absolutism, see Gianfranco Poggi, *The Development of the Modern State* (London: Hutchinson, 1978). On the relation of state formation to other long-term social processes including monetarisation, taxation and economic development, the taming of warriors and decline in violence, and the curbing of affects and related changes in habitus that constitute the 'civilising process', see Norbert Elias, *The Civilising Process* (Oxford: Blackwell, 2000).

2   Max Weber was the first to insist that what characterised the modern state was its claim to the monopoly over the use of force: the army for its potential use against enemies outside the state's territory, and the police for its use against those within. See Max Weber, *The Theory of Social and Economic Organization*, ed. and trans. A. Henderson and T. Parsons (New York: Free Press, 1964), p. 154. However, state domination is primarily attained through law which Weber saw as the guarantee of conformity through physical and psychological coercion, enacted by a special staff of people employed for that purpose. See Max Weber, *Law in Economy and Society*, ed. M. Rheinstein (Cambridge [MA]: Harvard University Press, 1954), p. 5. Habermas follows on from this and emphasises the connection between law, coercion and bureaucratically organised domination, see Jürgen Habermas, *The Theory of Communicative Action*, vol. II (Cambridge: Polity, 1987), p. 358.

3   Weber, *Economy and Society*, p. 54.

4   As Berger notes:

> The ultimate and, no doubt, the oldest means of social control is physical violence. . . Even in the politely operated societies of modern democracies the ultimate argument is violence. No state can exist without a police force or its equivalent in armed might. This ultimate violence may not be used frequently. There may be innumerable steps in its application, in the way of warnings and reprimands. But if all the warnings are disregarded, even in so slight a manner as paying a traffic ticket, the last thing that will happen is that a couple of cops show up at the door with handcuffs and a Black Maria. (Peter Berger *Invitation to Sociology* [Harmondsworth: Penguin, 1966], p. 84.)

5   As Poggi puts it, 'one can visualize the whole state as a *legally* arranged set of organs for the forming, application and enforcement of *laws*', see Poggi, *Development of the Modern State*, p. 102.

6   See Christopher Pierson, *The Modern State* (London: Routledge, 1996).

7   Marxist-orientated scholars see the state as a relatively independent but necessary instrument of class domination and exploitation. They provide a limited understanding of what happened in the Kerry babies case. Habermas has emphasised how certain legitimation and motivation crises – such as provoked in the Republic of Ireland by the conflict in Northern Ireland – can undermine the state. In particular, he emphasised how people could lose faith in the political system (Jürgen Habermas, *Legitimation Crisis*, trans. T. McCarthy [London: Heinemann, 1976], pp. 69, 75).

8   See Habermas, *Theory of Communicative Action*, p. 358; Jürgen Habermas, *The Structural Transformation of the Public Sphere* (Oxford: Polity, 1989), p. 55. It would appear that Habermas sees positivity as the basis of positive law, but how positive law relates to positivism is not clear.

9   Formal contract law is perhaps the most rational and calculable. The aim, as Weber said, is to remove 'emotionally colored ethical postulates such as "justice" and "human dignity"' from interfering with the process (*Economy and Society*, vol. II, p. 886).

10   'Modern compulsory law, sanctioned by the state, becomes an institution detached from the ethical motivations of the legal person and dependent upon abstract obedience to the law.' (Habermas, *Theory of Communicative Action* II, p. 174).

11   *Ibid.*, p. 309.

12   'The juridification of social relations requires a high degree of value generalization, and extensive loosening of social action from normative contexts, and a splitting up of concrete ethical life into morality and legality. . . . Cultural tradition must already have thawed to the point where legitimate orders can do without dogmatic foundations firmly fixed in tradition.' *Ibid.*, p. 317.

13   Wolfgang Schluchter, *The Rise of Western Rationalism* (Berkeley: University of California Press, 1981), p. 114.

14   See Breathnach, *The Irish Police* (Dublin: Anvil Press, 1974), pp. 178–9.

15   Joseph Lee, *Ireland 1912–1985: Politics and Society* (Cambridge: Cambridge University Press, 1989), pp. 479–80; Derek Dunne and Gene Kerrigan, *Round Up the Usual suspects: Nicky Kelly and the Cosgrave Coalition* (Dublin: Magill, 1984), pp. 73–8.

16   Conor Cruise O'Brien, *Memoir: My Life and Times* (Dublin: Poolbeg, 1998), p. 355. O'Brien notes the he refrained from telling this story to two other ministers, Garret FitzGerald and Justin Keating, because he thought it would worry them. Derek Dunne and Gene Kerrigan claim that that the suspect was interrogated in Naas Garda Station by two members of what became known as the 'heavy gang' (Dunne and Kerrigan, *Round Up the Usual Suspects*, p. 97).

17   Garret Fitzgerald, *All in a Life: An Autobiography* (Dublin: Gill & Macmillan, 1991), p. 313.

18   See Ciaran McCullagh, *Crime in Ireland: A Sociological Introduction* (Cork: Cork University Press, 1996), pp. 30–9; C. Wouters 'Changing Patterns of Social Controls and Self–Controls: On the Rise of Crime since the 1950s and the Sociogenesis of a 'Third Nature', *British Journal of Criminology* 39 (3) 1999: 416–32.

19   This is based on the argument that the conflict in Northern Ireland led to a general increase in violence and brutality in Irish society, see Brewer *et al.*, *Crime in Ireland*, p. 35.

20   *Ibid.*, pp. 248–90.

21   See H. Franke 'Violent Crime in the Netherlands: A Historical-Sociological Analysis', *Crime, Law and Social Change* 21 (1994): 73–100.

22   The operation of the Special Branch and the Murder Squad could not be deemed to prove the existence of a police state in the Republic from the 1970s. See Brian Chapman, *Police State* (London: Macmillan, 1970), p. 137.

23   G. Kerrigan, 'The Kerry Babies Case', *Magill*, 30 May 1985, p. 20.

24   Ronan Bennett, *Double Jeopardy: The Retrial of the Guildford Four* (London: Penguin, 1993), p. 32. Roger Shuy analysed the tapes of interrogation of a murder suspect and compared them with the final written confession. He found several differences between what the suspect (Carter) said in the taped interrogation and what he was alleged to have said for the written statement. He described many examples of where, although Carter appeared to be agreeing with statements of the police officer, the words in the confession were those of the police officer and not Carter's. As Shuy notes, 'we should keep in mind that Officer A testified under oath that he wrote down only Carter's own words and sentences. Roger Shuy, *The Language of Confession, Interrogation and Deception* (London: Sage, 1998), p. 100.

25   For a detailed background to the events leading up to the O'Briain Committee, see Joy Joyce and Peter Murtagh, *Blind Justice* (Dublin: Poolbeg, 1984), pp. 120–7.

26   Report of the Committee to Recommend Certain Safeguards for Persons in Custody and for Members of An Garda Síochána, 1978, p. 14. Wrightsman and Kassin estimated that in the 1990s 50 per cent of cases in London and Birmingham, 47 per cent of cases in Los Angeles, 68 per cent of cases in New York City, were accompanied by confessions (L. Wrightsman and S. Kassin, *Confessions in the Courtroom* (Newbury Park [CA]: Sage, 1993), p. 1).

27   Committee to Recommend Certain Safeguards, p. 6.

28   *Ibid.*, p. 9.

29   *Ibid.*

30   *Ibid.*, p. 12.

31   *Ibid.*, pp. 15–16.

32   See Dunne and Kerrigan, *Round Up the Usual Suspects*, pp. 131–41.

33   *Ibid.*, pp. 100, 270.

34   *Ibid.*, p. 234.

35   *Ibid.*, p. 9.

36   Quoted in Bennett, *Double Jeopardy*, p. 2.

37   *The Irish Times*, 20 Jan. and 20 June, 1984.

38   *The Irish Times*, 30 Nov. 1984.

39   *The Irish Times*, 12 Dec. 1984.

40   *The Irish Times*, 22 Oct. 1985.

41   *The Irish Times*, 22 Oct. 1985.

42   Fred Inbau, John Reid and Joseph Buckley, *Criminal Interrogation and Confessions*, 3rd edn (Baltimore: Williams & Wilkins, 1986), pp. xiv–xvii, 5, 35.

43   *Ibid.*, pp. 77–126.

44   The students were asked to type letters on a computer system as quickly as possible. They were warned not to touch a certain key which, they were told, would cause the system to crash. After a minute the system was deliberately designed to crash. Videotapes of the process made it clear that none of the students had pressed the key. An accomplice was brought in to swear that he had seen each subject press the forbidden key. The researcher asked each student to sign a prepared statement of guilt. If they refused to sign after two requests, they received an angry phone call from the researcher. Eventually, almost two-thirds of the students signed the statement (Shuy, *Language of Confession*, pp. 45–6).

45   See Inbau *et al.*, *Criminal Interrogation and Confessions*, 176–8.

46   Shuy, *Language of Confession*, p. 43

47   P. O'Mahony, 'The Kerry Babies Case: Towards a Social Psychological Analysis', *Irish Journal of Psychology* 13 (2) 1992: 223–38. See also, S. Milgram, *Obedience to Authority* (New York: Harper, 1974); R. Lifton, *Thought Reform and the Psychology of Totalism* (New York: Norton, 1963).

48   See O'Halloran, *Lost Innocence*, pp. 49–50.

49   For a description of this protest, see McCafferty, *A Woman to Blame*, pp. 96–130.

Chapter 13 The media

1   Although there have been numerous instances of investigative journalism making an important contribution to the creation of a mature, democratic society in Ireland, there has as yet been no adequate historical review and analysis of this role of the media. See for example, John Horgan, *Irish Media: A Critical History Since 1922* (London: Routledge, 2001).

2   The relationship between the media, the public sphere and the creation of a mature, democratic society is complex and has been the subject of much theorising, research and debate. For a good overview of these issues, see John Keane, *The Media and Democracy* (Cambridge: Polity, 1991); Peter Dahlgren, *Television and the Public Sphere* (London: Sage, 1995); J. Curran, 'Rethinking the Media as a Public Sphere' in P. Dahlgren and C. Sparks (eds), *Communication and Citizenship* (London: Routledge, 1991), pp. 28–57; N. Garnham, 'The Media and the Public Sphere' in P. Golding, G. Murdock and P. Schlesinger (eds), *Communicating Politics* (Leicester: Leicester University Press, 1986), pp. 37–53.

3   *The Irish Times*, 16, 19 and 25 Apr. 1984.

4   For his account of how he became involved in the Case, see Barry O'Halloran, *Lost Innocence: The Inside Story of the Kerry Babies Case* (Dublin: Raytown Press, 1985), pp. 172–7.

5   O'Halloran, *Lost Innocence*, p. 175.

6   On the strategies journalists use to convey objectivity, see G. Tuchmann, 'Objectivity as Strategic Ritual: An Examination of Newsmen's Notions of Objectivity', *American Journal of Sociology* 77 (4) 1972: 660–79.

7   Pat Mann told the Tribunal that Kathleen Hayes reported rough treatment and slapping to him on 2 May 1984 (TT, 33/53). Mr Justice Lynch concluded that he was unable to determine whether any allegations of physical abuse were made by any member of the Hayes family to Pat Mann in or about the month of May, 1984, but that, if such complaints were made, they 'were made for the purpose of protecting the family reputation in Mr. Mann's eyes and of inducing Mr Mann to believe in their case' (TR, p. 79).

8   In February 1977 *The Irish Times* published a series of articles about the alleged existence of a Heavy Gang within the gardaí. It was based on a number of interviews with people who said that they had been abused and beaten by members of the Gang while they were in custody. The Minister for Justice, Patrick Cooney, denied that such a gang existed.

9   On the role of the media as the social conscience of Irish society, see T. Inglis, 'Irish Civil Society: From Church to Media Domination' in T. Inglis, Z. Mach and R. Mazanek (eds), *Religion and Politics: East–West Contrasts from Contemporary Europe* (Dublin: University College Dublin Press, 2000), pp. 49–67.

10   *Magill*, Nov. 1985, pp. 16–34.

11   *Ibid.*, p. 18

12   During the programme, Joanne Hayes said that in general she felt that she and her family had been treated fairly by the media. This reiterated what she wrote in her book (Joanne Hayes, *My Story* [Dingle: Brandon Press, 1985], pp. 162–4).

13   *Magill*, Mar. 1986, p. 22.

14   *Ibid.*, pp. 26.

15   *Ibid.*, pp. 22, 24.

16   *Ibid.*, p. 23.

17   *Ibid.*, p. 24.

18 *Ibid.*, pp. 24–5.

19 *Ibid.*, p. 27.

20 *Irish Independent*, 7 Nov. 1989.

21 See Keane, *Media and Democracy*, pp. 17–20.

22 See J. Curran, 'Mass Media and Democracy: A Reappraisal' in J. Curran and M. Gurevitch (eds), *Mass Media and Society* (London: Edward Arnold, 1991), pp. 97–8.

23 McQuail points out that the ability of the media to protect the public interest is dependent on people working in the media being committed to freedom, justice/equality and order/solidarity. See D. McQuail, 'Mass Media in the Public Interest: Towards a Framework of Norms for Media Performance' in Curran and Gurevitch (eds), *Mass Media and Society*, pp. 72–3. The notion of the media challenging the state's 'monopoly of legitimate symbolic violence' and its power to name and proclaim the truth, is derived from Bourdieu (Pierre Bourdieu, *Language and Symbolic Power* [Cambridge: Polity, 1991], pp. 239–40).

24 See Craig Calhoun (ed.), *Habermas and the Public Sphere* (Cambridge, MA: MIT Press, 1992).

25 Keane notes that some of the ways the state interferes with and censors the media are (a) through enacting emergency powers to protect social order, (b) through establishing police and military apparatuses whose operations are kept secret – as would seem to have been the case with the so-called 'heavy gang', and (c) through lying about, deliberately distorting, and covering up its errors and mistakes. See Keane, *Media and Democracy*, pp. 94–103.

26 On the censorship of the media in Ireland, see M. Kelly and B. Rolston, 'Broadcasting in Ireland: Issues of National Identity and Censorship' in P. Clancy, S. Drudy, K. Lynch and L. O'Dowd (eds), *Irish Society: Sociological Perspectives* (Dublin: Institute of Public Administration, 1995), pp. 563–92. On section 31 of the Broadcasting Act, see B. Purcell, 'The Silence in Irish Broadcasting' in B. Rolston (ed.), *The Media and Northern Ireland* (London: Macmillan, 1991), pp. 51–68.

27 On the influence and operation of libel law in Ireland, see Marie McGonagle (ed.), *Law and the Media: Views of Journalists and Lawyers* (Dublin: Round Hall Press, 1997); Kevin Boyle and Marie McGonagle, *Press Freedom and Libel* (Dublin: National Newspapers of Ireland, 1988).

28 On the relevance of news factors to the stories that get told in the media, see J. Palmer, 'News Production' in *The Media: An Introduction*, ed. A. Briggs and P. Cobley, Harlow: Longman 1998, 377–391; J. Galtung, Johan and M. Ruge, 'Structuring and Selecting News' in S. Cohen and J. Young (eds), *The Manufacture of News* (London: Sage, 1981), pp. 52–63; T. Harris and D. O'Neill, 'What is News? Galtung and Ruge Revisited', *Journalism Studies* 2 (2) 2001: 261–80. On crime as a news factor and how it is handled by the media, see Richard Ericson, Patricia Baranak and Janet Chan, *Representing Order: Crime, Law and Justice in the News Media* (Milton Keynes: Open University Press, 1991).

29 See James Curran and Jean Seaton, *Power Without Responsibility*, 3rd edn (London: Routledge, 1988), pp. 78–133; Jeremy Tunstall, *Newspaper Power: The New National Press in Britain* (Oxford: Clarendon, 1966), pp. 7–94. In relation to Ireland, see D. Bell, 'Communications, Corporatism and Dependent Development in Ireland', *Journal of Communication*, 45 (4) 1995: 70–88.

30 Given that this was one of the first public investigations of sexual transgression in Ireland, it would be interesting to compare the way the story was covered in the tabloids and the broadsheets, particularly during the early days of the Tribunal.

31   On the objectivity of journalists, the work of journalists, and the way news is constructed, see Gaye Tuchmann, *Making News: A Study in the Construction of Reality* (New York: Free Press, 1978); M. Schudson, 'What is a Reporter? The Private Face of Public Journalism' in J. Carey (ed.), *Media, Myths and Narratives* (London: Sage, 1988), pp. 228–45; and J. Lichtenberg, 'In Defence of Objectivity' in J. Curran and M. Gurevitch (eds), *Mass Media and Society* (London: Edward Arnold, 1991), pp. 216–31.

32   See for example, G. Murdock, 'Class, Power, and the Press: Problems of Conceptualisation and Evidence' in H. Christian (ed.), *The Sociology of Journalism and the Press* (Keele: Sociological Review Monograph, 1980), pp. 37–70; J. Westergaard, 'Power, Class and the Media' in J. Curran, M. Gurevitch and J. Woolacott (eds), *Mass Communication and Society* (London: Edward Arnold, 1977), pp. 95–115; D. Ruccinski, 'Personalized Bias in News; The Potency of the Particular', *Communication Research* 19 (1) 1992: 91–108.

33   This is an argument developed by John Waters and Desmond Fennell. See for example, John Waters, *Everyday Like Sunday?* (Dublin: Poolbeg, 1995), p. 284; Desmond Fennell, *Heresy: The Battle of Ideas in Modern Ireland* (Belfast: Blackstaff, 1993), pp. 186–212.

34   See Justin Lewis, *The Ideological Octopus* (London: Routledge, 1991); R. Fowler, 'Hysterical Style in the Press' in D. Graddol and O. Boyd-Barrett (eds), *Media Texts: Authors and Readers* (Milton Keynes: Open University Press, 1994), pp. 90–9.

35   One of the classic texts on the relation between journalists and sources is Herbert Gans, *Deciding What's News* (London: Constable 1980). For a comprehensive study on the relation between journalists and police, see Richard Ericson, Patricia Baranek and Janet Chan, *Negotiating Control: A Study of News Sources* (Milton Keynes: Open University Press, 1989), pp. 91–171.

36   On the way police leak stories and lead journalists see R. Ericson, 'Patrolling the Facts: Secrecy and Publicity in Police Work' *British Journal of Sociology* 40 (1989), 205–26; Ericson *et al*, *Negotiating Control*, pp. 123–52.

Chapter 14   Unruly bodies

1   See Tom Inglis, *Moral Monopoly: The Rise and Fall of the Catholic Church in modern Ireland*, 2nd edn (Dublin: University College Dublin Press, 1998); Tom Inglis, *Lessons in Irish Sexuality* (Dublin: University College Dublin Press, 1998); A. Greeley and C. Ward, 'How "Secularised" Is the Ireland We Live In?' *Doctrine and Life* 50 (1) 2000: 581–603.

2   There was an ongoing struggle between taken-for-granted 'traditions' and newly emerging, highly organised meaning systems which had very different understandings of women and sex. See A. Swidler, 'Culture in Action: Symbols and Strategies', *American Sociological Review* 51, 1986: 278.

3   For an overview of these struggles, see Chrystel Hug, *The Politics of Sexual Morality in Ireland* (London: Macmillan, 1999).

4   See Frances Finnegan, *Do Penance or Perish: A Study of Magdalen Asylums in Ireland* (Pilltown [Kilkenny]: Congrave Press, 2001); Mike Milotte, *Banished Babies: The Secret History of Ireland's Baby Export Business* (Dublin: New Island Books, 1997).

5   Nell McCafferty, *A Woman to Blame* (Dublin, Attic Press, 1985) p. 13.

6   Foucault insists that chance and power go together.

> To begin with there must have been a play of circumstances which, contrary to all expectations, brought down on the most obscure individual, on his mediocre life, on his ultimately fairly ordinary shortcomings, the gaze of power and the explosion of its wrath: a throw of the dice which saw to it that the vigilance of the authorities or the institutions, doubtless destined to efface all disturbance, detained this person rather than that person, this scandalous monk, this battered woman, this inveterate and raging drunkard, this quarrelsome merchant, and not so many others, beside them, whose disturbance of the peace was no less great.

See Michel Foucault, 'The Life of Infamous Men' in M. Morris and P. Patton (eds), *Michel Foucault: Power, Truth, Strategy* (Sydney: Feral, 1979), p. 81.

7   M. Foucault, 'The Dangerous Individual' pp. 125–51 in L. Kritzman (ed.) *Michel Foucault, Politics, Philosophy, Culture: Interviews and Other Writings 1977–1984* (London: Routledge, 1998), pp. 128, 131.

8   See M. Foucault, *The History of Sexuality* vol. 1 (New York: Vintage, 1980), p. 31.

9   See A. O'Connor, 'Images of the Evil Woman in Irish Folklore: A Preliminary Survey', *Women's Studies International Forum*, 11 (4) 1998: 281–5; A. O'Connor, 'Women in Irish Folklore: The Testimony Regarding Illegitimacy, Abortion and Infanticide' in M. O'Dowd and M. McCurtain (eds) *Women in Early Modern Ireland* (Edinburgh: Edinburgh University Press, 1991), pp. 304–17.

10   See McAvoy, 'The Regulation of Sexuality', p. 264. Groneman argues that the notion of female class contamination was prevalent among social commentators at the beginning of the twentieth century. There was a growing fear that middle- and upper-class women would become like working-class women 'who were perceived as inordinately lustful and as sexual opportunists' (C. Groneman, 'Nymphomania: The Historical Construction of Female Sexuality' *Signs* 19 (2) 1994: 358).

11   Edward Said, 'Afterword' to *Orientalism* (Harmondsworth: Penguin, 1995), p. 332.

12   See Foucault, *History of Sexuality*, p. 37.

13   Dollimore points out that sexual transgressives or 'queers' are at the heart of individualism because, in Oscar Wilde's terms, they despise uniformity of type and conformity to rule; two conditions that are not only at the heart of individualism, but to cultural resistance and social change. See Jonathan Dollimore, *Sexual Dissidence: Augustine to Wilde, Freud to Foucault* (Oxford: Clarendon Press, 1991), pp. 229, 8.

14   Michel Foucault, *Language, Counter-memory, Practice: Selected Essays and Interviews by Michel Foucault*, ed. D. Boucard (Cornell [N.Y]: Cornell University Press, 1977).

15   See R. Kearney, 'Myths and Scapegoats: The Case of René Girard' *Theory, Culture and Society* 12, 1995: 1–14.

16   Michel Foucault, *Power–Knowledge: Selected Interviews and Other Writings 1972–77*, ed. C. Gordon (New York: Pantheon, 1980), p. 193.

17   Said, 'Afterword', p. 332.

18   Edward Said, *Orientalism* (Harmondsworth: Penguin), p. 311.

19   *Ibid.*, 312.

20 René Girard, *The Scapegoat* (London: Athlone, 1986), p. 15.

21 *Ibid.*, p. 17.

22 *Ibid.*, p. 14.

23 Bourdieu, like Foucault, sought to rehistoricise sexuality by linking sexual relations and, more generally, relations between the sexes, to the 'long and partly immobile history of the androcentric unconscious.' (Pierre Bourdieu, *Masculine Domination* [Stanford: Stanford University Press, 2001], p. 103). The constitution of women as sexually deviant or transgressive is part of their symbolic domination which

> is exerted not in the pure logic of knowing consciousness but through schemes of perception, appreciation and action that are constitutive of habitus and which, below the level of the decisions of consciousness and the controls of will, set up a cognitive relationship that is profoundly obscure to itself. (p. 37)

24 See for example, Melanie Klein, *The Writings of Melanie Klein.* London: Hogarth Press, 1952: Dorothy Dinnerstein, *The Mermaid and the Minator* (New York: Harper & Row, 1976); Nancy Chodorow, *The Reproduction of Mothering* (Berkeley: University of California Press, 1978); Ann Ferguson *Blood at the Root* (London: Pandora, 1989).

25 See Mary Condren, 'Sacrifice and Political Legitimation: The Production of Gendered Social Order' in J. Hoff and M. Coulter (eds), *Irish Women's Voices: Past and Present.* Special Issue of *Journal of Women's History.* 6 (4) and 7 (1) 1995: 160–89; Inglis, *Moral Monopoly,* pp. 178–200.

26 Diane Purkiss, *The Witch in History: Early Modern and Twentieth Century Representations* (London: Routledge, 1996), p. 97.

27 Quoted in *The Irish Times,* 17 Jan. 1985; 23 Jan. 1985; 24 Jan. 1985.

28 McCafferty, *A Woman to Blame,* p. 28.

29 *Ibid.,* 76.

30 *Ibid.,* 152.

31 *Ibid.,* 154.

32 The extent to which witch-hunting can be conflated with woman–hunting and, more broadly, the social control of women is a contentious one; see C. Larner, *Enemies of God: the Witch-Hunt in Scotland* (Baltimore, MD: Johns Hopkins University Press, 1981), pp. 92–100. The more contentious argument is that the witch-hunts persecuted women for their sexuality. See Marianne Hester, *Lewd Women and Wicked Witches* (London: Routledge, 1992), p. 114.

33 H. R. Trevor-Roper, *The European Witch-Craze of the Sixteenth and Seventeenth Centuries* (Harmondsworth: Penguin, 1969), p. 8.

34 *Ibid.,* p. 119.

35 *Ibid.,* p. 120.

36 Anne Barstow, *Witchcraze: Our Legacy of Violence Against Women* (London: Pandora, 1994), p. 23.

37 Quoted in Barstow, *Witchcraze,* p. 135.

38 *Ibid.,* p. 29; Hester, *Lewd Women,* p. 199.

39 Barstow, *Witchcraze,* p. 138.

40 Hester, *Lewd Women,* p. 196.

41   Carol Karlsen, *The Devil in the Shape of a Woman: Witchcraft in Colonial New England* (New York: Norton, 1987), pp. 138–42.

42   O'Connor, 'Women in Irish Folklore', p. 309.

43   *Ibid.*, p. 311.

44   Barstow, *Witchcraze*, pp. 26–7.

45   Hester, *Lewd Women*, p. 200.

46   Barstow in *Witchcraze* gives explicit details of some of these confessions, many of them featuring infanticide, and the torturing techniques used to extract them.

47   Trevor-Roper, *European Witch-Craze*, p. 42.

48   *Ibid.*, p. 46.

49   James Sharpe, *Instruments of Darkness: Witchcraft in England 1550–1750* (London: Hamish Hamilton, 1996), p. 218.

50   Trevor-Roper, *European Witch-Craze*, pp. 50–1.

51   Barstow, *Witchcraze*, p. 148.

52   Joanne Hayes, *My Story* (Dingle: Brandon Press, 1985), pp. 84–6.

53   See Barstow, *Witchcraze*, p. 82; Hester, *Lewd Women*, p. 197.

54   See Jane Kenny, 'How has the figure of the witch, already known in pagan antiquity, taken on new characteristics in modern-day society?' Unpublished MSocSc. thesis, University College Dublin, 1998, pp. 31–2. See also Sean O'Súilleabháin, *Irish Folk Custom and Belief* (Dublin: Mercier Press, 1977).

55   Mr Justice Lynch also contrasted the local support for Joanne Hayes with the abusive phone calls made by residents of Abbeydorney to Mrs Moloney, the wife of the local guard (TR, p. 147).

56   Hester, *Lewd Women*, p. 199.

57   Sharpe, *Instruments of Darkness*, pp. 9, 182–3.

Chapter 15   Conclusion

1   In November 1985, Fintan O'Toole, as editor of *Magill*, called on Michael Noonan the Minister for Justice to reject the Tribunal Report produced by Mr Justice Kevin Lynch. He noted:

> Nobody sets out to create a police state, not even the police. All that is needed is the acceptance of expediency, whether for the detention of suspects, the extraction of confessions, or a refusal of politicians to act as watchdogs because it is more trouble than it is worth. (*Magill*, Nov. 1985).

2   For an overview of the changes in the position of women in Irish society, see Pat O'Connor, *Emerging Voices: Women in Contemporary Irish Society* (Dublin: Institute of Public Administration, 1998). For an overview of the development of the Irish Women's Movement, see Linda Connolly, *The Irish Women's Movement: From Revolution to Devolution* (Basingstoke: Palgrave, 2002).

3   'She [Joanne Hayes] tried to get Jeremiah Locke to desert his wife and the one lawful child which he then had and to set up house with herself.' (TR, p. 146)

4   Joanne Hayes, *My Story* (Dingle: Brandon Press 1985), p. 34.

5   In the aftermath of the Kerry babies case, the Murder Squad was effectively disbanded. Five of its members were transferred to desk jobs, one of them, Superintendent Courtney, at his own request. See Gene Kerrigan's analysis of members of the Murder Squad being made scapegoats in *Magill*, 14 Nov. 1985.

6   In July 1997, Dean Lyons made a detailed confession about how he stabbed two women to death in Grangegorman in Dublin. Subsequently, Mark Nash also confessed to the same murders, but provided crucial corroborating evidence that made it convincing that he perpetrated the crime. Expert assessment indicated that Lyons confessed because he was highly suggestible – particularly since he was probably suffering from heroin withdrawal effects. The Director of Public Prosecutions eventually dropped the charges against Dean Lyons, who died in England four years later. See *Magill*, Feb. 2001; *Sunday Tribune*, 27 May and 3 June 2001.

7   Parrhesia, or speaking freely and frankly without distortion or dissimulation, that is making a direct connection between speech and reality, words and the world of things, was at the centre of Foucault's life work. It is a care for the truth, often at a risk both to the listener and to the speaker. It is the opposite of rhetoric and speaking to impress. For an analysis of parrhesia and how this was central to the work of Max Weber and Michel Foucault – and how they both relied heavily on Nietzsche – see Arpád Szakolczai, *Max Weber and Michel Foucault: Parallel Life-Works* (London: Routledge, 1998), 179–86.

8   Foucault claimed that 'Christianity is a confession', that every Christian has the duty to know not just his own faults and the temptations to which he has been exposed, but what is happening to him, and to declare these things to other people. See Michel Foucault, 'The Hermeneutics of the Self' in *Religion and Culture by Michel Foucault*, ed. J. Carrette (Manchester: Manchester University Press, 1999), pp. 169–70.

9   This is an adaptation of Foucault's argument. See Michel Foucault, *The Order of Things: An Archaeology of the Human Sciences* (New York: Vintage, 1973).

10   The more that psychologists emphasise the importance of culture, and the more that sociologists emphasise issues such as experience, emotions and identity, the more the gap between the disciplines appears to be closing. Benson describes cultural psychology as the examination of 'how people, working together, using a vast range of tools, both physical and symbolic . . . make meaningful the world they find, make meaningful worlds and, in the course of doing all these things, construct themselves as types of person and self who inhabit these worlds'. See Ciarán Benson, *The Cultural Psychology of Self: Place, Morality and Art in Human Worlds* (London: Routledge, 2001), p. 11.

11   See Pierre Bourdieu, *The Logic of Practice* (Cambridge: Polity, 1990), pp. 30–41.

12   On ethnographic 'thick description', see Clifford Geertz, *The Interpretation of Cultures* (New York: Basic Books, 1973). On developing an understanding of participants' feel for the game, see Bourdieu, *The Logic of Practice*, pp. 80–97. For an example of thick description linked to the development of an understanding of social structure and long-term processes of social change in Ireland, see Laurence Taylor, *Occasions of Faith* (Dublin: Lilliput, 1995).

13   Bourdieu refers to this as the intellectualist bias or the scholastic fallacy. See Bourdieu and Wacquant, *An Invitation to Reflexive Sociology* (Cambridge: Polity, 1992), pp. 39–40; Pierre Bourdieu, *Pascalian Meditations* (Cambridge: Polity, 2000), pp. 48–84.

14   A more fundamental problem with the intellectualist bias of sociologists is that social scientific rationality becomes part of the symbolic domination of others, particularly the marginalised and oppressed. See Bourdieu, *Pascalian Meditations*, p. 83.

15   Benson, *Cultural Psychology of Self*, p. 45.

16   See Richard Kearney, *Postnationalist Ireland: Politics, Culture, Philosophy* (London: Routledge, 1997), pp. 108–21.

Appendix

Survey results

In 1997, Eoin O'Mahony (Research Assistant) and I carried out a small survey to discover what, if anything, people remembered of the Kerry babies story. We sent a postal questionnaire to a random sample (generated by the Economic and Social Research Institute) of 120 people selected from the national register of electors. Where possible we followed up these letters with phone calls, and when necessary conducted an interview over the phone. We replaced those who had died or migrated with other names randomly selected. We obtained 58 replies – a response rate of 48 per cent. The response was higher among females: 39 of the 58 respondents. There was also an imbalance in the age of the respondents. Only 10 were aged 18–30 years, 24 were aged between 31–50, and 24 were over 51 years.

The majority (46) of the 58 respondents remembered the case. However, what they remembered and how precisely varied significantly. Eighteen of the respondents remembered either Joanne Hayes's first or second name. Eighteen mentioned that she was an unmarried mother. Twenty-seven referred to one or two babies, abandoned or killed.

Joanne Hayes had a baby but other baby found off cliff and she and her family blamed for first baby's death. She had a baby which was found buried on the farm. Saw pictures of the boyfriend who was married and worked in the same place. (Female, 31–50 years, third-level education, living in a city)

Joanne Hayes, baby found on beach, how unfortunate for the people involved. Symptomatic of attitudes in Ireland at the time of being pregnant and the stigma. Connected with Lovett incident. People should have minded own business and should not have been brought into national arena. Irish solution was disregard. (Male, 31–50 years, third-level education, living in a city)

My feelings, well I think the guards put the Hayes family through hell. They wanted to solve the case! I will never forget the names Joanne Hayes and Jeremiah Locke. (Female, 31–50 years, second-level education, living in a city)

A feeling of sorrow and regret of the woman in question. My heart went out to her. She had to go to court: the media went to town on it. A tragedy that happened to her and her family. Remorselessly dragged out. (Male, over 51 years, primary education, living in a town)

As a way of trying to probe their memories, we then asked respondents if they could remember any of the events, outcomes, or people involved. Twelve of the respondents mentioned an Inquiry, Tribunal or court case. Eight made reference to media coverage or books being written. We also asked respondents if anyone was to blame for the incident. Nine of the 47 respondents who remembered something about the case, said that Irish society or attitudes at the time were to blame. For example:

The attitudes of those who believe it is wrong to have an illegitimate child. The lady involved probably was pressured to act the way in which she did because of the attitude of people in her area at the time. (Female, 18–30 years, third-level education, living in a city)

Irish society, lack of education perhaps. The mothers I think must take some of the blame. Perhaps responsibility would be a kinder word than blame. (Female, 31–50 years, third-level education, living in a town).

Rural attitudes to unmarried mothers. (Female, over 51 years, second-level education, living in a town)

Society in general in this so-called 'modern/Christian' Ireland and also the attitudes of the Catholic Church at the time to unmarried mothers. (Female, over 51 years, primary-level education, living in a city)

No back up system, department for advice. No support, social services. (Male, over 51 years, primary-level education, living in a city)

Finally, we asked respondents for their main memory or feeling about what happened. Fourteen mentioned a general sense of sadness, sorrow and tragedy.

This is a selection of responses to this question.

Particularly outraged at police reaction. Questioning of the senior counsel. (Male, over 51 years, second-level education, living in a city)

Initial reaction gross miscarriage of justice; nothing came about, no impartiality. (Male, 31–50 years, third-level education, living in a town)

A pity that the Special Unit was brought into a domestic affair. Was not suitable. Feel sorry for the people. (Male, 31–50 years, third-level education, living in a town).

Bit of a scandal. We were not sure what, but we were more inclined to blame her. (Male, over 51 years, third-level education, living in a city)

Terrible for the baby, deserved life. (Male, 18–30 years, primary-level education, living in a rural area)

Index

Printed in the United Kingdom
by Lightning Source UK Ltd.
9829100001B/49-510